An Introduction to Sophocles

An Introduction to Sophocles

T. B. L. WEBSTER

Methuen & Co Ltd
11 NEW FETTER LANE LONDON EC4

First published 1936 *by Oxford University Press*
Second edition 1969 *by Methuen & Co Ltd*
11 *New Fetter Lane, London EC*4
© 1969 *by T. B. L. Webster*
Printed in Great Britain by
Fletcher & Son Ltd, Norwich

SBN 416 4184 6

Distributed in the U.S.A. by
Barnes and Noble Inc

To R. W.

*Les grands littérateurs n'ont jamais
fait qu'une seule œuvre.*

PROUST

Preface to the First Edition

IT appeared to me soon after I started to work on Sophocles that I could only interpret a passage to my own satisfaction by comparing it with other passages of the same kind. This necessitated my using the analytical and comparative method, and gave me the main divisions of this essay into thought, characters, plot, songs and style. But this procedure made it necessary to assume the order of Sophocles' plays and difficult to discuss his development. I therefore decided to begin with a chapter on the life of Sophocles and the chronology of his plays and to end with a general account of his development.

I have tried to quote the authorities that I have used, but I am very conscious that ideas which now seem to me to be mine may have come to me from others whom I have forgotten. In particular I feel that I am more indebted to Pohlenz's *Griechische Tragödie* than my notes show. Tycho von Wilamowitz's *Dramatische Technik* has influenced me greatly, although the more I have studied Sophocles the further I have moved from his position. Nestle's *Euripides* showed me the possibility of a chapter on thought. Of the books which have come out while I have been working, Weinstock has been helpful for character, Reinhardt for plot, Kranz' *Stasimon* for song, and the relevant volume of Schmid-Stählin for style.

In conclusion I should like to thank Mr. C. Bailey, Lady Barlow, Mr. C. M. Bowra, Professor E. S. Forster, and Professor Hermann Fränkel for reading my manuscript, Mr. K. G. D. Cave for making the *index locorum* and reading my proofs, and Mr. Robert Willis for much salutary criticism.

Manchester, 1935.   T. B. L. W.

Preface to the Second Edition

THIS book was written more than thirty years ago, but I hope that it still serves its modest purpose of providing a sort of comparative grammar of Sophoclean drama. Various kinds of evidence have made the early stage of Sophocles' development clearer, and I have added a new Appendix on this. Asterisks by page numbers refer the reader to addenda and corrigenda listed at the end of the book.

Two extremely useful general works should be mentioned first. Albin Lesky's *Tragische Dichtung der Hellenen* (first published 1956, second edition 1964, and a third revision promised) contains an excellent fifty pages on Sophocles, in which all the major problems are discussed in the light of modern scholarship. (A more general account, but with very good bibliography, is available in English in his *History of Greek Literature*, Methuen 1966.) The scholarship of Sophocles from 1939–1959 is reviewed in 200 pages by Holger Friis Johansen in *Lustrum* 7, 1962, 94 ff. This discusses critically and penetratingly in English 844 articles and books concerned with Sophocles. For three widely differing general books on Sophocles I should quote C. M. Bowra, *Sophoclean Tragedy*, Oxford 1939; A. J. A. Waldock, *Sophocles the Dramatist*, Cambridge 1951; C. H. Whitman, *Sophocles*, Harvard 1951.

Stanford, 1968.   T. B. L. W.

The publishers are grateful to the Clarendon Press, Oxford, for permission to reproduce the text of the 1936 edition.

Contents

X CONTENTS

I. Life

SOPHOCLES was born some five years before Marathon; as a youth he led the chorus which celebrated the victory of Salamis; he died in the year before the fall of Athens. His lifetime covers the most glorious century of Athenian history. He was growing up during the Persian wars, he saw the Delian league turn into empire and the empire into tyranny, and the tyranny falling to ruin in the Peloponnesian war. The ancient 'Life' and passing references in other authors show that he took a full part in this Athenian history both as poet and as citizen. Although the evidence is meagre, we can form some idea of his early life, his dramatic career, his friends, his public life, and of his old age.

He was born in 497/6 at Colonus. Nothing is known of his father, Sophillus, except that he owned a weapon factory. The 'Life' says that Sophillus cannot himself have been a carpenter or a smith, because a smith's son would never have been elected general, nor would he have been left unscathed by the comic poets. Pliny is following the same tradition when he tells us that Sophocles was born in the highest station.[1] We shall find more evidence to bear this out.

In his youth Sophocles was given prizes for athletics and for his school work. He was taught music by Lamprus. Plutarch classes Lamprus with Pindar and Pratinas as a writer of good music and contrasts them with Philoxenus and Timotheus.[2] His music was sober and restrained

---

[1] See Blumenthal, *R.E.* iii *a*, 1041. Pliny, *N.H.* xxxvii. 40 'principi loco genito'.   [2] See Note A, at end, p. 179.

rather than wild and realistic. We can see the same contrast between the choruses of Sophocles and the later choruses and arias of Euripides who was much influenced by Timotheus. The only other record of Sophocles' youth that has survived is the statement that he led the chorus of thanksgiving after the battle of Salamis, partly perhaps because of his personal beauty, which was famous. But we may surely assume that he would not have been chosen unless he had also been well born.

His dramatic career started in 468, when he won his first victory with the *Triptolemus*. According to Plutarch[1] his first victory coincided with his first production. This was the beginning of his long and successful life as dramatist in the course of which he won no less than eighteen victories and was never third in the contest. The total number of his plays was one hundred and twenty-three; this makes thirty-one trilogies, and therefore he must have written on an average a trilogy every other year.[2]

The certain dates of his dramatic career are the following:

468. *Triptolemus.*
467. No production.
443 or 441. *Antigone.*[3]
438. First prize.
431. Second prize.
428. No production.
415. No production.
409. *Philoctetes.*
406. Chorus in mourning for Euripides at the *proagon*.
401. *Coloneus*, produced posthumously.

[1] Plutarch, *Cimon*, 8. (Cf. however, Schmid-Stählin, p. 313.) The *Triptolemus* is dated to this year by Pliny, *N.H.* xviii. 65. The years when he did not produce are fixed by our knowledge of the first and second prizewinners (Sophocles was never third).

[2] See Note B, at end, p. 179.

[3] Dated by the first argument to the vicinity of the Samian war; Euripides was victorious in 442.

We can, however, add to this calendar with a considerable degree of confidence. The *Nausicaa* and *Thamyras*
were very early, if, as we are told, Sophocles himself acted
in them. The choregic inscription of Aexone[1] records the
name of a *Telepheia* which was probably produced in the
thirties; of the known titles the *Aleadae*, *Mysians*, and
Assembly of Achaeans would best compose such a trilogy.
The *Tereus* has been connected with a passage in Thucydides where the historian, writing of the year 431, distinguishes carefully between Tereus the husband of Procne
and Teres the father of Sitalces, the king of Thrace with
whom the Athenians made an alliance in that year. On
account of this passage Zielinsky dates the play to the time
of the Peloponnesian war.[2] The connexion is convincing,
but not the dating. If Sophocles was chiefly responsible
for popularizing the Tereus legend, his play must have
given rise to the confusion between Tereus and Teres. This
can only have arisen when the Athenians were interested
in Teres, and therefore the play must have been produced
before 431, though probably not long before.

Of the surviving plays, the *Ajax* must be early on the
internal evidence of technique and language. References
to outside events are doubtful[3] and quotation does not
afford much help. But although the *Ajax* cannot con-
clusively be proved either earlier or later than the Telephus trilogy of Euripides (438), the Polyxena scene of the
Hecuba, produced about 425, certainly recalls Tecmessa's
appeal.[4] In the *Acharnians*, also produced in 425, where

---

[1] See Note C, at end, p. 179.

[2] Zielinsky, *Iresione*, i, p. 449; Gernet, *Mélanges Navarre*, p. 207; Thuc.
ii. 29.   [3] See Note D, at end, p. 180.

[4] For parallels with Euripidean plays of 438, compare *Aj.* 1102 with
fr. 722 of the *Telephus*, 1295 with the *Cretan Women*; see Schmid-Stählin,
p. 329, n. 3, for the conflicting views. Compare 485, 489, 858 with *Hec.*
349, 357, 411.

Lamachus sees Dicaeopolis in his shield, Aristophanes is parodying the end of the Menelaus debate and he has a reminiscence of the third *stasimon* in one of the choruses. The *Ajax* was certainly written before 425 and probably before 440.[1]

The *Trachiniae* has no references to outside events and is quoted by no comedy. A considerable number of Euripidean parallels have been noted. They cover a period from 438 to 417, but in no case can it be said with certainty which poet is the borrower.[2] *Trachiniae* and *Tereus* must have been very much alike. Both had the diptych form; both dealt with the tragedy of a cultured woman married to a wild husband; in both the woman bewailed the lot of women. And there is close correspondence both of metre and thought between the choric fragments of the *Tereus* and the *parodos* of the *Trachiniae*. If we add the internal evidence of language and technique (of which more later), we can assign to the *Trachiniae* also a date before, but perhaps not long before, 431.

For the *Tyrannus* the case is rather better. The description of the plague, although it has literary ancestors in the *Eumenides* and the *Iliad*, must be inspired by the Athenian plague at the beginning of the Peloponnesian war. This puts the upper limit at 430.[3] Euripides appears to have

[1] 1142 ff. with *Ach.* 1128 ff.; 1192 ff. with *Ach.* 979 ff.; perhaps also *Ach.* 319–20 is modelled on 727–8.

[2] Prologue with *Andromache*; 139 with *H.F.* 339f.; 163 with *H.F.* 462; 383 with *Med.* 83; 416 with *Suppl.* 567; Hyllus' messenger speech with the messenger speech in the *Medea*; the nurse's speech with *Alc.* 158 ff.; the entry of Heracles with *H.F.* 1042 ff. See Schmid-Stählin, p. 375, for literature; Reinhardt, op. cit., p. 256. For parallels with *Tereus* see Appendix.

[3] Cf. also *O.T.* 873 f. with Thuc. ii. 47. 4, 53. 4. See Schmid-Stählin, p. 361. It does not, however, seem to me safe to go farther and equate Apollo's demand for the expulsion of Oedipus with the Spartans' demand for the expulsion of Pericles. For reminiscences of the *Eumenides* see Hirst, *C.R.* 1934, p. 170.

borrowed from the *Tyrannus* for the *Hippolytus*, which was produced in 428. Creon's self-defence is closely parallel to Hippolytus' self-defence, and the scene with the Corinthian messenger and Iocasta is the model for the scene in which the nurse discloses Phaedra's love to Hippolytus. These parallels are unusually convincing, and if they are accepted, date the *Tyrannus* to 429.[1]

The comic poets afford additional evidence that the *Tyrannus* was produced in the early twenties. Aristophanes has two reminiscences of the *Tyrannus* in the *Knights* which was produced in 424 and one in the *Acharnians* which was produced in 425. In addition to these references, Athenaeus has a curious story about the *Tyrannus* and the *Medea* which may have some bearing on the chronology.[2] He says that Callias wrote an alphabetical tragedy from which Euripides and Sophocles borrowed for the *Tyrannus* and the *Medea*. If it is allowed that this story places the *Tyrannus* near the *Medea*, it is slight confirmatory evidence for dating the *Tyrannus* to 429.

The limits for dating the *Electra* are given by Aristophanes. In the *parabasis* of the second edition of the *Clouds*, which must be later than 418, he writes, 'This comedy came seeking like that Electra ('Electra in the play'—Rogers) . . . for she will know her brother's lock'. 'That Electra' is the Electra of the *Choephori*, and the reference would be obscure if Sophocles had already produced his play. In the *Gerytades* Aristophanes parodied a line of Sophocles' *Electra* and the *Gerytades* can be dated to 408. Sophocles' *Electra* must have been produced between 418 and 408.[3]

---

[1] *Hipp.* 1013 f. with *O.T.* 583 f.; see Zielinsky, *Iresione*, i, p. 307, n. 2, and below, ch. iv, p. 92. *Hecuba*, 1255 f. recalls the Tiresias scene.

[2] See Note E, at end, p. 180.

[3] *Clouds*, 534; *Gerytades*, fr. 168. See Geissler, *Philol. Untersuch.* 1921, pp. 61 ff.

The limits can be further narrowed by a consideration of Euripides' *Electra*, *Orestes*, and *Helen*. A great deal has been written on the relation of the two *Electras* and most of the arguments have not led to any certain result. But Euripides wrote another play about a later stage in the same story, the *Orestes*, produced in 408. Bruhn[1] has shown that it is a continuation of Sophocles' *Electra*. Euripides has forgotten the marriage of his own Electra to the peasant and he names the third sister, Chrysothemis, who appears in Sophocles' play but is not mentioned in either the *Electra* or *Iphigenia in Tauris* of Euripides. This argument is sound, and in the absence of contrary proof we are bound to date Sophocles' *Electra* between Euripides' *Electra* and *Orestes*. Bruhn goes farther. He rightly notes some remarkable parallels between Sophocles' *Electra* and Euripides' *Helen* which was produced in 412. Euripides' *Electra* was produced in 413. Bruhn assumes that Euripides borrowed from Sophocles in the *Helen* and that he borrowed during rehearsal, since the two plays must have been produced in the same year. But it is just as likely that Sophocles was the borrower. If so, the limits for the *Electra* are 411–409. Of these years 409 is unlikely because the *Electra* is so like the *Philoctetes* in structure.

We can, then, with some probability draw up the following calendar for Sophocles' dramatic career. It could be enlarged by including the lost plays which can be dated by internal evidence, but that evidence must be set out in full elsewhere.

468. *Triptolemus*.
467. No production.
Very early. *Thamyras* and *Nausicaa*.
443 or 1. *Antigone*.
    Ajax near and perhaps earlier.
    Telepheia near and perhaps later.

[1] See Note F, at end, p. 181.

438. First prize.

Before 431. *Trachiniae* and *Tereus*.

431. Second prize.

429. *Tyrannus.*

428. No production.

415. No production.

411 or 410. *Electra*.

409. *Philoctetes*.

406. Chorus in mourning for Euripides.

401. *Coloneus* posthumously.

We have two pieces of evidence that Sophocles was interested in the theoretical as well as the practical side of dramatic art.

The 'Company of the educated' which, according to the 'Life', Sophocles formed in honour of the Muses, may have been in part a religious institution.[1] Although in the 'Life' this statement immediately follows the section on acting, the writer is here epitomizing different sections of a longer work and the meaning of the 'educated' should not be restricted to the actors who had been trained by Sophocles. The 'Company' was probably a society of educated Athenians which was founded by Sophocles to discuss problems of literature and drama; such a society would begin their meetings by sacrificing to the Muses. Perhaps the 'Company of Muses' which in the *Thesmophoriazusae* is helping Agathon compose his choruses[2] is the same society.

Suidas in his notice of Sophocles tells us that he wrote a book 'on the Chorus'. As Aly points out,[3] 'Chorus' was the official name for tragedy, and a book on the chorus would deal with all branches of the poet's art.

[1] See Θίασος in Liddell and Scott, 'A religious guild or confraternity'. 'Fellow sacrificers to the Muses' occur on a Boeotian inscription.

[2] Aristophanes, *Thesm.* 41. Blumenthal suggests that 'the educated' are actors, *R.E.* iii *a.* 1049. Contrast Köhler, *Rh. Mus.* 1884, p. 295.

[3] *Philologus, Suppt.* xxi. 3, p. 93.

Sophocles' book has parallels in such contemporary works as *Scene-painting* by Agatharchus, *The Parthenon* by Ictinus, *Symmetry* by Polyclitus, and *Painting* by Parrhasius. The sayings[1] of Sophocles that have survived, his criticism of Aeschylus, his comparison of Euripides' characters with his own and his account of the development of his own style, presumably come from this book. Sophocles may well have written it for and read it to the 'Company of the educated'. It is, however, more important that the existence of such a book by Sophocles is external evidence for that conscious and careful craftsmanship which we shall discuss when we come to analyse the style and composition of his plays.

In Plutarch's accounts of Sophocles' first victory we find further evidence for Sophocles' position in Athenian society. Plutarch tells us that popular feeling ran so high that the archon, instead of appointing the usual judges, ordered Cimon and his brother generals to give judgement, and they adjudged the victory to Sophocles in preference to Aeschylus. It is tempting to argue from this that Sophocles was one of Cimon's friends or, considering their relative positions, that Cimon was the patron of Sophocles. The inference becomes more plausible when we remember that Cimon and Sophocles had three common friends— Archelaus, Polygnotus, and Ion.

Archelaus, besides being an important thinker and the teacher of Socrates, was the poet who celebrated Cimon's victories. Sophocles wrote an elegiac poem[2] to him. It is very possible that this poem was not written until Sophocles and Archelaus were campaigning together in the Samian war, but even if this is true, the poem is still evidence that Sophocles was the friend of a friend of Cimon.

---

[1] Athenaeus, i. 22 *a*; Aristotle, *Poet.* 1460^{b}33; Plut. *de prof. in virt.* 79 B.

[2] *Anth. Lyr.* i, p. 67.

Another close friend of Cimon was the painter, Polygnotus. A possible connexion between him and Sophocles can be built up out of fragments of information. According to the 'Life' there was a picture of Sophocles holding a lyre in the *Stoa Poikile*, painted because Sophocles took up a lyre and played it in his *Thamyras*. The *Thamyras* was an early play; the Stoa was built by Cimon's brother-in-law, Peisianax, soon after 457, and certainly contained pictures by Polygnotus. It is suggested that Polygnotus painted Sophocles as Thamyras.[1] Polygnotus painted a Thamyras in Athens to which several vase-paintings can be traced back. He also painted a Thamyras in Delphi and a fragment of Sophocles' play tallies with Pausanias' description of this picture. This is the evidence for the connexion. If it is accepted, we can go a stage farther and suggest that two other scenes in early Sophoclean plays, the discovery of Odysseus in the *Nausicaa* and the oath scene in the *Ajax of Locri*, inspired Polygnotan pictures. This connexion between poet and painter seems the more likely when we remember that according to the ancient authorities both had the same object, both were primarily delineators of character. Perhaps we should find an allusion to Polygnotus in a remark of Sophocles quoted by Ion of Chios.[2] Sophocles said that if a painter painted Apollo's hair golden and not black, he would make a worse picture. It would appear from this that Sophocles preferred the restricted palette of Polygnotus to the rich style that came in during the second half of the fifth century

[1] For literature and illustrations see Séchan, *Études sur la trag. gr.*, p. 193; Zielinsky, *Iresione*, i, p. 448, states the connexion between Sophocles and Polygnotus as fact, thence argues to the connexion with Cimon. It is not fact, but plausible conjecture. For the Thamyras in Delphi see Pausanias, x. 30. 8. Cf. Sophocles, fr. 244. For the *Nausicaa* see Séchan, p. 167. For the *Ajax* see Appendix.

[2] Athenaeus, xiii. 603 *e*; see the account in Bruns, *Literarische Porträt*, p. 50 f. Cf. also Steven, *C.Q.* 1933, p. 154.

and which we know from the gold and white effeminates
of the Meidias painter. If Polygnotus and Sophocles were
friends, this friendship is another link between Sophocles
and the circle of Cimon.

The third and strongest link is Ion of Chios. Ion certainly met Sophocles when Sophocles came to Chios as
general in 440, but, as Ion may have been in Athens as
early as 470 and certainly won a victory at the Dionysia
between 452 and 449, it is likely that the two poets already
knew one another; the fragments of Ion's tragedies are
strongly marked by the influence of Sophocles. Ion was
also a friend of Cimon, and in his *Epidemiae* compared
Cimon and Pericles to the disadvantage of Pericles.[1]
Pericles' manner in company was arrogant and ill bred;
he was haughty and scornful of others. Ion preferred
Cimon's taste and culture and natural grace in society.
He also shared Cimon's love of Sparta. In Ion's account
of the dinner-party in Chios at which both poets were
present, Sophocles shows that very culture and natural
grace which Ion praises in Cimon.

All these indications are slight in themselves, but taken
together they seem to show that Sophocles belonged to
that aristocratic, cultured, philospartan circle which during the first half of the century was led by Cimon and
which welcomed such distinguished foreigners as Ion and
Polygnotus. This environment would suit Sophocles' own
cast of thought so far as that can be deduced from his plays.

Another distinguished foreigner must be added to the
list of Sophocles' friends, a later arrival in Athens, Herodotus. Sophocles wrote an ode to Herodotus of which a
line and a half are preserved;[2] 'Sophocles made an ode for

---

[1] Plutarch, *Pericles*, 5.

[2] *Anth. Lyr.* i, p. 67. Jacoby, *R.E. Supplt.* ii, p. 233, supposes that this
Herodotus is not the historian. Contrast Rasch, *Commentationes Jenenses*,
x. p. 4.

Herodotus when he was fifty-five.' Sophocles was fifty-five in 441/2. We know that Herodotus went to Thurii about this time and he may well have come to Athens on his way. The close connexion between the works of the two writers is best explained by a personal acquaintance.

The public life of Sophocles begins for us with the year 443/2. The inscriptions of this year preserve the name of Sophocles as Hellenotamias, or president of the imperial treasury.[1] It is usually assumed that this Sophocles was the poet, and there is no reason to doubt the identification, although the fact is not mentioned in any literary source. This was always a post of great responsibility, as the Hellenotamias was in control of the finances of the empire, and especially of the tribute from the allies. In this particular year, in addition to the ordinary business, the tribute was rearranged.

In 440 Sophocles was elected *strategos*. He served with Pericles in the Samian war and went with the detachment which was sent to collect help from Chios and Lesbos. At Chios he met Ion and related at dinner that Pericles said that he was a good poet but a bad general. On the same expedition both Pericles and Sophocles were defeated by the philosopher Melissus. This generalship in the Samian war is well supported by the evidence.[2]

The 'Life'[3] in speaking of Sophocles' colleagues in the generalship couples Thucydides and Pericles as 'the first men in the city'. The only Thucydides who could be so described is the son of Melesias, who was Cimon's brother-in-law and led the opposition to Pericles. As he was in

---

[1] *Suppl. Epigr. Graecum*, 5, 1931, xii. 36.

[2] *Life*, 1; Ion *ap.* Athenaeum, loc. cit. (cf. Cic. *Off.* i. 144); Thuc. i. 116. 1; Plut. *Pericles*, 26; Suidas, s.v. *Melissus*.

[3] See Note G, at end, p. 181.

exile from 443 to 433,[1] he cannot have been general in the Samian war. Unless there is a confusion in our source, Sophocles must have been general with Thucydides in another year. We are told that Thucydides was general in 444/3 and Sophocles may have been his colleague then.[2] Or Thucydides may have been again elected general after his ostracism and Sophocles may have served with him in the year 428.

The further statement of the 'Life' about Sophocles' generalship in the war with the Anaeans contains a chronological confusion. Either the figure for Sophocles' age is wrong and this generalship is in fact the Samian generalship of which we have already spoken (and some at least of the Anaeans were Samian refugees); or the date is wrong and Sophocles was general in the Anaean war of 428[3] (it will be remembered that he produced no plays that year).

There remains the generalship with Nicias, attested by Plutarch. This cannot coincide with the generalship with Thucydides because Sophocles could not be the oldest on any board that contained the son of Melesias, who was born in 500 or earlier. As Plutarch expressly calls Sophocles the poet, it is wanton to suppose that he has confused him with the other Sophocles. It has also been suggested that Aristophanes in the *Peace*[4] is referring to the other Sophocles when he says that 'Sophocles will put to sea on a sieve for money'. But as Aristophanes goes on to speak of the poet Cratinus, he also certainly means the poet Sophocles.

[1] Wade-Gery, *J.H.S.* 1932, p. 206. The Thucydides who was general in the Samian war cannot have been either the son of Melesias or the historian (Thuc. i. 117. 2).

[2] Mr. Wade-Gery doubts this generalship of Thucydides, but on no convincing grounds (op. cit., p. 222).

[3] Thuc. iii. 32. 2. Σαμίων τῶν ἐξ ’Αναίων; Thuc. iii. 19. 2. the Anaean war; cf. Blumenthal, *R.E.* iii a. 1044.

[4] Schmid-Stählin, p. 319, n. 1, suggests this confusion in Plutarch; Drew, *Cl. Rev.* 1928, p. 56 in Aristophanes.

We can take the two references together and assume that Sophocles was general in one of the years in which Nicias was general, 426–3. Both the Anaean war and the earlier Samian war mentioned by the scholiast to the *Peace* seem too distant to justify Aristophanes' gibe.

But another possible interpretation of the passage in the *Peace* must be mentioned. According to Dicaeopolis in the *Acharnians* ambassadors as well as generals 'profiteered' in the Archidamian war. The 'Life' says that Sophocles served on embassies, and it is possible that he was ambassador and not general when he sailed upon a sieve for money. In any case we have evidence for considerable public service between 441 and 421.

This public service may have continued till Sophocles' extreme old age. Aristotle tells a story of Sophocles in the *Rhetoric* which shows that he was one of the ten *probouloi* chosen to manage the affairs of Athens after the failure of the Sicilian expedition. It seems quite likely that the poet, who had had, as we have seen, considerable experience, was one of the 'older men' who were chosen in this crisis. Aristotle also speaks twice of a trial in which Sophocles was involved.[1] It has been suggested that in all three passages another Sophocles and not the poet is meant. But as Aristotle certainly refers to the poet on eight other occasions in the *Rhetoric*, and as he gives no indication that he does not mean the poet whenever he says Sophocles, the onus of proof is on those who deny the identification. It is pleasant to believe that the poet who had served his country as Hellenotamias and on embassies and at least three times as general, was called out again in his extreme old age to serve her in her hour of need.

[1] Sophocles, *Proboulos*; Aristotle, *Rhetoric*, iii. 1419ᵃ25 (cf. Thuc. viii. 1. 3). See Wilamowitz, *Aristot. u. Athen*, i, p. 102, n. 6. Objections: Cope in his Commentary on *Rhet*. i. 14. 3; Swoboda in *R.E.* iii *a*. 1095. Minor references; *Rhet*. iii. 1416ᵃ15; *Rhet*. i. 1374ᵇ36.

The 'Life' says that Sophocles was exceedingly religious, and supports this assertion by the following story. Heracles informed Sophocles in a dream where a stolen wreath was to be found. Sophocles was rewarded by the people with a talent for this information. He then founded a shrine to the Informer Heracles. He performed a more important religious service in connexion with the cult of Asclepius. The *parados* of the *Tyrannus* has a vivid description of a plague which must have been founded on the great plague at the beginning of the Peloponnesian war. One of the consequences of this plague was the introduction of the cult of Asclepius into Athens in the year 420. Sophocles received the god into his private house until the official quarters were ready and wrote a paean in his honour. For these services he was honoured after his death as the hero Dexion. He was also priest of Halon, a minor deity connected with Asclepius.[1]

A famous story of Sophocles' old age has survived in various accounts.[2] According to this story Sophocles was sued for madness by his son Iophon. Iophon was his son by his lawful wife, Nicostrate; he had another son, Ariston, by the Sicyonian *hetaira*, Theoris. Iophon charges Sophocles with lavishing all his affection on Ariston's son, the younger Sophocles. The old man proved to the jury that he was not mad by reciting verses from the *Coloneus*. These are the main lines of the story but the details vary in different sources. Probably the whole is a fiction. The 'Life', in telling this story, says that Sophocles put Iophon into a play; in this play Iophon was jealous of the younger Sophocles and accused his father to the *phratores*. The 'Life' then goes on to quote Satyrus for Sophocles' self-defence. Satyrus, as we know from the fragments of his

[1] Sophocles honoured as Dexion: *Etym. M.* p. 256. 6. The paean: *Anth. Lyr.* i, p. 67. Halon: see Schmid-Stählin, p. 319. 7.
[2] See Schmid-Stählin, p. 321, for literature.

'Life of Euripides', is a quite untrustworthy source and
went to the poets of the old comedy for his information.
A comedy may well have provided him with this story.
For, although no one will believe that Sophocles put
Iophon into a play, a comic poet may very well have put
both Sophocles and Iophon into a play. Now Iophon is
said to have accused Sophocles to the *phratores* and Leucon
produced a play called *Phratores* in 421.[1] If we assume that
Sophocles read in his defence verses from the *Tyrannus*,
not the *Coloneus*—and Satyrus only says the *Oedipus*—
this play may be Satyrus' source. Some scholars have
nevertheless accepted his story and seen the reflection
of these private troubles of Sophocles in the Polynices
scene of the *Coloneus*. Others have used it to reconstruct
Sophocles' family tree.[2] Both procedures are quite without justification. The only members of Sophocles' family
for whom there is any evidence are Iophon and Iophon's
son the younger Sophocles.

By good fortune we have a true account[3] of Sophocles'
old age to put against this fiction. Dionysus in the *Frogs*,
which was produced in the year that Sophocles died, refuses to summon Sophocles from the dead, because he
wants to see what Iophon can do without his father. This
proves that father and son were working happily together
till the end. Nor can the story of the dispute be recon-
ciled with the epitaph which has survived from Phrynichus' *Muses*: 'Blessed Sophocles who lived long and died
happy and wise when he had written many beautiful
tragedies. He ended well, having suffered no ill.' Aristophanes' epithet 'content', by which he describes Sophocles
elsewhere in the *Frogs*, and the picture which Plato draws

---

[1] See Note H, at end, p. 182.

[2] *Polynices scene*: e.g. Robert, *Ödipus*, i. 470 f.; Turolla, *Saggio*, p. 196.
Family tree: e.g. Blumenthal, *R.E.* iii a. 1042.

[3] Aristophanes, *Frogs*, 78, 82; Phrynichus, fr. 51; Plato, *Rep.* 329 B.

at the beginning of the *Republic*, agree with this epitaph. Sophocles died a contented and peaceful old man.

The happy temperament of which Aristophanes and Phrynichus speak was famous. 'In a word', the 'Life' says, 'he had such charm of character that he was beloved by all.' We can see a reflection of it in the satyr plays. Sophocles shows the southerner's ability to throw off the serious side of religion, and he adopts the tone and feeling of the Homeric hymns. The *Ichneutae* is best known to us. Apollo's proclamation, the hunt of the satyrs, their horror at the sound of the lyre, the riddling dialogue with the nymph and her indignation that her son should be regarded as a thief are all in the spirit of the hymn to Hermes. We can catch something also of the atmosphere of the *Inachus*, of the arrival of Hermes in his cap of darkness, the piping of Argus, and the account of the entry of Wealth.

Ion's story of the dinner-party at Chios shows the same grace and charm in Sophocles' behaviour. We are fortunate in having this contemporary portrait. Ion tells us nothing of the careful artist whose perfectly constructed plays won no less than eighteen victories, nor of the religious citizen who was thought worthy to receive Asclepius in his house and who was honoured as a hero after his death. But we see something of Sophocles as a man. Here is the evidence for that sensitiveness to beauty and colour which we feel behind the magic lines in the prologue of the *Electra*,[1] 'See already the sun's bright lamp awakes the birds and tunes their morning voices, and sable starry night has vanished.' And Ion's closing picture shows us Sophocles' place in the life of fifth-century Athens. 'In state business he was neither clever nor energetic, but like one of the Athenian nobles.' Knowing Ion's political affinities, we can interpret these words. Sophocles had

[1] 17 f. (tr. Robert Willis).

not the quickness and the cunning of a Themistocles; the *Tyrannus* gives his verdict on this kind of intelligence. Nor had he the meddlesome energy which was the prized virtue of the Athenian democrat; but he had that 'quietness', which is praised by the Just Argument in the *Clouds* and which is accounted a virtue in Greek aristocratic thought from Pindar to Plato.[1] He served Athens when she needed him and loved her so much that no invitation from foreign courts could tempt him, like Aeschylus and Euripides, to leave her. He was like one of the Athenian nobles—Cimon or Thucydides, son of Melesias.

[1] *Clouds*, 1007; for history of this idea see Wade-Gery, *J.H.S.* 1932, p. 224.

II. Thought

SOPHOCLES was 'like one of the Athenian nobles'.
He was religious as they were. He served his country
when she needed him. He was open to the cultural influences of his time, but was not clever in the Themisto-
clean sense. Our present task is to consider how far this
picture is substantiated by the evidence of the plays and
fragments. We shall then be able to say both what
Sophocles himself thought and what thinkers influenced
him.

It may, however, be argued that Sophocles is a dramatic
poet and not a philosopher, and that the views expressed
in his plays are the views of his characters in their particular
situation and not his own views for all time. But we know
from the *Frogs* of Aristophanes that in the fifth century
the poet was regarded as a teacher, and Sophocles himself
said that he represented men as they ought to be represented.[1] The dramatist did not need to be an original
thinker, but he was expected to use his play as a means of
conveying ideas and ideals to his public.

His instruction is contained partly in the significant
utterances of characters and chorus and partly in his whole
treatment of the story. For instance, in the *Antigone*
Creon's speech about anarchy and the song of the chorus
about the dangers of intellect have a significance beyond
the play. Nor can one doubt that the doxology sung by
the chorus at the end sums up Sophocles' view of the story.

[1] Cf. Jaeger, *Paideia*, p. 355 f.

'Wisdom is the chief part of happiness. There must be no irreverence towards the gods. The great words of the proud pay a price of great blows and teach wisdom in old age.' Ideas such as piety, modesty, nobility run through the plays like the *leitmotifs* of a Wagnerian opera and must have been virtues which Sophocles himself valued.[1]

Sophocles' approach to a traditional story can be seen most clearly from his *Electra*. Besides the earlier accounts of Homer and Pindar, the *Choephori* of Aeschylus and the *Electra* of Euripides both survive and both are probably earlier than Sophocles' play. The central problem of this story is the matricide and its religious and personal consequences. Aeschylus has a further play, the *Eumenides*, in which to present his solution; Euripides allows his characters to criticize the morality of Apollo's oracle and repent after the deed. Sophocles transfers the emphasis to the character of Electra. The climax of his play is the recognition scene; the murders are placed in the unemphatic position at the end and neither is reported in a messenger-speech. Clytemnestra is painted as black as possible; no Cassandra gives her a pretext for vengeance; she has instituted a festival on the day of Agamemnon's death, and she prays to Apollo to kill her own children. Therefore her death and Aegisthus' death can be represented as justifiable and pious acts. In proportion as the importance of the murders decreases, the importance of Electra increases. The whole plot is designed to make the spectator identify himself with Electra and to show her character from the greatest possible number of aspects. Sophocles' innovations are directed to two ends: the justification of Apollo, who has given the command to punish the criminals, and the portrayal of Electra, a noble lady living in complete isolation in the house of her father's murderers.

[1] See, for detailed references, p. 107, n.

The theme of Sophocles' innovations[1] could be pursued further, but we can see from his treatment of the Electra story that he moulded his stuff with a definite purpose and that he had definite ideas and ideals which he wanted to communicate to the public. We are therefore justified in searching the plays for his views on the religious and human problems of his time and in attempting to discover what thinkers particularly influenced him and what is his position in the history of Greek thought.

The ordinary Athenian accepted the Homeric mythology and the popular religion; the intellectual rejected them, whether he became a sceptic or interpreted the gods in terms of allegory or philosophy. Sophocles stands between the two extremes, and we must try to define his middle position. His choruses pray to the gods of popular religion. When the women of Trachis hear of Heracles' victory they sing a paean to Apollo and Artemis just as they might in the fifth century. The human gods of Homer and the Homeric hymns reappear in the satyr plays, Apollo and Hermes in the *Ichneutae*, Hermes and Iris in the *Inachus*; and we may conjecture that other gods were handled in the same way in the *Eris* and *Crisis*. But the satyr plays were burlesques and had different conventions from tragedy. The only god or goddess whom Sophocles brings on the stage in the surviving plays is Athena in the *Ajax*. Here the contrast with the Homeric Athena is instructive. In Homer Odysseus is the personal friend or favourite of Athena. In Sophocles her protection is based on the character of Odysseus. He is 'modest', and the gods love the modest. Sophocles has purified and moralized the Homeric Athena, who only survives in the diseased imagination of Ajax.

Purification and moralization of the Homeric mythology and popular religion is characteristic of the whole

[1] See Note I, at end, p. 182.

religious thought of Sophocles.[1] We have already seen it in the *Electra*. Apollo's command to Orestes to kill his mother, and Orestes' subsequent punishment, do not redound to the god's credit. Sophocles therefore suppresses and emends. Other poets from Solon to Euripides, including the pious Pindar, may criticize myths and discuss the origin of the gods; but for Sophocles such matters are too holy to be discussed and he does his emendation silently.[2]

Having defined Sophocles' general position, we can proceed to consider what he tells us about the gods' nature and their powers.[3] Zeus is supreme. He is 'the steward of things to come', just as he is the steward of war in Homer. 'The dice of Zeus always fall well.'[4] Sophocles' noblest and most complete expression of this idea is in a chorus of the *Antigone*: 'Thy power, O Zeus, what human transgression can restrain? It neither sleep, which ages all, nor the unwearied months of the gods conquer; but a ruler unaged by time, thou dwellest in the flashing light of Olympus.' The sublimity of language reminds us of Aeschylus and Pindar; the thought is nearer to Xenophanes and Heraclitus than to the popular religion.[5] But

---

[1] Cf. Nestle, *Griechische Religiosität, II*, p. 83.

[2] He only once comes near to such explicit criticism. In an early play, the *Trachiniae* (498 f.), the chorus sing, 'I pass over (παρέβαν) the things of the gods and I do not tell how Cypris deceived the son of Cronus or dark Hades or Poseidon the earthquaker.' This exception to Sophocles' usual silence may be due to the form of the song, since, as Kranz has seen (*Stasimon*, p. 217, 254), this chorus is Pindaric in form and *parabasis* of this kind is common in Pindar.

[3] He often speaks of the gods or god without naming a particular god, cf. Weinstock, *Sophokles*, p. 272; Wehrli, λαθὲ βιώσας, p. 98, particularly n. 3.

[4] Fr. 590, cf. Δ 84. Fr. 895 cf. Simonides, fr. 63; Pindar, *P*. ii. 90.

[5] 604 f. (cf. *O.C.* 607). For the language, cf. Aesch. *Suppl*. 91 f.; Pindar, *P*. ii. 91. For the thought, cf. Xenophanes, fr. 23–5; Heraclitus, fr. 102.

although Sophocles may have been influenced by the philosophers, he nowhere, like Euripides, alludes directly to philosophic conceptions of God.

Zeus himself and Apollo as the son of Zeus can see everything. They can communicate their foreknowledge to men through the medium of oracles, omens, and dreams. This is the common belief of the poets from Homer onwards. In the plays of Aeschylus oracles, dreams, and omens are quoted and have their fulfilment. But Sophocles regards them as something more than a part of the traditional religion. They are the justification for the traditional religion. If they are not true, there is no reason for believing in the gods. The chorus sing in the *Tyrannus*,[1] 'I will not go to worship at the inviolate navel of the earth . . . if these (oracles) do not come true, clear for all men to show. . . . For Laius' old prophecies are fading and men thrust them aside, and nowhere is clear honour paid to Apollo but religion is perishing.' Here Sophocles clearly states his own belief and as clearly criticizes the unbelief of his contemporaries. Even where the oracle is part of the story, the dramatist need not emphasize it; Sophocles shows his belief in oracles by making them the framework of his plots. The *Trachiniae*, *Tyrannus*, *Electra*, *Philoctetes*, and *Coloneus* all begin with the announcement of an oracle and end with its fulfilment, and the oracle is one of the leading motives in all these plays.

Oracles come true, though not always in the expected sense. At the end of the *Trachiniae* Heracles discovers the truth of the oracle which he had misinterpreted; he thought that release from toil meant happiness, whereas in fact it meant death. Oedipus went into exile to avoid killing his father and marrying his mother, and by going into exile fulfilled the oracle. The nearest parallels to both these

[1] 897, cf. *El.* 498 f.

stories are in Herodotus;[1] Cambyses was told that he should die in Ecbatana, but he never thought that there was an Ecbatana in Egypt. Croesus dreamt that his son should be killed by a spear wound and took every precaution to prevent it, but the dream nevertheless came true. Herodotus uses prophecies as a framework for these stories in exactly the same way as Sophocles. Sophocles' whole position is summed up in a fragment of Heraclitus,[2] 'The lord, whose oracle is in Delphi, does not speak out or conceal, but gives a sign'.

In the *Tyrannus* both Apollo and his ministers are triumphantly justified and the scepticism of Iocasta and Oedipus condemned. Sophocles is supporting the traditional religion against contemporary attacks. Criticism of oracles was particularly common at the time of the Peloponnesian war. False oracles were produced in large quantities, and the oracle-monger became a figure for the comic stage. Thucydides tells us that only one of the prophecies about the Peloponnesian war had come true, and Euripides in his *Philoctetes* (produced in 431) said that prophecy was a mere delusion.[3] In this atmosphere Sophocles wrote the *Tyrannus* to defend what was for him, as for Socrates, one of the basic facts of religion.

We have dwelt at some length on Zeus and Apollo because they are of supreme importance for the religious thought of Sophocles. Cypris and Eros are in a rather different position. It might almost be said that they are not personalities but mythological names for the power of love. Sophocles' Aphrodite has none of the personal ill-will of the goddess in the *Hippolytus*. When the chorus in the *Trachiniae* sing that 'Cypris is shown to be the

[1] iii. 64; i. 34. Perhaps the oracle of the ship turned to stone in the *Odyssey* is the prototype of the oracular framework.

[2] Fr. 93; cf. Soph. fr. 771.

[3] Euripides, fr. 793. See Nestle, *Protagoras*, p. 21.

doer of these things', Cypris is not a personal goddess wilfully leading men astray, since from another standpoint love can be called a disease.[1] Cypris and Eros are used interchangeably; they are love in the same sense that Ares is war and Hephaestus is fire. In the *Antigone* not only gods and men but fish, beasts of the field, and wild animals are said to be victims of Eros. The equation of the force which compels animals to mate with the love of gods and of men seems to belong to the fifth century and probably comes from the philosophers. Our earliest reference to the love which attacks beasts as well as men is in the *Supplices* of Aeschylus. But the closest parallel to the passage in the *Antigone* is a fragment of Empedocles,[2] where Cypris 'leads the unmusical tribe of prolific fish'. The thought of the philosophers has influenced Sophocles and the personal and prejudiced goddess of Homer has become something more like a cosmic force.

The Fates, the Furies, and other figures are rather below the gods in rank. Fate has changed in the same direction as Cypris. Sophocles never speaks of three Fates, nor does he give them their names. For him fate is another way of looking at the will of the gods. In the *Philoctetes* the chorus speak of 'the destiny (πότμος) of the gods', just as Pindar speaks of the fate of the gods. Later Philoctetes says that he is being conveyed by 'the mighty fate and the wisdom of friends and the all powerful god who brought these things to pass'. Zeus is the agent, mighty Fate is his will, and he works through the wisdom of friends. Empedocles is expressing the same relation between the gods and fate when he speaks of 'an utterance of fate, an ancient decree of the gods'.[3] This interpretation of fate holds even for a passage in the *Antigone*, where there seems at

---

[1] *Trach.* 860; *Trach.* 544 = fr. 149.
[2] *Ant.* 782; Aesch. *Suppl.* 999; Empedocles, fr. 74.
[3] *Phil.* 1116, 1466; Pindar, *O.* ii. 37; Empedocles, fr. 115.

first sight to be a conflict between Fate and the gods as
in the *Prometheus* and once in Herodotus.[1] But when
Sophocles says that Ares cannot escape Fate, Ares is not
the god but simply War.

Two other figures have, like Fate, some share in the
governing of the world, Fortune and Time. The lyric
poets speak of Fortune as a force in the ordering of human
affairs and Empedocles made her a first cause. Euripides
carries on this tradition.[2] Democritus, however, thought
that Fortune was invented by men to cover their own
folly. This may well have been the view of Sophocles; in
two passages where Fortune is said to rule human affairs
the speakers are a homely messenger and the sceptical
Iocasta.[3] Sophocles' world is ruled by the gods and the
changes are normally ascribed to them; Fortune is only
called in by the uneducated and the sceptical. But in the
later plays of Euripides the force in the background is
Chance, and Fortune governs the world.

Time is another of these abstract concepts which attain
personality in the mouth of the poet. Ajax, for instance,
begins his monologue, 'Time gives birth to things unseen
and when they have appeared hides them again'. It has
been suggested that Sophocles is following the Orphics in
his personification of time. This may be true ultimately.
But for Sophocles Pindar and Heraclitus are more obvious
sources; Pindar speaks of 'crafty Time, hung over men's
heads, complicating the course of life'.[4] Sophocles sees
Time as a person and therefore can speak of the agency of

[1] *Ant.* 951; Aesch. *P.V.* 517 f.; Hdt. i. 91.

[2] Archilochus, fr. 8; Bacchylides, xiv. 3; Pindar, *O.* xii. 1; Empedocles,
A 48; Euripides, *Hec.* 491, *Hel.* 1137, *Tro.* 1203, *H.F.* 480; cf. Pohlenz,
Gr. Trag., p. 413 f.

[3] *Ant.* 1158, *O.T.* 977, cf. fr. 575; Democritus, fr. 119; cf. Sheppard,
Oedipus Tyrannus, pp. 157, 161.

[4] *Aj.* 646, *O.T.* 1213; Pindar, *I.* viii. 28; Heraclitus, fr. 52; cf. Schmid-
Stählin, p. 462; Sheppard, op. cit., p. 140.

Time. But this agency is different in kind from the agency of gods and men. It is symbolical rather than real.

We have seen that the Fates have lost their position as independent and ancient powers and have become a personification of the will of the gods. Something of the same transmutation overtakes the Furies. Originally the Furies are goddesses who pursue wrongdoers, particularly murderers, and a kinsman could call down a Fury on a kinsman who had sinned against him. The belief in Furies goes back to Homer and the idea is still present in Herodotus and Euripides. Herodotus speaks of Vengeance (τίσις) and not of Furies; the Vengeance of Demaratus attacks Leotychidas and Cleomenes. In the *Hercules* of Euripides the chorus think that the Penalties (ποίναι) of Lycus are destroying the house of Heracles.[1] Aeschylus describes the Furies, 'not women but Gorgons, and yet I will not liken them to the Gorgon mould. . . . These are wingless, black, utterly horrible'. They are grim demons of a more primitive religion who terrify their beholders and are spurned from the converse of the gods. In Sophocles they are not described, except that in the *Ajax* they are 'holy and swift-footed' and in the *Electra* 'many-handed, many-footed', and 'bronze-footed'. They are not the grim demons of Aeschylus, but 'holy daughters of the gods', who are coupled with justice. They are no longer independent powers but ministers of the gods' justice. Here again Sophocles reminds us of Heraclitus, who speaks of the Furies as 'allies of justice, finding out the sun, if he passes beyond his bounds'.[2]

We see the same advance from a more primitive religion when we examine the attitude of the gods to virtue and vice. In the *Coloneus* Oedipus tells Theseus to 'believe that the gods look upon the pious man and look upon the

[1] Hdt. vi. 72. 1, 84. 3; Euripides, *H.F.* 889, &c.
[2] See Note J, at end, p. 183.

impious, but that no unholy man ever escaped'.[1] The
gods punish vice, but the sins which the gods punish are
referred to in general terms—impiety, injustice, unholi-
ness, &c. Sophocles does not insist on a holiness which is
merely formal. In Homer, however, the omission of sacrifice is always punished, and later writers follow him. The
gods had every reason to be angry, since they got their
sustenance from the savour of the sacrifice. It is surprising
to find this belief still surviving in Aeschylus.[2] The en-
lightened Athenians of the later fifth century abandoned
it, and it is ridiculed in the *Birds* of Aristophanes.[3] Some
thinkers went farther and threw over the whole idea of
divine punishment. Euripides was among them. For, although some of his characters believe in divine justice, his
own position is rather represented by a fragment of
Melanippe:[4] 'Do you think that the crimes fly on wings
to the gods and then some one writes them in Zeus' folded
tablets and Zeus reads them and gives judgement to men ?'
Sophocles, however, remains in the tradition of Hesiod
and Pindar,[5] but purifies and generalizes the old belief.

The gods administer justice in accordance with their
laws. In the *Antigone* they are 'unwritten and sure laws
of the gods not for yesterday or to-day, but eternal'; in
the *Tyrannus* the chorus sing of laws which are 'set forth
high footed, born in the heavenly aether, of which Olympus alone is father, nor did the mortal growth of men bear
them, nor will forgetfulness ever put them to sleep'.[6]
They are partly moral commands such as 'bury the dead',
'avenge the dead', 'commit no injustice', and partly univer-
sal principles such as the danger of excess and the changes

---

[1] *O.C.* 278; cf. *Aj.* 132, *O.T.* 892, *El.* 1382.
[2] Aesch. *Cho.* 255. [3] Ar. *Birds*, 1516 ff.
[4] Euripides, fr. 508.
[5] Hesiod, *Op.* 280, 320 f.; Pindar, *O.* iii. 70.
[6] *Ant.* 454 f., *O.T.* 865 f., *Aj.* 1130, *El.* 1095, *Ant.* 611, *Trach.* 126.

of human fortunes. For both there are analogies in other
writers from the time of Hesiod onwards, and Sophocles
is writing in a well-established tradition.¹ Hesiod's Zeus
appointed this law for men, that the beasts should eat
each other but men should have justice. Empedocles, in
phraseology which recalls the *Tyrannus*, says that 'the law
of all (not to kill the living) is stretched through the wide
ruling heaven and the unapproachable light'. The Aeschylean divine law, that the doer shall suffer and the suf-
ferer learn, is rather a cosmological principle than a moral
law. Similarly, for Heraclitus the law of god is the principle on which the universe works and 'to speak wisely a
man must arm himself with it as a city with a law and
much more strongly. For all human laws are nourished
by the one divine law.' Sophocles is perhaps nearest in
phrasing and idea to Heraclitus and Empedocles.

But there is another tradition which is completely opposed to the Sophoclean. This tradition can be traced
back to a fragment of Pindar, where law which is the king
of gods and men justifies the act of violence. It is the will
of a tyrant. The next stage is the Zeus of the *Prometheus*,
who is a tyrant and 'rules lawlessly by new laws'. Later
still Thucydides in the Melian dialogues makes the Athenians state the right of the stronger as an eternal law, and
the wording suggests that it is an intended travesty of
Sophocles' description of the divine laws in the *Antigone*.
Yet another development from the fragment of Pindar
can be seen in a passage of Euripides' *Hecuba*,² where Hecuba speaks of the law which rules the gods: 'for it is by

¹ Hesiod, *Op.* 276; Empedocles, fr. 135; Aesch. *Ag.* 1563, 177; Heraclitus, fr. 114; cf. Aesch. *Eum.* 171, 391; Gorgias, fr. 6; Thuc. ii. 37. 3,
iii. 82. 6; Euripides, *Hipp.* 98; cf. Nestle, *Class. Phil.* v, p. 137.
² Pindar, fr. 152; Aesch. *P.V.* 150; Thuc. v. 105; Euripides, *Hec.* 798;
Critias, fr. 25. I have left Pindar at the beginning of this succession, but
I am not satisfied that the fragment has yet been interpreted correctly.

law that we believe in them and live differentiating right and wrong'. Some of the sophists regarded belief in the gods as a human convention, and Euripides is here quoting them. It is interesting to find this complete inversion of the Sophoclean conception in a play which was produced within a few years of the *Tyrannus*.

Now that we have considered the general conception of the divine laws, we must consider their content more closely. The commands to bury the dead and avenge the dead are commonplaces of Greek thought, and parallels are unnecessary. The principle that excess is dangerous is also a commonplace, but there are two opinions as to the source of the danger. The excess itself may be of various kinds: excessive physical strength, excessive pride, or excessive cleverness.[1] The danger comes either from the gods who are jealous of man's success or from man himself who is tempted by his power or wit to commit a crime.

The jealousy of the gods is stated clearly by Herodotus: 'god is wont to dock everything that stands out.'[2] But the only characters in Sophocles who quote it are Aegisthus and Philoctetes.[3] Aegisthus is a tyrant and Philoctetes is embittered by suffering. In both cases the jealousy of the gods is not Sophocles' own interpretation of the situation, but the private opinion of a wrong-headed character.

Sophocles' own view is stated by the chorus of the

[1] *Physical strength*, *Aj.* 1250; *pride*, *Ant.* 473; *cleverness*, *Ant.* 331 f. Note particularly the familiar command not to 'talk big'—Soph. *Aj.* 386, *El.* 830.

[2] Hdt. vii. 10, ε cf. i. 32. 1, iii. 40. 2; Pindar, *P.* x. 30; Aesch. *Pers.* 354, *Ag.* 750; Euripides, *H.F.* 840. Svend Ranulf, *The Jealousy of the Gods*, has made a useful collection of passages but fails to recognize that the divine punishment of arrogant boasting is not an instance of divine jealousy.

[3] *El.* 1466 (cf. Wehrli, op. cit., p. 98, n. 1), *Phil.* 449.

Antigone.[1] It is an eternal law of the gods 'that nothing very large comes into the life of men without *ate*', for men conceive hopes which lead them astray. The gods are only responsible in so far as they have made the principle that excess is dangerous, that anything big is in the region of *ate*. But man is responsible for the act of *hybris* which brings on the *ate* or infatuation. The words *ate* and *hybris* are as old as Homer, and the doctrine can be traced through Hesiod and Solon to Pindar and Aeschylus who give it its classical form.[2] Man becomes too proud and commits an act of *hybris*; god sends *ate* upon him and he becomes infatuated; then he falls and learns sense by suffering. Pindar's Ixion learnt clearly in what he had sinned, for '*Hybris* drove him into *ate* and soon he had a fitting punishment'. This doctrine is a keystone of the Aeschylean theology, and he distinguishes his position clearly. In the *Agamemnon* he says in effect that others may believe in the jealousy of the gods, but he has a view of his own. Not wealth, but the impious deed, the act of *hybris*, meets with punishment. Sophocles is repeating this Aeschylean idea in the chorus of the *Antigone* which we have quoted. Creon is a dramatization of it. When he perceives his disaster, he says that his own folly has caused his son to perish.[3] 'I have learnt my bitter lesson. It was a god that smote me then with crushing weight.' His decree was an act of *hybris*; his acts during the play have been heaven-sent infatuation; now he has learnt by suffering. Sophocles stands very near to Aeschylus, and the difference between them is not a difference of thought

---

[1] 613, cf. Theognis 321; Democritus, fr. 173.

[2] Homer, 1 505 f., T 86 f.; Hesiod, *Op.* 213; Solon, i. 33 f.; Pindar, *P.* ii. 45; Aeschylus, *Ag.* 177 with 750 f.

[3] *Ant.* 1272 with 620. Cf. Ajax: he commits *hybris* by attempting to murder the generals, Athena maddens him (51), then he sees his fault in the monologue (646 f.). Probably the *Tereus* had the same idea (fr. 592).

but a difference of dramatic emphasis. Sophocles is more interested in Creon himself than in Creon's *hybris* and its results.

Although Sophocles inherited the *hybris* theory from Aeschylus and believed with him that the gods punish crime, he apparently did not also believe that the punishment could continue from generation to generation, a view held by other thinkers both before and after Aeschylus.[1] Sophocles undoubtedly knew it, and two passages in the *Antigone* and one in the *Electra*[2] could be interpreted as expressions of it. But more probably Sophocles is using the terminology of the inherited curse to express the simpler notion of a succession of woes in a single house. In another place in the *Antigone* the chorus say that Antigone has inherited her father's fierce spirit, which looks like a rationalization of the inherited curse. Although the inherited curse was a leading motive in Aeschylus' Theban trilogy, there is no trace of the idea in the *Tyrannus*. In the *Coloneus*[3] Oedipus says, '*Perhaps* the gods have long been angry with the race'; he recognizes that the inherited curse is a possible explanation of his troubles, but rejects the explanation. If this reading of Sophocles is correct, he is again purifying, moralizing, and clarifying the ancient idea, not only in the interests of religion, but also in the interests of the personality of his characters.

The last of the divine laws is a cosmological principle. Zeus has ordained that all human affairs are subject to change. This change is often compared to natural phenomena and usually described as circular. For instance,

---

[1] Aesch. *Suppl.* 433, *Cho.* 61, 1065, &c.; Hesiod, *Op.* 284; Solon, i. 25 f.; Theognis, 203 (contrast 731 by another poet); Hdt. i. 91, vii. 137; Euripides, *Hipp.* 820, 831. [2] *Ant.* 582, 856; *El.* 504.

[3] *Ant.* 471, cf. Euripides, *H.F.* 1261, which should probably be interpreted as a rationalization. *O.C.* 965; Weinstock, op. cit., p. 198, overlooks the 'perhaps' which seems to me emphatic.

when Ajax declares that he will submit to the gods and
yield to Agamemnon, he compares his change of position
to the succession of winter and summer, night and day,
wind and calm, and sleep and waking.[1] Ultimately the
comparison of human fortunes to natural phenomena goes
back to Homer, who says that human fortunes are like the
leaves, some grow, some fade away. From him the comparison passes to the lyric poets. Archilochus for the first
time has the idea of continual motion, but with him it is
the ebb and flow of the tide and not the circular motion
of the *Ajax*. Circular motion is found again in Herodotus and Euripides. Herodotus speaks of a circle of
human affairs whose swing does not allow the same always
to be fortunate. Euripides says that the fruitful plants
of the earth and the race of men have the same circle.[2]
The circle must have been introduced at some time
between Archilochus and Sophocles. Probably the philosophers were responsible; the Ionian physicists made everything rise from a single element and return to it again.
Sophocles' source may well have been Heraclitus. One of
his fragments reminds us of the beginning of Ajax' solilo-
quy, 'these things having changed are those things, and
those things having changed are these things'.[3]

Man must take up some attitude to the gods and adopt
some line of conduct when faced with these vicissitudes.
A broad distinction may be drawn between two attitudes,
the pessimistic and the optimistic. Both can be found in
the plays of Sophocles, but the balance is in favour of
optimism. The extreme form of pessimism is not found

[1] Cf. *Trach.* 129; fr. 871; cf. Schmid-Stählin, p. 311, n. 6, who assumes
a Pythagorean origin; cf. also Pearson to fr. 871.

[2] Homer, Z 146; cf. Pindar, *P.* viii. 132; Sophocles, fr. 593; Archilochus,
fr. 67; Hdt. i. 207.2; Euripides, fr. 419.

[3] Heraclitus, fr. 88 (cf. *Aj.* 646–7), fr. 103; Anaximander, A. 14;
Xenophanes, fr. 27; Empedocles, fr. 17, 26.

in Sophocles. Theognis once states that man is not responsible for his actions because he is powerless before the gods, and Priam implies it when he tells Helen that not she but the gods are responsible for the siege of Troy.[1] Less extreme in its pessimism is another view which is also found in Homer and has a long history after him, the view that a man cannot expect better from the gods than a mixed lot.[2] This again is not directly stated in Sophocles, but it lies behind the pessimism of Odysseus, when, looking on the mad Ajax, he makes the common comparison, 'All we that live are nothing but images or a light shadow.'[3] But though Odysseus is pessimistic, Sophocles' own view is rather expressed by Athena when she tells Odysseus to draw the lesson of modesty from Ajax' troubles. Nor must Sophocles himself be accounted pessimistic when in the *Coloneus* he quotes a sentiment from Theognis, 'Not to be born best solves the riddle'.[4] The chorus are old and depressed by the troubles of Oedipus, and a pessimistic song is needed at this point in the plot.

Sophocles is not pessimistic; it is even an over-statement to call him resigned. When the chorus sing at the end of the *Trachiniae* that 'none of these things is not Zeus', they are making the gods responsible for all human joys and sorrows; in the same spirit the victors of Salamis ascribe their victory to the gods.[5] This recognition of the omnipotence of the gods does not abolish human responsibility and free will. Religious determinism and free will

[1] Theognis, 133; Homer, Γ 164; cf. Hdt. i. 45. 2, cf. Rohde, *Psyche*, ii, p. 236.

[2] Homer, ω 525; Mimnermus, fr. 2, 16; Simonides, fr. 10; Hdt. vii. 203. 2.

[3] For the image, cf. Pindar, *P*. viii. 135; Aesch. *Ag*. 1327; Euripides, *Medea* 1224. For the thought, cf. *O.T*. 1186, fr. 13, 945.

[4] *O.C*. 1224; Theognis, 425, cf. Bacchylides, v. 160; Euripides, fr. 287, cf. 452; Hdt. i. 31 (Cleobis and Biton).

[5] *Trach*. 1278, cf. *O.C*. 394, fr. 646; Hdt. vii. 139. 5.

are not incompatible. They may be the two sides of the
same act seen from the point of view of the gods and from
the point of view of man. From the standpoint of the
gods Zeus brings weal and woe upon men; from the
human standpoint man is free to act and is responsible
for his actions.[1] We have quoted the evidence for the
divine standpoint; the evidence for human responsibility
can be given very briefly: Antigone, Creon, and Philoctetes are all told by the chorus that they are responsible
for their misfortunes.[2] The belief in free will is already
found in Homer, 'Mortals blame the gods . . . but they
themselves by their own folly suffer ills beyond their fate'.
In Aeschylus,[3] in spite of the potency of the ancestral
curse the individual is responsible for his acts, Agamemnon
for the murder of Iphigenia and Clytemnestra for the
murder of Agamemnon; but Aeschylus is more interested
in the working of the ancestral curse than in the personality of his characters. In the later fifth century some
thinkers held that man's free choice was limited not by
the power of the gods but by the strength of his own
lower nature. Several times in Euripides the passions are
said to be stronger than the will.[4] In these passages he is
stating one form of the antithesis between nature (*physis*)
and law (*nomos*), which was a famous topic of discussion
during the second half of the fifth century. Sophocles'
interpretation is diametrically opposed to that of Euripides,
and where, as in the *Antigone*, the two are contrasted,
physis is the nobler and not the baser antagonist, not the
lower but the higher nature of Antigone.

A further distinction makes the compatibility between

[1] Turolla (*Saggio sulla poesia di Sofocle*, p. 25 f.) denies this. Wehrli
(op. cit., p. 100) sees both but finds them logically incompatible.
[2] *Ant.* 875, 1259; *Phil.* 1318; cf. *O.T.* 819.
[3] Homer, α 33; Solon, 8; Aesch. *Ag.* 218, 1505, *P.V.* 268.
[4] e.g. *Hipp.* 358, fr. 837, 912. *Physis* is discussed more fully below.

religious determinism and free will easier to understand.
Sophocles distinguishes between the motive and the act.
The motive comes from the agent's will, and for this he is
responsible; the act may not fulfil or may even directly
contradict his intentions, and for this he is not responsible.
When Deianira has sent Heracles a poisoned robe, she is
told that 'for them whose errors do not come from the
will anger is soft'.[1] The separation of motive from act is
a great ethical advance which seems to have been made
at the beginning of the fifth century or at the end of the
sixth; for us it appears first in Simonides.[2]

The recognition of the god's omnipotence does not
abolish human responsibility, but leads man to a definite
standard of conduct, which we have termed the optimistic
attitude to life. Man must stay within the bounds imposed on him by the gods, and he must endure the lot
which the gods have sent him. We may call these two
rules the negative and the positive side of his faith. The
negative side is expressed neatly in a fragment, 'mortal
growth should have mortal thoughts'. The idea occurs
elsewhere,[3] but Sophocles introduces the word (*physis*)
which implies that man's conduct towards the gods should
be regulated by the difference in their 'growth'. Two passages in Heraclitus and Pindar[4] which may well have influenced Sophocles illustrate his conception. Heraclitus
says that 'god calls man an infant, as man a child'. In
Pindar 'the race of men and gods is one but strength keeps
them apart . . . we are like the immortals in some way
either in mind or in growth'. In both these passages
god and man have the same *physis*, but god is at a more

---

[1] *Trach.* 727, cf. *O.C.* 548, fr. 665, 746; cf. Sheppard, op. cit., p. xxx f.
[2] Simonides, fr. 4. 20; cf. Bowra, *Class. Phil.* 1934, p. 230 f.
[3] Fr. 590, cf. 524; cf. Epicharmus, fr. 263; Aesch. *Pers.* 820; Alcman,
fr. 1. 50; Pindar, *O.* v. 53 f. Cf. also Democritus, fr. 3.
[4] Heraclitus, fr. 79; Pindar, *N.* vi. 1 (cf. Myres, *Political Ideas*, p. 156).

advanced stage of growth. Gods are greater than men, and the man who does not accept what they send is as foolish as the Homeric hero who seeks to overcome them in battle.[1]

Positively, it is the duty of man to endure what the gods send him. This duty can be traced back to Homer but has its most classical expression in Pindar, 'For one good thing the gods apportion men two bad. Fools cannot bear them decently but good men can, turning the fair outside.'[2] The pessimistic theory that the gods give man more bad than good is made the basis of the optimistic duty of endurance. Man should endure bad fortune. Oedipus says, 'Endurance has been taught me by sufferings and length of days and thirdly by my nobility'. The demand for fortitude is common in Greek literature, but it is interesting to see to what different writers ascribe the power to endure; for Archilochus endurance is a gift of the gods; for Pindar and Sophocles it depends on birth; Pericles ascribes it to education; and for Euripides it comes from the perception that misfortune is one of the necessities of our nature.[3] In good fortune man should remember that the gods dispense bad as well as good, and this remembrance gives rise to a sane and cautious outlook on life. 'You cannot tell the life of men until one dies whether it is bad or good in anything.'[4] Therefore man should get what pleasure he can out of his position. 'Our life would not be bad even in this state if we are happy.'[5] More than

---

[1] Fr. 196, cf. Homer, Z 128, &c.

[2] *P*. iii. 145; cf. 188; Archilochus, fr. 7. 5; Aesch. *Pers*. 293; Hdt. i. 87. 4.

[3] *O.C.* 7, cf. fr. 319, *Aj*. 319, *Trach*. 1074; Archilochus, loc. cit.; Pindar, loc. cit. ('good' implies birth); Thuc. ii. 61. 4; Euripides, fr. 757.

[4] *Trach*. 2; cf. *O.T*. 1528, *Phil*. 505, fr. 646, 845; Aesch. *Ag*. 928; Hdt. i. 32; Euripides, *Andr*. 100; Thuc. ii. 44. 1.

[5] *O.C.* 798; cf. *El*. 354, fr. 593; Pindar, *P*. viii. 137; Aesch. *Pers*. 840; Euripides, *H.F.* 503; Democritus, fr. 189, 191.

that, man should do what he can to better his position. 'Fortune does not help the despairing.'[1]

Our discussion of Sophocles' religion has inevitably led us beyond its proper bounds into the sphere of ethics. When Oedipus says at the beginning of the *Coloneus* that he has been taught to bear misfortune, he names as the third, and therefore most important of his teachers, 'nobility'. We shall have to consider whether the nobles of Athens had certain standards and methods of behaviour of their own, and whether Sophocles is advocating these standards in his plays, as we believe he associated with the nobles in his daily life. If we read Pindar, the *Clouds* of Aristophanes, and the earlier books of the Republic, we become aware of a continuous tradition of aristocratic thought; its high ethical ideals are opposed to a more realistic theory of conduct for which we have evidence in other writers, particularly Thucydides and the fragments of the sophists, as well as in the possibly biased accounts of their opponents.[2] The keywords of the aristocratic thinkers are quietness (*apragmosyne*), safe-mindedness (*sophrosyne*), and honour; the keywords of the realists are meddling (*polypragmosyne*), cleverness, and self-seeking.

Meddling is the ideal of the Athenian democrat in Thucydides. Euripides shows us clearly the contrast between meddling and quietness; Medea hopes that no one will think her quiet, but of the other sort, stern to foes and kind to friends; Amphion, the type of the cultured young Athenian aristocrat, prefers the quiet man to the daring navigator or ruler.[3] Echoes of this opposition

---

[1] Fr. 927, cf. *Phil.* 1419, fr. 308, 407.

[2] For the evidence connecting Pindar and Plato and a general account of the aristocratic tradition see Wade-Gery, *J.H.S.* 1932, p. 224 f.

[3] Thuc. i. 70, &c. Euripides, *Medea*, 808. Contrast Euripides, fr. 194 (Amphion), Democritus, fr. 3, 80; Hdt. i. 8; Aristophanes, *Clouds*, 1007, *Birds*, 44, 1321. See Nestle, *Philologus*, 1925, p. 129.

can be found in Sophocles and he clearly believes in quietness.[1]

Cleverness which has the single aim of ministering to the self-seeking of its possessor is a dangerous thing. Sophocles was conversant with the intellectual ideas of his time and could allude to them when he wished. But he sees the dangers of intellect alone; 'in the contriving of his art he has a thing clever beyond all hope; sometimes his path is evil and sometimes good.'[2] Intellectual cleverness is the salient characteristic of the Athenian democrat and of Themistocles in the first book of Thucydides. It lacks the moral element which for a Greek makes the difference between intellect and intelligence. Sophocles demands the moral element of *aidos* which Pindar and other writers couple with 'good counsel'. The man who has *aidos* cannot tell lies, and Sophocles believes that lies will not in the end prevail. Neoptolemus like the Spartan Brasidas would rather conquer by force than by fraud.[3] A reflection of Sophocles' attitude to lies has rightly been seen in his use of intrigues and plots;[4] Medea, Iphigenia, and most of the other Euripidean plotters are successful in carrying out their plots; but in the *Trachiniae* Deianira achieves the opposite of her intention, and in the *Electra* and *Philoctetes* Orestes and Neoptolemus fail to carry their intrigues through to the end.

Intellectual cleverness will use any means to gain its

---

[1] *Trach.* 616; cf. *Ant.* 68; *O.T.* 767; *El.* 155; fr. 81, 82, 83.

[2] *Ant.* 365. Schmid-Stählin (op. cit., p. 310) describes this chorus as a *parabasis* in the Aristophanic sense. Cf. Sheppard, op. cit., p. 140, on the parallel between Oedipus and Themistocles.

[3] *Intelligence and intellect*: Heraclitus, fr. 40; Democritus, fr. 65; cf. Aesch. fr. 390. Mr. C. M. Bowra points out to me the parallel in Euripides, *Bacchae*, 395–6. *Aidos and good counsel*: Pindar, *O.* vii. 80; Hdt. vii. 210; Thuc. i. 84; Democritus, fr. 179; Euripides, *Hipp.* 78. *Lies do not prevail*: *O.T.* 613, cf. fr. 62, 834. *Neoptolemus and Brasidas*: *Phil.* 90; Thuc. iv. 86. 6.   [4] See Solmsen, *Philologus*, lxxxvii, p. 1.

ends, but Sophocles condemns fair words when they cover foul deeds. Parallels can, of course, be found in earlier literature, but unscrupulous eloquence was particularly a problem of the second half of the fifth century, when Protagoras was teaching how to make the worse appear the better reason, when Gorgias was practising rhetoric, 'craftsman of persuasion', and when Aristophanes and Euripides found common ground in condemning the demagogue.[1]

Against the purely intellectual cleverness of the realists Sophocles sets the aristocratic ideal of *sophrosyne*, safe-mindedness. The prologue of the *Ajax* will serve us as a starting-point for discussing this virtue. Athena says to Odysseus,[2] 'Seeing these things, never yourself speak a boastful word to the gods, nor be puffed with pride, if your hand is heavier than another's or your coffers deeper. For in a single day all human things may set and rise again. The gods love the *modest* and hate the wicked.' Modesty (*sophrosyne*) consists in the recognition of the limits of human possibilities and a sane and cautious attitude to the changes of life; it is, in fact, that right attitude to the gods and the fortunes sent by the gods which we have already described. It should guard a man against stubbornness and self-will, unreasoning anger, and misleading hope,[3] all of which are dangers for great personalities such as Sophocles' heroes.

---

[1] *Ant.* 495, *El.* 1039, *O.C.* 782, &c. Protagoras, A 21, 21 *a*; Gorgias, A 28. Aristophanes, *Ach.* 370, &c.; Euripides, *Medea*, 576, &c.

[2] *Aj.* 127 f. Cf. Mette, μηδὲν ἄγαν, for the history of this idea. Cf. also Weinstock, op. cit., p. 59 f.; Sheppard, op. cit., p. lxi f.; Schadewaldt, *Aias u. Antigone*, p. 103 f.

[3] *Stubbornness*: e.g. *Ant.* 1028; further Sophoclean references in ch. iii. Cf. Homer, Ι 255; Aesch. *P.V.* 1034. *Anger*: e.g. *Trach.* 552; cf. Homer, Σ 107; Euripides, *Medea*, 447; Democritus, fr. 298 *a*. *Hope*: e.g. *Ant.* 615; cf. Hesiod, *Op.* 498; Bacchylides, ix. 18; Pindar, *N.* xi. 59, &c.; Thuc. ii. 62. 5, &c.

If the doxology of the *Antigone* be compared with the passage from the *Ajax* which we have just quoted, it appears that wisdom (φρονεῖν) and modesty can be used interchangeably, and elsewhere in the *Antigone* the same virtue is called good counsel (εὐβουλία).[1] *Sophrosyne* then has both a moral and an intellectual side; morally it means modesty and the avoidance of excess; intellectually it means the recognition of the limits of human possibility. In view of the double nature of *sophrosyne* we are not surprised to find that in a fragment Folly is called the true sister of Vice. The equation of virtue and wisdom which we associate particularly with Socrates is also found in the *Palamedes* of Gorgias. But Homer already has it in germ when he says that the suitors are neither wise nor just.[2]

A little more can be gained from a brief study of the two most important names for this virtue, *sophrosyne* and *euboulia*. The word *sophrosyne* is first used in its Sophoclean sense by Theognis, but the idea goes back to Homer. In Hesiod and the lyric poets it is expressed by 'moderation'. In Aeschylus and other fifth-century writers modesty is the opposite of all forms of *hybris* and passion. Two passages are of particular interest in view of our interpretation of Sophocles. Thucydides calls *sophrosyne* the distinguishing characteristic of the aristocratic form of government, and Heraclitus connects modesty with acting according to the commands of nature (*physis*).[3] Good

[1] φρονεῖν. ἐπιστήμη in *Ant.* 720 (cf. with this Hesiod, *Op.* 293, Hdt. vii. 10). *Good counsel: Ant.* 1050, &c.

[2] Soph. fr. 925; Gorgias, fr. 11 a (26); Homer, β 282. For further connexions between Sophocles and Socrates see Wolf, *Platos Apologie*, p. 65 f., 81 f.

[3] Theognis, 753. The word in Homer means 'caution'; for the idea cf. ψ 13. *Moderation* (μέτρον &c.) in early poets: Hesiod, *Op.* 306, &c.; Archilochus, fr. 22; Pindar *O.* xiii, 67. *Sophrosyne* in fifth-century writers: Aesch. *Sept.* 568, &c.; Euripides, *Med.* 635; *Hipp.* 79, 995; Antiphon, fr. 58; Democritus, fr. 210, 211; Thuc. ii. 40, iv. 18. *Sophrosyne* and aristo-

counsel (εὐβουλία) is used in the Sophoclean sense by other writers of the fifth century. In Thucydides the Spartan king Archidamus couples it with *sophrosyne* and *aidos* and explains it as obedience to law.[1]

When we consider the gulf between the aristocratic *sophrosyne* and the unscrupulous cleverness of the realists, we understand the bitterness with which Sophocles portrays the sophistic rhetorician in the Odysseus of the *Philoctetes* and the Creon of the *Coloneus*. The charge against the rhetorician is that whatever he says, his real aim is personal advancement. This attitude must have been common in the second half of the fifth century, since covetousness is a first cause of human action for both Thucydides and Gorgias.[2] Sophocles has embodied the contrast between his own ideal and the sophistic rhetorician of the Athenian democracy in the Neoptolemus and Odysseus of his *Philoctetes*. Odysseus was born with the desire to conquer in everything, Neoptolemus prefers an honourable failure to a dishonourable victory.[3]

Neoptolemus' sense of honour involves a high ideal of conduct. In a passage which we have already quoted Medea contrasts the quiet man with those who are stern to foes and kind to friends. That it was as right to harm foes as to help friends, is a common assumption of Greek ethics from the time of Homer to Plato's Polemarchus. But in Sophocles the characters who regard it as their duty to harm enemies and who pray to the gods to harm their enemies are the angry characters, Antigone and Creon, Electra, Philoctetes, and Oedipus. When Philoc-

---

cracy: Thuc. iii. 82, 8; cf. Aristophanes, *Clouds*, 962, 1006. *Sophrosyne* and *physis*: Heraclitus, fr. 112 (MSS. σωφρονεῖν).

[1] Pindar, *Paean II*, 50; Aesch. *Pers.* 749, *P.V.* 1035; Hdt. vii. 10; Thuc. i. 84; Aristophanes, *Birds*, 1539.

[2] Gorgias, fr. 11a (19); Thuc. iii. 82, 8. N.B. Sophocles' account of the dangers of wealth in *Ant*. 295.   [3] *Phil.* 1052, 94.

tetes tries to shoot his enemy Odysseus, Neoptolemus prevents him, saying, 'It is not honourable for you or me'.[1] Neoptolemus implies that the just man ought not to harm any one, and this is the quiet man's theory which Medea rejects. Democritus is writing in the same tradition when he says that justice is to do one's duty and the wronger is more unhappy than the wronged. Pindar shows the beginning of this ideal when he says, 'He bade him praise even the foe if he acted justly'. It finds its complete expression in Plato. In the first book of the *Republic* Polemarchus puts up the old view that it is just to harm enemies and Socrates destroys it by his contention that the just man cannot intentionally harm any one.[2]

It is at first sight surprising to find Odysseus saying in the very scene where he refuses to be a party to the mal-treatment of Ajax' dead body, 'For whom is it more likely for me to labour than for myself?' The egoism seems to conflict with his altruism. But probably such passages should be explained by the duty to follow the dictates of *physis* and realize each his own nature.[3] Euripides, for instance, says, 'Whoever manages best his own nature, is wise with regard to advantage'. The doctrine is an antici-pation of Aristotle's 'love of self'.

The ideal of which we have been speaking can be traced back to Pindar and is therefore in part the ideal of the Dorian hero. It carries with it the Dorian hero's view that glory and honour are preferable to riches and even to life itself. Deianira says that life with ill repute is

---

[1] *Phil.* 1304; cf. *O.T.* 314, *Aj.* 1334-5.

[2] Democritus, fr. 45, 46, 256; Pindar, *P.* ix. 170; N.B. in the second book of the *Republic* Glaucon and Adeimantus put up the realist theory of complete injustice for Socrates to destroy (perhaps their source is Antiphon cf. *Ox. pap.* 1364). Socrates' final definition of justice is 'to do one's own job and not to meddle'.

[3] *Aj.* 1365 (cf. Weinstock, op. cit., ad loc.), *O.T.* 594, *Phil.* 926, *O.C.* 309. Euripides, fr. 635, cf. Pindar, *N.* i. 37. See Jaeger, *Paideia*, p. 35.

intolerable.[1] There is no need to quote parallels for this commonplace of Greek aristocratic thought. Death is welcome in misfortune. The direct opposite of this heroic view is the Ionian desire to live under any conditions rather than die. The unheroic view is only held by the aged in Sophocles, such as the old Creon and the old chorus in the *Antigone* and the old Acrisius.[2]

In the heroic view death is the end of troubles. 'The dead have no toils.' Death makes no distinction of persons; he is 'a god who does not know equity or favour but loves simple justice'.[3] But though there is no pain in death, Sophocles believes in some sort of after life. Antigone wants to please the dead, because she will lie among them for ever, and Oedipus asks with what eyes he would look at his father and mother when he reached Hades. But these passages do not imply more than the shadowy existence of the Homeric underworld. Sophocles never refers to the contemporary theories of immortality, such as the Orphic's prison-house of the soul, the transmigration of the Pythagoreans, the air to air and earth to earth of the philosophers, although we find their traces in Pindar, Aeschylus, and Euripides. He once speaks of the after life of the initiated, but the fragment probably comes from the *Triptolemus*, where the foundation of the mysteries was an essential part of the story. Sophocles remains in the traditional belief which was probably held by the normal Athenian of his day.[4]

[1] *Trach.* 721, cf. *El.* 989, *O.T.* 518, &c. See Gerlach, ἀνὴρ ἀγαθός, p. 50 ff.

[2] *Ant.* 220, 580, fr. 66, 67. Cf. Homer, I 401, λ 489; Mimnermus, fr. 2, 10; Anacreon, fr. 44; Hdt. vii. 46; Euripides, *Or.* 1082, &c.

[3] *Trach.* 1173, fr. 770; cf. *Ant.* 519, *El.* 1170, *O.C.* 955; Homer, I 320, Aesch. *Suppl.* 802, fr. 161.

[4] For modern views of death see Pindar, *O.* ii. 105 f., fr. 114–5; Aesch. *Suppl.* 230; Euripides, *Suppl.* 531, fr. 639. The reference to the mysteries by Sophocles is in fr. 837 (in *O.C.* 681 f., 1049 f., he also refers to them but says nothing of the rites or beliefs).

We have still to consider the relation of man to the state
and the relation of man to the family. Politically, the
Greek tragedian is bound to represent the conditions of
society which he imagines as obtaining at the time of
which he is writing, the Homeric kingship; but this does
not prevent his transferring to that time his own political
sentiments and his role of teacher makes this almost im-
perative. Two of the ideas which we have considered in
discussing Sophocles' ethics have also a political application, *sophrosyne* and *apragmosyne*. In the *Republic* when
the state is founded each of the classes within it keeps in
its own place because of its *sophrosyne*. Sophocles demands
a similar obedience to ruler and laws from his citizens. 'If
he obeys the laws of the land . . ., he will be high in his
city', sing the chorus in the *Antigone*. Ajax calls this
obedience to the rulers modesty.[1] Sophocles' demand is,
of course, nothing new. The demand for a strong ruler
goes back to Homer; Aeschylus has the same political
application of modesty, the duty to obey the laws is called
lawfulness (*eunomia*) by the lyric poets, and Pindar speaks
of modest lawfulness. Heraclitus says that the people
should fight for the law as if it were their city wall.[2] The
subject obeys because the ruler rules for his good. Oedipus cares for his people in their distress and calls them 'my
children', like Homer's Odysseus, who was kindly as a
father. In the same spirit Pindar calls on Arcesilas to
handle a wound gently, and the Aeschylean ruler will not
act without his people.[3] The presupposition of the sub-

[1] *Ant.* 368 (cf. Simonides, fr. 4, interpreted by Bowra, *Class. Phil.* 1934,
p. 230 f.). *Aj.* 668 f. (cf. fr. 683). Other references in Sophocles: *Aj.* 1071,
1352, *Phil.* 925, 1010, *Ant.* 661 f. (cf. Aesch. *Sept.* 224; Antiphon, fr. 61).

[2] Homer, B 204 (cf. Thuc. ii. 37, 3; Euripides, *Andr.* 479); Aesch. *Eum.*
520 f. (cf. 690 f.; Euripides, fr. 628); Pindar, *Paean I*, 10 (cf. *P.* v. 90;
Solon, fr. 3. 30; Bacchylides, xii. 186); Heraclitus, fr. 44.

[3] *O.T.* 58 f.; Homer, λ 689; Pindar, *P.* iv. 480; Aesch. *Suppl.* 398.

jects' obedience is that the ruler not only rules for their good, but knows what that good is. He rules by an art surpassing all other arts.[1] *Apragmosyne* also has its political application. In the *Republic* Socrates states the principle that no one rules willingly. Creon in the *Tyrannus* draws a picture of the quiet man who does not wish to rule. The passage is closely followed by Euripides in the *Hippolytus* and *Ion*.[2]

Sophocles' political thought leads on to Plato. But there was another theory which corresponds to the realistic theory in ethics. According to this theory the ruler rules because it is a law of nature that the stronger should rule the weaker. It is put most clearly in a passage of the Melian dialogue which we have already quoted and in which Thucydides is parodying a speech of Antigone: 'it is a necessity of human nature that man should rule whatever he possesses; we did not make this law nor are we the first to use it, it was in existence when we received it and we shall leave it existing to eternity'. From here it is an easy step to Thrasymachus' belief that justice is the advantage of the stronger.[3]

Sophocles knew this theory and puts it into the mouth of Creon in the *Antigone* and Oedipus in the *Tyrannus*. Both claim absolute power over Thebes. Creon is told that the tyrant can use any law he pleases, like the Zeus of the *Prometheus*. Oedipus thinks only of his private advantage when he condemns Creon. *Hybris*, as the chorus of the *Tyrannus* say, is part of the nature of this kind of ruler.[4] The tyrant denies the elementary rights of free

[1] *O.T.* 380; *Phil.* 138–9. Perhaps a reference to the political art taught by Democritus and Protagoras.

[2] *O.T.* 584 f.; cf. Euripides, *Hipp.* 1013 f., *Ion* 621 f.

[3] Thuc. v. 105 (cf. *Ant.* 454); cf. Gorgias, fr. 11 (6); Thrasymachus, A. 10.

[4] *Ant.* 738, 213 (cf. Aesch. *P.V.* 188). *O.T.* 624 f., 873 (cf. *Aj.* 1350). See Sheppard, op. cit., p. xli f.

speech and equality of opportunity which are claimed
for the Athenian democracy. Both Tiresias and Creon
demand their right to a fair hearing.[1] Sophocles could not
believe, like Thrasymachus, that the city was to be used
solely for the ruler's advantage. He held that there
should be equality of opportunity of the kind advocated
by the Syracusan Athenagoras. 'The small would best
be saved with the great and the great by the small.'[2]
Co-operation is more consistent with the good of both
small and great and therefore with the good of the
whole state than the self-seeking of either the tyrant or
the demagogue.

Finally we have to consider the relation of man to the
family, and by this relation I mean all that can be included under the word *physis*. Our discussion of Sophocles'
moral and religious thought has already shown us the importance of this conception. *Physis* originally meant process of growth. But besides meaning stages of growth
and kinds of growth—a usage to which we shall return
later—it means something very like nature in the sense
in which we say it is a man's nature to do this or that.
This nature may be either lower nature or higher nature,
and the thinkers of the fifth century are divided along
these lines. Although both Euripides and Thucydides
reflect more than one view in their writings, it would in
the main be true to say that Euripides, Thucydides, and
the sophists stand on one side, Sophocles, Pindar, and
Aristophanes on the other. For Euripides and the sophists,
the realist school, *physis*, besides meaning the growth of
the whole world, means man's lower nature, his passions.
'*Physis* willed it who has no care for laws.' The most striking expression of this outlook is in a fragment of the
sophist Antiphon, where he says that most of the rights

[1] *O.T.* 408, 544; cf. Euripides, *Suppl.* 433; Thuc. ii. 37.
[2] *Aj.* 160–3, cf. Thuc. vi. 39.

established by law are enemies of nature.[1] Law and convention are forces which restrict nature. The gulf between these thinkers and Sophocles is clearly seen when it is remembered that high and low birth are for them among the conventions.

For Sophocles the derivation of the word *physis* implies that the growth comes from a seed which was sown by some one. He, like Aeschylus, regards the seed as sown by the father and not by the mother. Euripides, who is learned in the latest biological theories, thinks that the mother joins with the father in the act of sowing.[2] Normally the child inherits the *physis* of the father, and the *physis* of the child consists of the characteristics inherited from the father. Neoptolemus has inherited his *physis* and his ideals from his father Achilles, and when he accepts the proposals of Odysseus he has left his *physis*. His *physis* is not only his inherited character, but also the highest standard of conduct to which he can attain.[3] Again Sophocles appears as a forerunner of Plato and a successor of Pindar; Pindar believes in breed above everything, Plato founds his state on the principle that each citizen is fitted by his inherited *physis* for a particular task.

[1] On the root meaning and development of *Physis* see Myres, *Political Ideas of the Greeks*, p. 154 f. The realistic view; Hippias, C. 1; Antiphon, *Ox. pap.* 1364; Thuc. i. 76. 3, iii. 45. 3, 82. 2, 84. 2, iv. 61. 5; Euripides, fr. 299, 837, 912. Schadewaldt (*Aias u. Antigone*) regards Ajax and Antigone as embodiments of the *physis-nomos* contrast. In a sense this is true, but in the Sophoclean sense of *physis*.

[2] Euripides, *Ion* 406, with Wilamowitz's note; but *Tro.* 135 closely corresponds with *Ant.* 569.

[3] *Inherited characteristics*: *Ant.* 471, *Phil.* 88; cf. Homer, Δ 370, β 271; Pindar, O. vii. 169, &c. See De Ruyt, *Rev. Belge*, 1933, p. 113. *Fixed characteristics*; fr. 808, cf. Pindar, O. xi. 20; Aristophanes, *Wasps*, 1457. The same idea lies behind Theognis, 183. *Departure from nature*: *Phil.* 902 (cf. *El.* 287, 341, *Aj.* 1093). For the principle cf. Heraclitus, fr. 112; Euripides, fr. 635.

If *physis* is fixed by birth, education is impossible, and
Pindar seems to believe this. But Sophocles does allow
physis to be changed in certain circumstances. Angry men
can be charmed out of their nature by their friends. The
unruly can be led astray by rhetoric; presumably they
have not grown properly and therefore have no fixed
physis. The young can be taught; according to Philoctetes Odysseus caught Neoptolemus when he was still ungrown, i.e. had not yet developed his fixed *physis*. One
of the influences on the young is the city in which they
live, and Theseus deplores the small effect that Thebes
has had on Creon.[1]

Besides meaning character in the sense which we have
been discussing, *physis* can be used for stages of growth
and kinds of growth. We shall then consider how Sophocles speaks of young and old, man and woman, slave and
free in terms of *physis*. It is a commonplace of Greek
literature that youth is headstrong and age is wise. In
Homer 'the young man's mind is light and his counsel
slender', and 'the old man knows ten thousand things'.
In terms of *physis* the young have not yet grown their
mind; Creon taunts the old Oedipus with not having
grown wits even at his age.[2] Women have a different
process of growth from men; Ismene says, 'We are women
grown and therefore cannot fight with men'.[3] The slave
also has a different process of growth, and although a slave
may have a free mind in spite of a slave body, Sophocles

---

[1] *Education*: Pindar, *N*. iii. 70. *Anger*: O.C. 1193, cf. the influence of
ὁμιλία which is stressed in Aeschylus and Euripides, e.g. *Pers.* 753, *Septem*,
599; Euripides, fr. 1052, &c. *The unruly*: *Phil.* 387. *The young*: *Phil.* 1014.
The city: O.C. 919, cf. Periclean Athens, an education to Greece.

[2] Homer, Ψ 587, β 16; Soph. O.C. 804, cf. 1229. O.C. 930 (age brings
emptiness of mind) is unique in Sophocles; cf., however, Herodotus, iii.
134. 3.

[3] *Ant.* 61, cf. *Trach.* 1062, &c. For proverbial remarks about women cf.
fr. 682, *Aj.* 293, &c.

believed with Homer that 'Zeus takes away half a man's virtue when he becomes a slave'.[1]

This theory of *physis* is essentially aristocratic and has a chivalry of its own. Oedipus will not chastise Tiresias because he is an old man. It carries with it an intense respect for the kinship which exists between father and children. Antigone buries her brother; she would not have buried her husband or her children in defiance of the city's law; she has the same theory of kinship as Apollo in the *Eumenides*.

Our survey of Sophocles' ideas is complete. We can now say what authors influenced him and what attitude he took up to the intellectual problems of his day. We start with Homer. Sophocles was called 'the most Homeric of poets', he was the tragic Homer just as Homer was the epic Sophocles.[2] There is no doubt that Homer is of the first importance as an artistic influence. Sophocles based whole plays on Homer, for instance the *Nausicaa*. In the surviving plays we can find many literary reminiscences, such as the reminiscence of Homer's Hector and Andromache in the scene between Ajax and Tecmessa. The index to Homeric quotations fills over a page of the Teubner text of the *scholia* to Sophocles. Besides these literary reminiscences, Sophocles' character drawing, prologues, technique of preparation, and language, all show the influence of Homer.[3] We have also had to trace many of his ideas back to Homer ultimately, but for his thought we must primarily consider writers who lived nearer Sophocles' own time.

[1] Homer, ρ 322. *Free mind and slave's body: Trach.* 52. It is significant that the pedagogue of the *Electra* is ἐσθλὸς γεγώς, not πεφυκώς.

[2] For a collection and assessment of the ancient evidence, cf. Cantarella, *Rivista indo-greco-italica*, 1926, p. 3.

[3] See the following and compare with Sophocles: *characters*, Bowra, *Tradition and Design in the Iliad*, p. 192 f.; *prologues*, Sheppard, *Pattern of the Iliad*, p. 13 f.; *preparation*, Drew, *A.J.P.* lii, p. 320; *language*, ch. vii below.

In the same way Sophocles knew the earlier lyric poets and used their technique, images, and phraseology, but the only lyric poet who greatly influenced his thought was Pindar. Pindar's post-Persian odes were written during the early years of Sophocles' manhood, and the two poets' periods of literary production overlapped by more than twenty years. Pindar's views on the gods and the right relation between man and the gods, on the aristocratic ideal, on modesty and good counsel, on law, and on *physis* are closely allied to the views of Sophocles. The two poets had much in common. Pindar had a definite connexion with Delphi; Sophocles had a particular veneration for Apollo and his oracle. Pindar was an aristocrat and believed in birth; Sophocles' sympathies were with the Athenian aristocrats. Pindar's friends in Athens belonged to the same class and held the same political views as Sophocles.[1]

Aeschylus was the greatest tragedian of the generation before, and Sophocles learnt the art of tragedy from him. Between Sophocles' first production and Aeschylus' death was a period of over ten years during which both were producing for the Athenian stage. The influence of Aeschylus is seen partly in literary reminiscences such as the Iole scene of the *Trachiniae*, partly in thought, technique, and language.[2] This influence is most easily detected, as one would expect, in the earliest plays. Ajax, Creon, and even Antigone herself, commit definite sins and suffer as the result. The moral is as clearly pointed as in the *Agamemnon* or *Persae*. But even here Sophocles shows a greater interest in the individual characters than in their faults and the resultant suffering. In thought two great differences separate Sophocles and Aeschylus, one political and one religious. Aeschylus is a democrat;

---

[1] Cf. Wade-Gery, op. cit., p. 205 f. For literary reminiscences of the lyric poets &c. see Schmid-Stählin, p. 311, n. 6.

[2] Some details are noted below in chs. v, vi, vii, viii.

in the *Eumenides* he gives the Areopagus its charter as a
murder court, not as the government of Athens, and in
the *Persae* he praises the Athenian democracy. He has
therefore no interest in birth or *physis*. The other difference is a difference of religious outlook. Aeschylus is in
the tradition of Hesiod and Solon, and though he purifies
their religion by a more philosophic conception of the
deity, his sense of the spectacular and his horror of crime
make him insist on the grimness of the Furies and the
certainty of punishment, if not for the sinner, then for his
children or, if not on earth, then in the underworld.
Sophocles, though he too is indebted to Hesiod, especially
for the personification of abstract ideas such as *aidos* and
nemesis, has a more cheerful religion and prefers to
emphasize reverent piety and the acceptance of the will
of god.

Sophocles' religion is the traditional religion which has
been handed down in literature and cult from Homer's
time, but it is nevertheless simplified and moralized by
philosophy. The works of Xenophanes and Heraclitus
were certainly known to him; of these Heraclitus was the
greater influence. He was an aristocrat and believed in
physis, in the divine laws governing the universe, in the
circle of human fortunes, in modesty, and in the main-
tenance of law and order; all these are to be found again
in Sophocles, and Heraclitus must have helped to form his
mind.[1] Whether Sophocles had himself read Democritus,
or whether the connexions of thought between them are
due to a common source such as Protagoras, who was certainly known to both, is hard to say. Another thinker
who may have influenced him is Archelaus, the friend of
Cimon, for whom Sophocles wrote an epigram. But our

[1] Schmid-Stählin, p. 491, suggests that Sophocles' preoccupation
with tragic irony arose from the contrast of knowledge and opinion in
Heraclitus.

knowledge of Archelaus is too fragmentary to enable us to assess the debt.

We now come to the sophists and the three writers who reflect their ideas, Herodotus, Euripides, and Thucydides. Of the sophists Protagoras is the most important and Sophocles was deeply impressed by his thought at the time that he wrote the *Antigone*. Like Protagoras, he ascribes the development of human culture to the intellect of man; he refers to Protagoras' theory of the impossibility of polluting the gods and to his opposed arguments on every topic.[1] But Sophocles makes his own position perfectly clear; he points out the dangers of intellect and puts the theory of pollution into the mouth of the angry Creon. His attitude to debating is equally clear. He has no use for a bad case dressed up in fair arguments.

We have also noticed allusions to theories of Antiphon and Thrasymachus. There may be further influence from the sophists. The several puns and etymologies perhaps owe something to Cratylus. The use of the same word by different characters in different senses, as for instance *sophron* by Electra and Chrysothemis, may reflect the *Synonyms* of Prodicus. Sophocles' position is well summed up by Busse:[2] 'Sophocles is completely in accord with the sophists in so far as they value the creativeness of the human spirit in the sphere of cultural progress, but he as definitely attacks their immorality when they regard the moral law as a human creation of man's caprice and without scruple set themselves above it'.

It is more difficult to determine the relation between Sophocles and Herodotus. The moral of many of Herodotus' stories is a moral with which Sophocles would agree.

---

[1] *Development of man*: *Ant.* 332 f. (Protagoras *ap.* Plato, *Protagoras*, 320 D ff.) *Pollution*: *Ant.* 1043 (cf. Nestle, *Class. Phil.* v, p. 138). *Two opposed arguments*: *Ant.* 687 (Protagoras, A 1).

[2] *N.J.B.B.* 1927, p. 135.

The acceptance of the god's will, the certainty of oracles, the circle of human fortunes are ideas which are common to both writers. The most important divergence in thought is that Herodotus, unlike Sophocles, believes in the jealousy of the gods and the punishment of later generations. Undoubtedly the two writers were personally acquainted. In some places we can be certain that Sophocles is borrowing from Herodotus, for instance, in his account of Egyptian customs in the *Coloneus*, which was written over twenty years after the final publication of Herodotus' history.[1]

The crux of this problem lies in the *Antigone*. In Antigone's last speech Sophocles refers to a story which is found in the third book of Herodotus.[2] The debate between Haemon and Creon agrees in thought, terminology, and imagery with Artabanus' speech to Xerxes and Mardonius in the seventh book. Antigone's speech has been condemned as an interpolation. But the arguments for believing it to be genuine are difficult to reject. Aristotle quotes it. It gives the intellectual justification of Antigone's action. It is introduced and rounded off in the common manner of archaic rhetoric ('By what law . . . by that law'). We must assume that Sophocles had heard the story of Intaphrenes' wife from Herodotus, possibly at a recital in Athens. But we can hardly also assume that Herodotus had composed the seventh book as early as 441. Of course we might suppose a common source, perhaps Protagoras. But that would not account

[1] *O.C.* 337; cf. further certain instances *O.T.* 981, *El.* 62, 421, *Phil.* 1207 fr. 473, 712. I am not certain about *O.T.* 975, *Phil.* 305: it may be that Sophocles originated these phrases in an earlier play.

[2] *Ant.* 904 f. with Hdt. iii. 119; see Jebb and Bruhn, ad loc.; Aly, *Volksmärchen*, p. 277 f.; Pohlenz, *Gr. Tr.* ii, p. 54; Jacoby, *R.E. Suppl.*, p. 246; Schmid-Stählin, op. cit., p. 318. See also below, ch. iv, for the bearing of this speech on Sophocles' character drawing. The other correspondence, *Ant.* 710 f. with Hdt. vii. 10, 2, 2 f., is almost as striking.

for the iambic rhythms which are prominent in this and
other speeches of Herodotus. I should prefer to regard
the borrowing as mutual and to say that Sophocles was
indebted to Herodotus for Eastern stories and customs,
and Herodotus to Sophocles for much of the moral and
religious colouring of his stories, and for some of the technique of his stories and speeches.

Sophocles took up, as we have seen, a definite attitude
to contemporary theories of religion, ethics, and politics.
Euripides and Thucydides recorded and reflected these
theories with little bias or partiality. In both writers we
can find characters who adopt the Sophoclean standpoint.
Of all the characters of Euripides Hippolytus is nearest
to the ideal of Sophocles; probably if we knew more,
we should see that Amphion in the *Antiope* belonged to
the same class. In Thucydides the Spartan king, Archidamus, is closest. This is perhaps significant in view of the
Laconizing tendencies of Cimon and the Athenian aristocracy. Much of the funeral speech is also near to Sophocles, but the Periclean ideal of intelligence, adaptability,
and readiness to interfere is essentially incompatible with
his thought.

The traditional religion tempered by philosophy, the
ideal of doing good, *sophrosyne* and *apragmosyne*, the belief
in personality and breed, these are the essentials of the
thought of Sophocles. We see them in Pindar before him
and in Aristophanes and Plato after him. It is the thought
of the Athenian aristocrats, Cimon and the elder Thucydides, and the circle of Socrates. Sophocles was 'like one
of the Athenian nobles'.

III. Characters

THE atmosphere in which Sophocles lived fostered his belief in breed and personality. He required two things of the story which he proposed to dramatize. It must have some positive religious value (or at least contain nothing discreditable to the gods) and it must have a hero or a heroine who could be made into a great character. The second requirement is even more important than the first, and Sophocles differs from the other two tragedians in directing his whole technique to the presentation of one or at most two great figures.

If we are to describe Sophocles' characters, which is our present object, we must make two assumptions.[1] Since Sophocles prided himself on his character-drawing, and was regarded by antiquity as a good draughtsman of character, we must assume that his characters are consistent, and that he did not sacrifice their consistency to the momentary effect of the particular scene. Secondly, we must assume that he has told us in the text all that he wishes to be known. Subtle psychological explanations which go far beyond the evidence of the text must be rejected.

Sophocles himself said that he created the sort of people one ought to create and Euripides created the sort of people that are.[2] He is an idealist, and Euripides a realist. We have

---

[1] The point is excellently put by Schadewaldt, *Aias u. Antigone*, p. 64. See ch. v, p. 101, n. 2, on T. von Wilamowitz's approach to Sophocles. Bruhn, on the other hand, seems to me often to read too much into the characters. Kamerbeek has excellent detailed studies of the characters of Electra, Philoctetes and Neoptolemus in his *Studiën over Sophocles*, pp. 88f., 36 f., 43 f.

[2] Aristotle, *Poetics*, 1460^{b}33. It seems more natural to supply ποιεῖν than εἶναι to Δεῖ. The interpretation is the same in both cases.

seen the standards of life and conduct which Sophocles demands. His idealism consists in creating characters who in the main conform to these standards and whose divergences, where they diverge, are clearly marked. Even the bad characters have some redeeming feature; Creon in the *Coloneus*, and Odysseus in the *Philoctetes*, are patriots according to their lights. A good commentary on Sophocles' remark about his characters is given by Robert Bridges, when he says of Shakespeare: 'In characterizing his people he wanted to make them interesting and beautiful, and the only reasonable course was to colour them with what he accounted most interesting and beautiful'.[1]

Sophocles' characters fall into several groups. The first is formed by the chief characters between whom there is a strong likeness.[2] They are Ajax (and with him we shall consider Teucer), Antigone, Creon (in the *Antigone*), Heracles, Oedipus, Electra, and Philoctetes. Two groups share some of the characteristics of these chief characters. These are the 'bad' characters—Agamemnon, Menelaus, Aegisthus, Odysseus (*Phil.*), Creon (*O.C.*)—and the 'good' characters—Odysseus (*Aj.*), Creon (*O.T.*), Theseus. The remaining groups are formed by the young men headed by Neoptolemus, the women headed by Deianira, the minor characters, and the choruses.

Of the chief characters two are women and the rest men. The norms which we expect are the manly man and the womanly woman, the masterful husband and the obedient wife. The two women both deviate from the norm. Antigone and Electra have the strength and firmness of purpose which a Greek associates with a man. But they have also the natural desires of a woman. Antigone

---

[1] Rothenstein, *Men and Memories*, I, p. 328. See Haussleiter's (*Fragen der Sittlichkeit*, p. 57 f.) analysis of the chief characters of Sophocles from this standpoint.

[2] See Wolff, *N.J.B.B.*, 1931, p. 394.

laments that she is to die, 'before ever I have known bridal
bed or song or had any portion in marriage or the nurtur-
ing of children', and Electra says that she is 'wasting away
without children and over me no kindly husband stands'.[1]
Neither are womanly women, but both are conscious of
the normal emotions of women.

The men have no need to emphasize their manliness.
Ajax and Oedipus behave to their wives like ordinary
Athenians. When Ajax tells Tecmessa that a woman's
glory is silence, he is neither brutal nor repressive according to Athenian standards.[2] Creon, however, and Heracles
lack control over their passions. Creon is both aware of
the attractions of women and terrified of yielding to them.
He warns Haemon never to lose his wits because of the
pleasure he takes in a woman. He himself, as a strong
man, will never yield to a woman. Heracles also scorns
feminine weakness when he says, 'A woman, a born woman
not grown as a man, slew me alone without a sword.' Yet
his passion for a woman could persuade him to destroy
her city, to wrong Deianira, and to over-ride his son's
objections to marrying Iole.[3] Heracles and Creon fall
short of the standard of manhood just as Antigone and
Electra rise above the standard of womanhood, but the
deviations from the standard are all clearly marked.

We have already spoken of Sophocles' belief in *physis*.
All the chief characters, except perhaps Creon, are conscious of their birth; as noble born they conform to
certain standards of life and action; as members of a
family they have a duty to be loyal to their parents and
a right to expect loyalty from their children. On these
duties, rights, and standards affection is based. Ajax is
afraid to return home without as much glory as his father
had won before Troy. He must show that he is Telamon's

[1] *Ant.* 917, cf. 813; *El.* 187, cf. 164.   [2] *Aj.* 293.
[3] *Ant.* 648, 484, 525; *Trach.* 1062, 460, and last scene *passim*.

true-born son, and he demands the same courage from his own son Eurysaces. And in spite of his resolute pursuit of his own ends he is not without affection for his son and Teucer, for his mother, and for Tecmessa. Teucer is like Ajax in his fear of his father and his love for his brother.[1]

Antigone believes that to please her kin is a duty which in the special case of her brother outweighs even her duty to the state. With it goes her strong affection, 'I was not born for hatred but for love'.[2] Electra has often been compared to Antigone, and she has the same deep affection for her kin. Like Antigone's, it is rooted in the duty to kinsfolk, 'He is a fool who forgets parents who have died in misery'. Therefore she despises Chrysothemis and hates Clytemnestra. Electra is more unfortunate than Antigone, because she has been living for years as a slave in her mother's house, and a slave's life is unworthy of her birth as a princess. She counts Clytemnestra mistress rather than mother.[3]

Oedipus is in an enigmatical position in the *Tyrannus*. He believes that he is the son of the king of Corinth, but doubts were expressed about his parentage and he went to Delphi to discover the truth. He feels the ties of kinship as strongly as any character. He is resolved to find out the secrets of his own origin, and when Tiresias speaks of his parents, he flashes out with 'What parents? Stay. Who of men begat me?' But still believing that he is the son of Polybus and Merope, he still loves his supposed parents in Corinth. In Thebes he has an affection for his brother-in-law Creon, which makes Creon's treachery all the more bitter, for Iocasta, whom he allows to over-persuade him and whom he tells all his fears, and for his

---

[1] Ajax: *relation to father*, 460 f.; *relation to son*, 545 f., cf. Weinstock, op. cit., p. 44; *affection*, 558, 562, 850, 652. Teucer: 1008, 991.

[2] *Ant.* 89, 907, 523.

[3] *Affection for Agamemnon and Orestes*, 1232. *Duty to kinsfolk*, 145. *Chrysothemis*, 365. *Clytemnestra*, 1194, 597.

children, particularly his daughters, whom he commends
to Creon's care at the end.[1]

He has the same affection for his daughters in the
Coloneus. Antigone, like Iocasta in the *Tyrannus*, can
over-persuade him. His daughters have won his affection
because they fulfil their duty to him; his hatred of his
sons and Creon is due to their disregard of this duty.[2]
In the *Coloneus* Oedipus knows that he is a noble Theban.
Nobility is a standard to which he can appeal and which
he must observe. His consciousness of nobility has en-
abled him to endure his misfortunes, and he demands the
same noble endurance from his daughters. He perceives
the same nobility in Theseus and is thereby drawn towards him. Oedipus feels that it is unnecessary to bind
Theseus with an oath, and he is prepared to listen to
Theseus' demand that he should receive Polynices.[3]

The friendship that grows up between Philoctetes and
Neoptolemus is very like the friendship of Oedipus and
Theseus. A common nobility draws the older and younger
man together. Philoctetes also finds it unnecessary to
swear Neoptolemus, and he also yields to Neoptolemus'
persuasion. Philoctetes and Neoptolemus speak the common language of the noble; they have the same ideal and
they admire and despise the same people. Philoctetes has,
like Ajax, a deep affection for his father. When he pro-
poses to kill himself he says that he is seeking his father.
Like Electra, he resents treatment which he regards as
unworthy of his rank; he says to Odysseus, 'Clearly our
father begat us to be slaves, not free'.[4]

Frankness, fortitude, and sensitiveness to shame also

---

[1] *Search for origin*, 437, cf. 787, 1058. *Affection for Polybus and Merope*,
998; *for Creon*, 85, cf. 551; *for Iocasta*, 772; *for children*, 1480.
[2] 1617; 1205; 337 f., 418, 1365; 770.　　　　[3] 8, 1640, 650, 1350.
[4] 811 (=O.C. 650), 1310 (=O.C. 1350); 475, 410 f.; 1210, cf. 492;
995. On Philoctetes and his father see Kamerbeek, op. cit., p. 39 f.

belong to this aristocratic ideal which Sophocles is drawing. Oedipus will have Creon's news published to all, Antigone and Electra scorn concealment of their designs. Heracles takes no pains to hide his mistress from his wife, and on the only occasion that he used guile against a foe paid heavily for it.[1]

Ajax and Heracles both regard it as dishonourable to lament in misfortune. But fortitude is most notable in Electra, Philoctetes, and Oedipus in the *Coloneus*. All three are suffering from continued physical and mental afflictions. Electra has been for years a slave in her father's house. Philoctetes has been abandoned on a lonely island with a gangrened foot. Oedipus has been driven into exile by his own sons. These evils affect their characters; they are all emotional, they cannot forget their present condition, nor forgive those who were responsible for it. But misfortunes cannot break their fortitude. Electra says that her life is pitiable but sufficient for her. Philoctetes' heroism shows itself in his account of his life on Lemnos and in his bearing when he is attacked by pain. Oedipus has been schooled to fortitude by his sufferings.[2]

Some evils are too great to bear. In their lowest depths of misery Creon, Oedipus, Heracles, and Philoctetes would rather die than live. Ajax has tarnished his honour by turning his sword against cattle, and death is the only cure for shame. Antigone is prepared to die rather than accept the dishonour of leaving her brother unburied. Electra wants to die because it is intolerable to her that she cannot do her duty by her father's memory, that she is treated like a slave, and has to behave like a rebel.[3]

---

[1] *O.T.* 93; *Ant.* 86; *El.* 1033; *Trach.* 480, 277.

[2] *Aj.* 319; *Trach.* 1072; *El.* 354; *Phil.* 535, 733; *O.C.* 5, 798. Cf. Reinhardt (*Sophokles*, p. 12) for the isolation of these characters.

[3] *Ant.* 1307, *Trach.* 1035, *O.T.* 1411, *Phil.* 1207; *Aj.* 361, 367; *Ant.* 461; *El.* 814 f., cf. 616.

Oedipus and Philoctetes are as sensitive as Electra. Oedipus is sensitive about his skill in guessing riddles, and particularly about the problem of his birth. In the *Coloneus* he resents any reference to his past crimes, and will not allow Theseus to touch him because of his pollution. Philoctetes is sensitive about his condition; he has become a savage and is afraid that the sailors may be unable to bear the stench from his foot.[1]

The standards, duties, and affections which are based on breed are less apparent in Creon and Heracles than in the other characters. Creon's duty to the state and Heracles' love for Iole outweigh the claims of kin. Heracles, however, shows a trace of the feelings of kinship. He demands complete obedience from his son when he commands Hyllus to build his pyre and marry Iole. He desires his mother and children to be present when he dies; and, like Electra and Philoctetes, he regards his present misery as unworthy of his divine birth. That Creon had any affection for his family can only be inferred from his lamentations. He demands absolute obedience from all his kin, particularly from Antigone and Haemon. But the state is far more important in his eyes.[2]

The political ideal of Sophocles is the ruler who rules in the interest of his people, and the subject who obeys him. All the chief characters of Sophocles, except Heracles in the *Trachiniae* and Oedipus in the *Coloneus*, offend in some way against this ideal, but though they offend, they are conscious of their obligation to rule well and to obey: Antigone and Electra both rate their duty to their kin higher than their duty to the state. Clytemnestra and Aegisthus are unjust usurpers, but Electra is conscious of her disobedience and knows that she is 'doing things beyond her bounds that do not befit her'. For Antigone

[1] *O.T.* 441, 1078; *O.C.* 515, 1132; *Phil.* 225, 473, 890.
[2] *Trach.* 1244, 1147, 1103; *Ant.* 1261, 486, 640.

the clash of duties is real, since Creon is her constitutional king. In the earlier part of the play she speaks scornfully of 'the good Creon', and says, 'I did not think your decrees were so strong that you, a mortal, could transgress the unwritten and sure laws of the gods'. But in her last speech she comes nearer to Ismene's standpoint, when she urges very special reasons for her disobedience, 'For never, had I been the mother of children, nor if my husband were mouldering in death, would I have undertaken this labour against the will of the citizens'.[1]

Ajax is at Troy in a double capacity, leader of troops, and himself under the leadership of Agamemnon. He is on terms of friendship with his Salaminians, but he is not prepared to obey his general. He does not accept the award of the court, but takes judgement into his own hands and tries to murder Agamemnon and Menelaus. In his monologue, however, he too, like Antigone, sees the need for order in the state, 'We shall learn to reverence the Atridae'. Philoctetes is like Ajax in his hatred of the Atridae; he too takes justice into his own hands when he tries, on recovering his bow, to shoot Odysseus. When he finally yields, he yields not because it is his duty to the Greek army, but because Heracles persuades him.

The fullest political portraits are those of the two kings, Creon and Oedipus. Creon is the simpler character. He believes that the good of the state comes before everything else, and so far he is a good ruler. But he further believes that this is attained by the rigid administration of Simonidean justice, good to friends and harm to foes, and by strong government, since nothing is worse than anarchy. He therefore regards the city as the property of the ruler. In the eyes of his citizens he is a tyrant; he can use any law he likes and his face inspires terror in the subject. Oedipus is different, though he also shows a streak of the

[1] *El.* 617; *Ant.* 31, 453, 905 (cf. 78).

tyrant, particularly in his dealings with Tiresias and Creon, and in his fears for his own safety. But normally he is the kind and considerate ruler. His subjects have tested him and found him 'pleasant in the city'. If he has saved them, he does not care about anything else, and it is for their sake that he extracts the truth from Tiresias. Oedipus is the good ruler in spite of his defects, and Creon the bad ruler in spite of his virtues.[1]

Besides the claims of family and state, men have a duty to the gods. The chief characters could be arranged in a scale from the pious Antigone to the sceptical Creon. It will serve our purpose here to note the most striking instances of their belief and unbelief. Both Antigone and Electra regard the honour which they pay to their dead kinsmen as a service to the gods, imposed on them by a law of the gods. Electra's joy culminates when she learns that Orestes' coming is due to the bidding of the gods. Antigone wavers once; she says in her last speech, 'Why should I look to the gods any longer?'[2] But this momentary weakness only sets off her steadfast certainty. Religious certainty and recognition of their own lack of *sophrosyne* distinguish Antigone and Electra from such Euripidean heroines as Medea. Antigone and Electra are essentially religious. Even their prayers for vengeance presuppose a belief in the justice of the gods.

Oedipus also is essentially religious. He goes into exile because he fears that the oracle will come true. He pursues the murderer of Laius in accordance with the oracle's instructions. In the *Coloneus* he makes careful sacrifice to the Eumenides. His belief only cracks in the depths of agony and in the height of anger. He refuses to believe in the skill of Tiresias, past or present, and when he hears of Polybus' death, he pours scorn on the oracle that told

---

[1] *Aj.* 348, 1069, 1243, 667; *Phil.* 1299; *Ant.* 666 f., 736 f., 213; *O.T.* 626 f., 510, 443.　　　　　[2] *El.* 1266; *Ant.* 922.

him he would murder his father. Similarly in his agony he loses his faith in divine justice and thinks that an evil spirit is torturing him. Two parallel passages give us the measure of Oedipus' religion. In the last scene of the *Tyrannus* he thinks that the stain on him is so great that all ordinary rules of pollution are over-ridden; in the *Coloneus* he will not allow Theseus to touch him for fear that he may be polluted. He only departs from the traditional religion in moments of extreme stress.[1]

The three soldiers, Heracles, Ajax, and Philoctetes, can be considered together. Heracles' ritual piety is emphasized; he is laying out a precinct for Zeus in Euboea during the early part of the play, and at the end he accepts the oracle as soon as he understands it. Ajax believes that he is strong enough to stand alone without the advice and help of the gods. When Athena has driven him mad and he has recovered his sanity, he admits that 'if god smites, the worse may escape the better'. He feels that Athena is a malignant force and her action has acquitted him of any obligation to the gods. Only in the monologue does he reach true reverence, when he says that he is going to purify himself of his stains. Philoctetes has been driven by his sufferings, and the sufferings of other good men, to believe that the gods are malignant and want the bad to triumph. Yet his prayers for vengeance imply that the gods are just, and he believes that they have shown themselves just in constraining Odysseus to come and seek him. At the end of the play he recognizes the omnipotence of god.[2]

Creon stands rather apart from the other characters. He transfers the strict Simonidean justice of his politics to the gods, and believes that they too reward the friends

[1] *O.T.* 133, *O.C.* 466 (cf. 189); *O.T.* 390, 964; 828; 1413, *O.C.* 1132.
[2] *Trach.* 237, 1159. *Aj.* 763 f.; 455; 587; 654, cf. 711. *Phil.* 446; 1036; 1467.

of the state and punish its enemies. But at the end of the play his misfortunes bring him to recognize the higher law of the gods in which Antigone believes. He is a mixture of superstition and scepticism. He carefully gives Antigone food in her tomb, stating that he is pure as far as she is concerned, but he does not care if the eagles carry the carrion of Polynices to the throne of Zeus.[1]

Sophocles regards the virtue of *sophrosyne* as second only to piety. His chief characters are not remarkable for it. But although they fall short of this ideal in various ways, their deviations are always noticed and sometimes they recognize their shortcomings themselves. Arrogance, violence, haste, inflexibility, and folly are all deviations from modesty. Ajax is the most arrogant of the chief characters; he prays that his son may be like him in everything but fortune.[2] All have a strain of cruelty and violence. Ajax and Heracles are rightly called 'fierce-hearted', and Antigone has inherited the fierce spirit of her father. Creon cruelly discusses Antigone with Ismene.[3]

Haste has many forms; it may be impatience, suspicion, or anger, but it may also be promptness and efficiency. Ajax, Oedipus, Electra, and Philoctetes are all impatient. The two kings, Creon and Oedipus, are ready to suspect bribery when they are thwarted, and flame into anger at any opposition. Oedipus still rages against his opponents in the *Coloneus*. Heracles throws Lichas over the cliff without asking whether he is innocent or guilty. The better side of haste is promptness and efficiency. These qualities are expected in the soldiers; no man was more 'forward

---

[1] *Ant.* 288; 1113; 775, 1040.

[2] *Aj.* 550, cf. 760 f. Cf. Teucer's taunts to Agamemnon and Menelaus, Antigone's first speech to Creon (469), Oedipus' pride in his own skill (*O.T.* 396 &c.).

[3] *Aj.* 885 (cf. 105); *Trach.* 975 (cf. 1133); *Ant.* 471 (cf. 546); 569. Cf. Oedipus' taunts to Tiresias (*O.T.* 371).

in spirit' than Ajax or 'braver to do what the moment needed'. But Antigone also shows no hesitation when she hears of Creon's decree, and Electra acts promptly when she tells Chrysothemis to throw away Clytemnestra's offerings, and when she plans to murder Aegisthus. Oedipus is the promptest of them all. In all the crises of his life—his flight from Corinth, his murder of Laius, his defeat of the sphinx, the plague, his search for his own origin—he is, like Ajax, brave to do what the moment needs.[1]

The modest man is prepared to listen to his friends, but these characters are too inflexible to yield easily. Ajax indignantly rejects the suggestion that he can be influenced, but his monologue represents a genuine change of attitude to the entreaties of Tecmessa and the chorus. Creon is unmoved by the entreaties of Ismene and Haemon, but he is finally moved by Tiresias. Oedipus is unmoved by the arguments of Creon, but is prepared to listen to Iocasta and the chorus. Odysseus says in the prologue that Philoctetes is inflexible, and in the course of the play Philoctetes himself gives ample evidence of this. Yet he is nearly over-persuaded by Neoptolemus and finally yields to Heracles.[2]

Lack of reason is clearly inconsistent with *sophrosyne*. Ajax' wish for suicide is judged by the chorus to be unreasonable, Antigone is in love with the impossible and has a fury in her heart, Creon always wears one habit of mind and is filled with bad counsel. Oedipus will not, like a reasonable man, assess the present by the past.

---

[1] *Impatience*: *Aj*. 540; *O.T*. 73; *El*. 169; *Phil*. 635. *Suspicion*: *Ant*. 289, 1033; *O.T*. 346, 385. *Anger*: *Trach*. 777. *Prompt efficiency*: *Aj*. 119; Teucer, 985; *Trach*. 160; *Phil*. 1299; *Ant*. 37; *El*. 431, 938; *O.T*. 794, 810, 48, 68, 1058.

[2] *Aj*. 594, 651; *Ant*. 569, 726, 1099, cf. 771; *O.T*. 669, cf. *O.C*. 1204; *Phil*. 103, 628, 1350, 1447.

Electra has no judgement and no caution, and Philoctetes' resistance is unreasonable.[1]

Arrogance, violence, haste, inflexibility, and folly are all faults, and so far it may be said that Sophocles is not drawing ideal characters. But these vices are closely connected with virtues which these characters possess, virtues such as spirit, energy, firmness, and idealism. The folly of Antigone and Electra is in the end justified.[2] Ajax and Creon discover the unreason of their actions. Heracles in the last scene of the *Trachiniae* realizes and accepts his position. Philoctetes finally yields to entreaty. Oedipus recognizes in his own hastiness the cause of his misfortunes. Sophocles does not condone these faults. Where the chief character does not recognize them himself, the chorus or another character points them out. Antigone, Creon, and Philoctetes are all told by the chorus that they have only themselves to blame for their misfortunes.[3]

In the foregoing description we have tried to show how far Sophocles' chief characters correspond with the ideal which he tried to draw. His view of life sets up certain standards of conduct towards family, state, and religion. Although the chief characters may often fall short of these standards they are usually themselves conscious of their shortcomings and the audience at least is left in no doubt. Shortcomings and virtues alike are typical in that they are all shared by several characters. In comparing these common elements we have tended to lose sight of the peculiar and distinctive combinations of them which constitute individuality. Our description must therefore be completed by a brief portrait of each.

Ajax is a soldier and justly confident in his valour. But his confidence has become arrogance which on the one

---

[1] *Aj.* 371; *Ant.* 90, 603; 705, 1052; *O.T.* 915; *El.* 213, 993; *Phil.* 1098.
[2] *Ant.* 904; *El.* 1089.
[3] *O.T.* 767; *Ant.* 875, 1260; *Phil.* 1095 (cf. 1318).

hand leads to brutality, and on the other to extreme sensitiveness to any slur on his honour or reputation.[1] Before his death he comes to understand these faults, so that his death is not only an escape but an atonement. Teucer has the efficiency and affection of his brother and a dash of his pride too.

Antigone believes that the burial of her brother is a duty to the gods, which transcends any duty which she may have to the state or to herself. She carries this out with unalterable purpose, and only in her last speech recognizes the existence of other duties and feels the need to justify herself. Creon is a king with a fixed view of the good of the state and a ruthless hatred of rebels. This view of the state pervades his whole life, his relation to his family and the gods, as well as his relation to his subjects. He has also a morbid fear of the influence of women.[2]

Heracles is a soldier like Ajax, quick to angry action and brutal when opposed. He is careful of ritual observances, and accepts his fate when he finds that it is in agreement with the oracle. But he is prepared to disregard all laws, human and divine, when he is in love.

Oedipus is a king with a deep affection for his people. He has confidence in his own intellectual powers and cannot tolerate any one who questions them. He has a deep affection for his supposed parents and for his wife and children, and therefore, as is natural, a passionate desire to find out the truth about his birth. In the aged Oedipus of the *Coloneus* the intolerance is even more marked, the affection for his daughters as strong as ever, and the sensitiveness which sent the young Oedipus to question the

---

[1] Cf. Wolff, *Platos Apologie*, p. 59 f.

[2] Wolff's characterization of Creon as a sententious sophist (*Sentenz u. Reflexion*, pp. 126 ff.) is mistaken. See T. von Wilamowitz, *Dramatische Technik*, p. 45. Creon's gnomes are due to the style of the early Sophocles.

oracle at Delphi has become a horror at the very mention of his past.

Electra has brooded for eight years over the murder of Agamemnon. She is obsessed by the affection in which she holds her father and brother, by the horror of her mother's crime, and by the indignity of her own position. Though she is conscious that it is wrong to kick against the pricks, she yet justifies her desire for vengeance as being in accordance with the laws of god.

Philoctetes is a sick man, outcast on a desert island, and cannot forget that he was abandoned by the Greeks. This colours his whole attitude; he comes to believe that the gods are malignant, and his dearest hope is that his enemies may suffer as he does. Yet he has the heroic virtue of fortitude in misfortune and, though inflexible to human appeals, accepts at once the guidance of Heracles.

The other characters can be treated at less length. We shall first describe the 'bad' characters and the 'good' characters, because they have the clearest affinities with the major characters. Menelaus and Agamemnon in the *Ajax*, Aegisthus in the *Electra*, Odysseus in the *Philoctetes*, and Creon in the *Coloneus* have some of the qualities of Creon in the *Antigone*. They all share his belief in the established order of the state. Menelaus and Agamemnon emphasize the need of obedience to commanders and laws. Aegisthus believes in his own absolute authority. Odysseus and Creon represent themselves as servants of their city.[1] Like Creon in the *Antigone*, they all disregard the laws of the gods in the pursuit of their immediate aims. Menelaus and Agamemnon are dishonouring the gods by refusing to bury Ajax. Aegisthus' death is the reward of his impiety. Odysseus is nominally pious, but his plea that Zeus commanded the return of Philoctetes is blasphemy, since, when he makes it, he knows that he is proposing to

[1] *Aj.* 1079, 1352; *El.* 1462; *Phil.* 1143, 1243; *O.C.* 737, 851.

deprive Philoctetes of his bow. Creon in the *Coloneus*
has no regard for the sanctity of suppliants.[1] These characters are also like Creon in the *Antigone*, in their mockery
of their foes and their ability to dress up base deeds in
fine words. Menelaus and Agamemnon insult the dead
Ajax and defend themselves by elaborate expositions of
political and military theory. Aegisthus insults the dead
Orestes, as he has insulted the dead Agamemnon, and yet
is prepared to make a speech in his own defence. Odysseus
makes light of Philoctetes' hardships and mocks him as he
leaves him; he believes that the tongue, not the hand, is
the leader in everything. Creon in the *Coloneus* has no
thought for the feelings of Oedipus when he describes his
condition and his past, and dresses up his endeavour to
control Oedipus' movements as a just summons to him to
return home.[2]

But for all their likenesses these characters are distinct
figures. Menelaus is a mere braggart, rejoicing in the
twist of fortune which has brought him to the top. Agamemnon is a soldier and is open to persuasion, even though
he may not change his mind. Aegisthus is the blackest;
tyrant, coward, and adulterer, he has not a word of pity
when he sees Clytemnestra's body, but thinks only of his
own safety. Odysseus is a subtle schemer whose only
interest is his own advancement. Creon in the *Coloneus*
is a fierce old man with no regard for the feelings or wishes
of any one.

Three characters, Odysseus in the *Ajax*, Creon in the
Tyrannus, Theseus in the *Coloneus*, are embodiments of the
modesty which the chief characters always recognize but
seldom attain. The basis of the characters of all three is
modesty, cautiousness, and awareness of human frailty.
Creon shows his caution when he refuses to make any

[1] *Aj.* 1129, 1343; *El.* 1383; *Phil.* 1051, 990; *O.C.* 823.
[2] *Aj.* 1091–2; *El.* 267, 1482; *Phil.* 16, 1060, 99; *O.C.* 745, 944, 761.

suggestion where he has not certain knowledge, and prefers the second position in the state. Odysseus' caution comes near to cowardice when he begs Athena not to call Ajax from his tent. All three understand the dangers of anger and the force of persuasion. All three pity human misfortunes and understand the fragility of human existence. Creon and Theseus both believe in the principle of equal rights in the state. All three reverence the gods. Odysseus acknowledges the direction of Athena and will not allow Agamemnon to transgress the divine laws. Creon refuses to allow Oedipus to leave the land until he has consulted Apollo again. Theseus persuades Oedipus to recognize Polynices' rights as a suppliant. This Odysseus, who is more moved by Ajax' nobility than his own hatred, is very different from the Odysseus of tradition, the liar and mocker whom Ajax knows and whom we see in the *Philoctetes*. Creon in the *Tyrannus* has nothing to do with the Creon of the *Antigone* or *Coloneus*. He too is noble and, when suspected of plotting against Oedipus, has no desire for long life with this repute upon him. Theseus' character is summed up in a line of the messenger speech: 'He in his nobility without lamentation consented to do this for the stranger'. If our interpretation of Sophocles' thought is correct, these three characters with their nobility and modesty come nearer than any to his ideal.[1]

According to Greek thought the young have not yet attained their true nature, and in particular they do not yet possess wisdom. Therefore Philoctetes defends Neoptolemus by saying that Odysseus caught him while he was still ungrown. Neoptolemus is disturbed by conflicting

---

[1] *Caution*: O.T. 569, 584; *Aj*. 74. *Anger and persuasion*: *Aj*. 1322, 1353; O.T. 605; O.C. 592, 1175. *Pity for misfortunes and awareness of fragility*: *Aj*. 121, O.T. 1473; O.C. 556, 566. *Reverence for the gods*: *Aj*. 35, 1343; O.T. 1438; O.C. 1179. *Nobility*: *Aj*. 1357 (contrast 103, 382); O.T. 518; O.C. 1636.

forces which, had he been grown up, would probably have
been brought into some ordered relation to each other,
whether the result had been an Odysseus or a Philoctetes.
Three forces are acting upon him. As the son of Achilles,
he has a belief in his own inherited characteristics and in
the standards which his birth demands. He feels it his
duty to do good and not ill, to reward benefactors, to be
truthful and refuse dishonourable success, and to win by
force rather than by fraud. As his father's son also, he
desires military glory and is easily tempted by the promise
that he shall take Troy; the same quality can be seen in
his reverence for Philoctetes' bow. Thirdly, as a member
of an army, he expects to obey his generals, just as he
expects obedience from his own crew. The conflict arises
when he is ordered by his commander Odysseus to deceive
Philoctetes; deceit is incompatible with his aristocratic
ideal. For the moment desire for military glory wins him.
But his meeting with Philoctetes brings a new force, pity,
into play, which finally, after Philoctetes' sickness, makes
concealment of the deceit no longer possible. The arrival
of Odysseus leaves him for a short time dumbfounded, but
afterwards he recovers himself and finally asserts his own
ideal as more important than his general's orders. When
he says, 'With justice on my side I do not fear your fear',
we feel that he has grown up and attained his nature.
Before, desire for glory could drive him in one direction
until pity drove him back again. Now he has decided to
live true to the heroic ideal. Euripides is portraying the
same kind of youth in Hippolytus and in the Achilles of
the *Iphigenia in Aulis*. But even in the first scene with
Odysseus Neoptolemus behaves naturally and lacks their
priggishness.[1]

[1] *Neoptolemus ungrown* : *Phil.* 1014. *Heroic ideal* : 88, 902; 1304; 672;
79, 580; 94; 90. Cf. also his religion, 192, 464, 841. *Glory* : 116, 352; 657.
Obedience : 93, 386, 1010; 141. *Pity*: 759, 965. *Final decision* : 1251.

Orestes is a slighter portrait on the same lines. He is inspired by the memory of his father Agamemnon, and has no doubt that his course of action is right because Apollo commanded it. He is therefore prompt and energetic in making his plans. But his plans involve the false report of his own death and, though he justifies this, he, like Neoptolemus, feels that he is acting against the heroic ideal of frankness and candour. When he hears Electra's lament and realizes that the broken slave woman before him is Electra herself, he, like Neoptolemus, yields to pity and confesses his identity. The excess of Electra's joy makes him recover himself, and for the rest of the play he is the calm and efficient son of Agamemnon.[1]

Haemon seems to be younger than either Neoptolemus or Orestes. His appeal to reason when trying to persuade his father has little relation to his own actions. It is true that his wish to obey his father in everything and his knowledge of opinion in Thebes are both real, but he would have neither known Theban opinion nor disobeyed his father, had he not been guided by his love for Antigone. It is this love that makes him throw off all restraint and flare up in anger against his father both on the stage and in the tomb. The Heracles of the *Trachiniae* must in his youth have been not unlike Haemon.[2]

Hyllus seems to be even younger than Haemon. He is intensely proud of his father and ready to do anything to help him. Therefore, when he has seen his father tortured by the fatal robe, he has no pity or understanding for his mother, and can justly be said to have forced her to suicide. His violent anger is followed by an equally violent repentance. His realization of his mother's innocence and his pity for her lot strengthens him to force his father also

[1] *El.* 33, 35; 38; 61; 1177; 1288.
[2] *Ant.* 685; 635, 692, 733; 648, 795; 766, 1231. I disagree with the recent interpretation of von Fritz, *Philologus*, 1934, p. 30 f.

to admit that she is not guilty of his death. But the sum of these sufferings is intolerable and he finds their cause in the 'mighty heedlessness of the gods'. Like Philoctetes, he abandons his belief in the justice of the gods because of their treatment of him. But what in Philoctetes is a cynicism ingrained by misery, in Hyllus is the momentary outburst of a boy.[1]

Polynices differs from the rest of these youths. He is harder and more formed, perhaps because he is older. His is the potentially noble character which has gone wrong. He has the heroic sense of honour but carries it to a further excess than Ajax and for less cause. He believes more in the right of primogeniture than the goodwill of the citizens. He believes that the good general should conceal bad news whatever effect it may have on the policy of his colleagues, and that retreat under any circumstances is dishonourable. He is truly shocked at his father's condition, but has never considered it until he needs his father's aid. But there is real nobility in his affection for his sisters and in his determination to face certain death.[2]

With the exception of Polynices who is more formed than the rest, the Sophoclean youths, though noble, are swayed by such emotions as pity or grief or love or desire for fame. The 'airy follies' of youth are still with them and they have not yet 'grown their wits'.

Women are weaker than men. Like the young, they are subject to gusts of passion, since their weakness is not only physical. The ideal is the modest woman who derives a quiet strength from her modesty and nobility. Tecmessa comes nearest to this ideal, but we shall start with Deianira, because she is the most carefully drawn of the women. She is a chief character but, as she is an obedient wife and not, like Antigone or Electra, a woman with a man's pur-

---

[1] *Trach.* 755, 1155, 1250; 734, 809, 932; 936, 1114; 1266.
[2] *O.C.* 1295; 1429; 1422; 1265; 1439.

pose, she has been reserved for treatment here. In spite of her one rash deed, her attempt to recover the love of Heracles, she has more affinities with Ismene than with Antigone. She has a woman's love for her husband and a woman's timorousness. But she has a quiet strength and nobility when she faces Lichas and when she goes to her death. She also has an initiative which distinguishes her from Euripides' Phaedra. Phaedra yields to the nurse's persuasion, but Deianira herself thinks of the charm and does not take much account of the cautioning of the chorus.

The two chief forces in her character are her love for Heracles and a timorousness which goes beyond *sophrosyne*. She loves Heracles and therefore cannot bear competition with the youthful Iole. Eros rules her just as he rules the gods, and she suffers bitter pangs when Heracles is away. Her one rash deed is an attempt to win him back, and when she commits suicide she dies in their bridal chamber.

Secondly, she is timorous; she feared her suitors; her life is continual misery, since she is always frightened for her husband or her children. When Heracles is announced victorious, she is afraid that he may fall. Although these fears are modest, yet, like the fears of Odysseus in the prologue of the *Ajax*, they seem to cross the border-line between modesty and cowardice. The chorus, who have true modesty, reproach Deianira with something like cowardice when they sing, 'I say that you should not destroy good hope'. But when she forces Lichas to tell her the truth, she shows her *sophrosyne*, 'I am not the sort of woman that does not understand human nature, that it cannot rejoice in the same things always'. Here Lichas rightly calls her 'a mortal with mortal thoughts and not unwise'. She cannot, however, preserve this attitude; her love for Heracles is too strong for her reason. Thus she

performs her one rash deed. She admits to the chorus
that she has never tried the charm with which she hopes
to win back the love of Heracles, and she feels her own
guilt when she says, 'Wicked daring may I neither know
nor learn. And I hate those that dare'. But as soon as
she learns the true nature of the charm, her nobility comes
out, and when she hears that the poison has had its effect,
she goes silently to death.[1]

Iocasta is like Deianira in her quiet nobility and her
love for her husband. She too goes silently to death when
she discovers her disgrace and shame. She too loves her
husband Oedipus. And she loved her former husband
Laius and calls upon him before she dies. No doubt she
loved her child too, and its exposure and her subsequent
disillusionment, when Laius was killed by robbers, are the
cause of her half-developed scepticism. She moves from
scepticism to credulity, as Deianira moves from timorousness to rashness. In a moment of triumph she is ready to
say that all human affairs are governed by chance, and that
an oracle can have its fulfilment in a dream. But though
she is scornful of oracles, she is at first careful to guard
herself by attributing the unfulfilled prophecy to the god's
minister and not the god himself. Her scepticism, like
Creon's in the *Antigone*, is not deep, since, when she is in
trouble, she prays to Apollo. Beyond this she is a queen,
and rates Creon and Oedipus for their unseemly quarrel-
ling when the city needs them.[2]

[1] *Love: Trach.* 545; 443, 41; 1138, 913. *Timorousness:* 7, 5, 150; 297
(cf. 303); 122. *Sophrosyne:* 439, 473. *Rashness:* 590, 582. *Nobility:* 721.

[2] *Love for Husband: O.T.* 862, 1061; 1245. Cf. Croiset, *Oedipe Roi*, p. 185
Love for child: 717; so Sheppard, op. cit., p. 155. *Scepticism:* 978, 981 (cf.
Croiset, op. cit., p. 147), 708; T. von Wilamowitz, op. cit., p. 81 f.,
denies that 708 and 852 can be interpreted by the psychology of the
speaker and derives them from the exigencies of plot construction; contrast, however, Weinstock's excellent treatment of the scene, op. cit.,
p. 180 f. *Credulity:* 712, 911. *Queen:* 634.

Clytemnestra, like Iocasta, is a woman of strong affections, embittered against her husband by his sacrifice of
her daughter. 'He did not travail when he begat her as
I did when I bore her.' And when she hears of Orestes'
death, for the moment she breaks down. Her strong
affection for her children accounts for her hatred of Agamemnon and her insults when he is dead. It accounts for
her hatred of Orestes and Electra because, though they
are her own children, they treat her as an enemy. This
strong physical affection also explains her alliance with
Aegisthus, with whom she finds peace, only disturbed by
Electra's threats. Like Iocasta, she is half a sceptic; she
fears no avenging spirit, but when she is in trouble, she
prays to the gods, though her prayer to Apollo is itself an
impiety. She is conceived rather in the same spirit as
Polynices, a noble character gone wrong. As a queen, she
has some sense of Electra's position and her own.[1]

Ismene and Chrysothemis are younger and unmarried.
Both have a real affection for their more ardent sister. But
both are conscious that they are women and cannot fight
with men, still less with the rulers of the city. Both try
to restrain their sisters from bringing ruin on themselves;
they believe that the dead will forgive them their careless-
ness. Here the similarity ends. Ismene refuses to help
Antigone at the beginning, but when the deed is done,
she recognizes the superior right of the divine law and
claims her share in the guilt. Her prudence is gone in her
distress and she is horrified at Creon's treatment of his
son's betrothed. Chrysothemis' compliance with the rule
of Clytemnestra and Aegisthus merits the reproach that
she is unworthy of Agamemnon's fatherhood. She recog-

---

[1] *Affection for children*: El. 532, 770. Cf. Reinhardt, op. cit., p. 164 f.
Hatred of Agamemnon: 277, 444. *Hatred of Orestes and Electra*: 289, 775.
Love of Aegisthus: 648. *Relation to gods*: 276, 793; contrast 637. *Queen*:
518, 612.

nizes that Electra is right, but neither the hope of marriage nor of glory will move her from her complacency.[1]

Three women, Tecmessa in the *Ajax* and the two sisters in the *Coloneus*, are of the same breed as Odysseus in the *Ajax* and Theseus. Tecmessa loves Ajax and is willing to die with him although she is a sword-won bride. Her capture was the will of the gods and therefore she accepts it, just as she later accepts Ajax' death as their will. Though she obeys Ajax in everything, she tried to stop him when he went out to murder the Atridae, and she tries to stop him when he threatens to kill himself. Both murder and suicide are acts of passion, and she is filled with *sophrosyne*. Of the other two Antigone is the fuller portrait. Both sisters love each other, their father, and their brothers. Antigone believes that god has willed the sufferings of Oedipus. She understands her father's and her brother's anger and tries to overcome them by her own calm reason. When Oedipus passes, she prays that she may die too. Of all the women in Sophocles this Antigone is nearest to the heroic maidens of Euripides, such as Macaria and Polyxena, but her heroism is unostentatious.[2]

The minor characters, who are only on the stage for a scene or two, are slightly drawn, but sufficiently to give them an independent existence. Only the 'messenger from the house' in the *Antigone* and the old man who arrives with Heracles in the *Trachiniae* are completely colourless, but it is possible that we have seen them both before. The 'messenger from the house' may have been

---

[1] *Affection: Ant.* 99; *El.* 374, 903. *Weakness: Ant.* 61, 63; *El.* 997, 340. *Restraint: Ant.* 49, 65; *El.* 330, 400. *Ismene's heroism: Ant.* 540, 564 (contrast 44, 79.) Cf. Schadewaldt, *Aias u. Antigone*, p. 89 f. *Chrysothemis' complacency: El.* 345, 970; 338, 1042; 958, 1006.

[2] *Tecmessa: Aj.* 490, 966, 392; 489, 950, 970; 529, 288, 585. *Antigone and Ismene: O.C.* 321, 324; 344, 445; 365, 420, 1414; 252, 1183; 1193, 1420; 1733.

the messenger of Haemon's suicide, who moralized on Fortune as a preparation for his narrative. The old man in the *Trachiniae* was probably the messenger of the first act; there he is only interested in his own advancement and therefore tells only the good news to Deianira; later when it suits his book he exposes Lichas. These two messengers have two of the ingredients in Sophocles' recipe for slaves—the tendency to moralize and the desire for gain. The tendency to moralize is most developed in the guard of the *Antigone* who has to be a match for Creon. The desire for gain may lead these slaves to meddle with disastrous results, as when the messenger exposes Lichas and the Corinthian[1] tells Oedipus of his origin. The third important ingredient is loyalty. Loyalty makes Lichas and the Theban herdsman attempt to conceal the truth, and loyalty enables the nurse in the *Trachiniae* and the pedagogue in the *Electra* to give their owners free criticism and advice. The messenger in the *Trachiniae* and the Corinthian herdsman in the *Tyrannus* have as important a function in the plot as the old slave in the *Ion*, but Sophocles does not distract attention from his chief character by a detailed portrait of the meddling slave; he only sketches them fully enough to make their parts intelligible.

Tiresias, in the *Antigone* and *Tyrannus*, is an old man unwilling to tell a disastrous truth. His care for the city in both plays forces him to speak. His age and blindness are stressed. He is a sketch for the full portrait of a blind and irritable old man which Sophocles later draws in the *Coloneus*.[2] Eurydice in the *Antigone*, timorous and honour-

---

[1] Sheppard, op. cit., p. 156, characterizes him as an eager rather vulgar busybody, full of his great news and delighted with his own cleverness. Saunders, *Greece and Rome*, iv, p. 14, notes the likeness of the *Antigone* guard, Corinthian herdsman, *Trachiniae* messenger, and merchant in the *Philoctetes*.   [2] So also Reinhardt, op. cit., p. 116.

able, the priest in the *Tyrannus*, asking help of Oedipus but remembering that Oedipus is man and not god, and the stranger in the *Coloneus*, disturbed but considerate, are sufficiently drawn for the parts they must play.

T. von Wilamowitz denies these minor figures all character; but if Eurydice is only introduced into the *Antigone* to commit suicide, and Tiresias to bring about the catastrophe, we may well ask why Sophocles has told us anything about them at all. As Weinstock says of Chrysothemis, Sophocles does not give the dramatic function to anybody but to that person whose peculiar quality naturally performs it.[1]

Finally we have to consider the character of the chorus. Some scholars regard this task as an impossibility; Kranz says that the choruses have no character, and Reinhardt compares their utterances to an orchestral accompaniment.[2] But their change of position can be regarded as evidence of the chorus' independence and therefore of their personality. To take an example, the ladies of Mycenae warn Electra to be careful when she unfolds her plan to Chrysothemis and after Chrysothemis' speech repeat their warning to Electra, but this is not inconsistent with their belief that she is essentially right and Chrysothemis wrong.[3]

In the *Ajax* and *Philoctetes* the chorus are soldiers who have sailed to Troy with their leaders, Ajax and Neop-

---

[1] Weinstock, op. cit., p. 17. Contrast T. von Wilamowitz, op. cit., p. 40 f. His account of the Tiresias scene in the *Tyrannus* is peculiarly unfortunate (p. 75 f.)

[2] Kranz, *Stasimon*, p. 220 f.; Reinhardt, op. cit., p. 193.

[3] *El.* 990, 1015, 1058. Cf. Untersteiner, *Rivista di Filologia*, 1933, p. 299 f., on the choruses of the *Ajax*, *Antigone*, *Electra*. Cf. Weinstock, op. cit., p. 14 (on the *Electra*), die Stimme des 'gesunden Menschenverstandes' zum Augenblick und aus dem Augenblick heraus; Helmreich, *Der Chor nach seinem Ethos betrachtet* (passim). Errandonea, *Mnemosyne*, l., p. 369 f., takes the same view but presses the characterization of the chorus too far.

tolemus. In both plays they express their dependence on their leaders; but in both plays they are free men with the right to express their own opinion. In the *Antigone* and the *Tyrannus* they are the nobles of Thebes and councillors of the city. In the *Antigone* they are old men with the old man's love of life, and loyal adherents of the house of Laius. In the *Tyrannus* they are deeply concerned for the distress of Thebes in the plague and deeply attached to Oedipus himself. In the *Coloneus* they are old men, citizens of Colonus, patriotic and loyal to Theseus. In the *Trachiniae* and the *Electra* they are women who sympathize with the heroine.[1]

It is undoubtedly intentional that the two choruses of women take little part in the action of the play. The exception when the chorus of the *Electra* tell Electra how to receive Aegisthus is hardly an exception. The choruses of men all make some contribution to the action. They are most active in the two latest plays. In the *Philoctetes* they support Neoptolemus in his speeches to Philoctetes, and while Philoctetes is asleep they suggest that Neoptolemus should steal his bow; during the *parodos* they have examined Philoctetes' cave. In the *Coloneus* they search for Oedipus when he is hidden in the wood, they instruct him how to sacrifice, and they do their best to hamper Creon when he tries to carry Oedipus off.[2]

Helpful and sympathetic, the chorus are also pious and modest. The doxologies of the *Antigone*, *Trachiniae*, and *Philoctetes*, the song on oracles in the *Tyrannus*, and the song on dreams in the *Electra* are sufficient evidence of the piety of the chorus. Their modesty can be seen in their readiness to criticize others for the lack of it. Here again

---

[1] Kranz, op. cit., p. 221, finds a contradiction between the hypothesis of the *Electra* χορὸς ἐπιχωρίων παρθένων and l. 234. But surely a παρθένος can be old enough to speak as a mother.

[2] *El.* 1437; *Phil.* 391, 507; 833; *O.C.* 118, 464, 829.

we need not accumulate examples; it is enough to note
that the chorus of Ajax' sailors say that both Teucer and
Agamemnon lack *sophrosyne*, and the Mycenaean ladies
tell Electra that her hatred of Clytemnestra pays no heed
to justice.[1] In the last two plays the choruses are more
active than in the others, and in the same way their outlook is less detached. The soldiers of Neoptolemus urge
him further on his false course, when he has the chance of
stealing Philoctetes' bow. The citizens of Colonus are
perhaps more fussy and inquisitive than becomes the truly
modest. But in general it would be true to say that the
chorus are sympathetic and helpful friends of the characters, with the sanity and religion of the ordinary man, and
perfect freedom to criticize any character at any moment.
They are therefore a valuable norm by which other characters can be measured.

The men and women of the chorus are ordinary people
living ordinary lives. They are therefore naturally pious
and modest, and their piety and modesty are subjected to
no strain.[2] The chief characters (and some of the other
characters too) have to face situations, caused by their own
personality or by external circumstances, in which their
piety and modesty may break down. In the main their
actions conform to the standards which we have discussed
in the last chapter; when they deviate, they are criticized.
In this sense Sophocles' claim to draw ideal characters
can be understood.

[1] *Aj.* 1264, *El.* 610; cf. *Ant.* 875, *Trach.* 122, *O.T.* 649, *Phil.* 1045, *O.C.*
1695.
[2] I owe this view of the chorus to Professor Hermann Fränkel.

IV. Character-Drawing

Arrangement of plot—long scenes—types of scene—character contrasts—references outside the play—change of outlook.

IN this and the following chapters we are no longer concerned with the life or thought or ideals of Sophocles, but with the details of his technique. His chief object in writing tragedy is to create and display great personalities, and therefore we shall deal with character-drawing before plot construction since that is to some extent determined by the character to be presented. The play gives a piece of the history of some person through the medium of actions and words. That person must have as complete a character as possible; the audience must see and hear him in the greatest possible number of different circumstances. His character is something more permanent than the piece of history which forms the play; it was there before the play began, and it will remain, even if modified, after the play is finished. This permanent quality also has to be communicated to the audience.

The Greek dramatist had complete freedom in the treatment of the traditional story, and Sophocles arranged his story to provide a large number of different situations for his chief character. We can compare his *Electra* with the handling of the same story by the other two tragedians. Electra is on the stage for almost the whole play. No ghost-raising, no skilful intriguing, no realistic detail or elaborate description distracts the attention of the audience from her tragedy. The whole arrangement of the plot—the Chrysothemis scenes, the long messenger speech, and the delaying of the recognition—is designed to give Electra's emotions the greatest possible scope, so that we see her in turn gloomy, scornful, elated, desperate, purposeful, sorrowful, joyful, and triumphant. In the

Coloneus also the plot is constructed to show a long and varied sequence of emotions in the hero. Oedipus' emotions are anxiety and then joyful acceptance of the omen in the prologue; in the first act indignation with the chorus and then anxiety, joy at Ismene's arrival, indignation at her story, agony during the short *kommos*, and warm friendship with Theseus; in the second act fury with Creon, anguish when Antigone is seized, scorn when Theseus arrives; in the third act joy at the return of his daughters, anger at the news of Polynices' request, submission to Antigone's appeal; in the later scenes fury with Polynices and agitation at the thunder, followed by something like exaltation when he leaves the stage.

In his later plays Sophocles makes his hero pass through a long and varied sequence of emotion within the limits of a single scene.[1] He builds long scenes of several parts, divided at most by a short strophe of lyrics followed after more dialogue by its antistrophe. The earliest scene with a considerable change of emotion is the Tiresias scene of the *Antigone*, where Creon passes from calm inquiry to fury and then, when Tiresias has angrily left the stage, to repentance. The second act of the *Trachiniae* is an intermediate stage before the really long scenes, such as the second act of the *Electra* and the first act of the *Philoctetes*. The first act of the *Philoctetes* is four hundred and sixty lines long and is only broken by a short strophe and antistrophe at two emotional points, the end of Neoptolemus' narrative and the end of Philoctetes' appeal. This long act is constructed to display a long series of emotions. Neoptolemus at the beginning is ready to play his part, but is gradually captured by the nobility of Philoctetes, until he is glad to have him for his friend and can make no use of the merchant's tale which Odysseus had con-

[1] On the development of the long scene, particularly in the second act, and on the divided strophe and antistrophe, see the next chapter.

structed to help him. Philoctetes is excited and joyful at
the sight of the Greeks, then full of self-pity; he pities
Neoptolemus because of Achilles' death; his pity changes
to anger against the Greeks who cheated Neoptolemus
and anger against the gods who only allow the bad to live;
then he makes his passionate appeal and is overjoyed by its
acceptance; he is furious again at the merchant's tale, and
ends in grateful friendship with Neoptolemus.

Inside the general scheme of the plot Sophocles chooses
certain types of scene to display character. The difference
between the methods of Sophocles and of Euripides may
broadly be stated thus. Sophocles displays his characters
by contrasting them with other characters, Euripides by
the situations which he makes them face and the mono-
logues which he makes them speak. A comparison[1] will
make the first point clear. When in the *Coloneus* Theseus
welcomes Oedipus to Athens, Oedipus is won by the
nobility and generosity of his host, and in the warmth of
Theseus' welcome he becomes a wise and kindly old man.
No one but Theseus or some one like Theseus could have
this effect on Oedipus. But when in the *Alcestis* Admetus forces Heracles to enter his house, Euripides shows
Admetus' sense of hospitality, not by contrasting him
with Heracles, but by the situation—the arrival of a guest
in the midst of his lamentations.

Typical scenes which Sophocles uses again and again
are appeals, persuasions, and debates.[2] All show the chief
character in contact with another character, and therefore,
besides furthering the story, either tell us something about
the chief character or identify our sympathies with him.

---

[1] *O.C.* 551 f., *Alc.* 476 f.
[2] e.g. *Appeal*: *Aj.* 485; *Ant.* 49, 544; *O.T.* 14; *El.* 947; *Phil.* 927; *O.C.*
1254. *Persuasion*: *Aj.* 1318; *Ant.* 988; *Trach.* 395; *O.T.* 634, 1119; *El.* 431;
Phil. 50; *O.C.* 1181. *Debate*: *Aj.* 1047, 1226; *Ant.* 450, 635; *O.T.* 532;
El. 516; *Phil.* 1004; *O.C.* 728, 897.

We learn Ajax' inflexibility when he will not listen to Tecmessa's appeal, and both the stubbornness and the affection of Oedipus when he yields ungraciously to Iocasta's persuasion. Creon bares his soul in his two debates with Antigone and Haemon. These types of scene are also used by the other·two tragedians, but not always for the same purpose.

The earliest scene of persuasion which has survived is the scene in the *Supplices* where Pelasgus is persuaded to accept the suppliants. This tells us nothing about the character of Pelasgus or the suppliants; it only shows the difficulty and importance of the task of persuasion. On the other hand, the scene in the *Septem* where the chorus try to dissuade Eteocles from meeting his brother, is the direct ancestor of the Sophoclean scene of persuasion. The only debate in Aeschylus is the trial scene in the *Eumenides*, and there the primary interest is in the verdict.[1]

All these types of scene were part of the tragedian's stock-in-trade when Euripides began to write, and he can use them all for the same purpose as Sophocles.[2] No one would doubt that we learn Hippolytus' character from the huntsman's attempt to persuade him to reverence Aphrodite, and Medea's from her debate with Jason. But often he has other objects. When Hecuba appeals to Agamemnon and Iphigenia persuades Thoas, the poet has no end beyond the furtherance of the action. Some of his debates, like the discussion on the relative merits of archers and foot-soldiers in the *Hercules*, are chiefly interesting for their matter and have little connexion with the subject of the play. Others are scenes from the law-court and consist of defence and prosecution before a judge, e.g. Eteocles *v.*

---

[1] *Suppl.* 333, cf. *Ag.* 905, *Cho.* 892, *Eum.* 794. *Septem* 677, cf. Prometheus and Oceanus, Prometheus and Hermes, Clytemnestra and Cassandra.
[2] *Appeal*: *Andr.* 920, *Or.* 640. *Persuasion*: *Hipp.* 88, cf. *Alc.* 280 &c. *Debate*: *Med.* 465, cf. *Alc.* 614.

Polynices before Iocasta.[1] The nearest approach to these legal scenes is the debate between Theseus, Creon, and Oedipus in the *Coloneus*, but it is no parallel, since the three speakers are evenly balanced and Theseus can in no sense be called a judge.

In all these scenes the effect on the hero depends on the quality of his antagonist, and therefore Sophocles chooses his minor figures with the greatest care. The poet is not more hampered in the treatment of his characters than in the treatment of his plot. Odysseus was given to Sophocles by tradition as wily and unscrupulous, and though he uses this tradition in the *Philoctetes*, the Odysseus of the *Ajax* is the type of *sophrosyne*. Nor when he has created a character, does he feel obliged to give the same person the same character in a later play. The three Creons of the *Antigone*, *Tyrannus*, and *Coloneus* are connected in little but in name. Nothing prevents the poet from creating his minor characters as foils to the major characters. The minor figure has its own individuality, but that individuality contains one essential quality which is either the opposite of some important trait in the major character and therefore throws that trait into relief, or is a quality possessed and valued by the major character and therefore makes a bond of sympathy between the two.

The technique of contrasted characters goes back to Homer. In the *Iliad* Hector and Andromache are contrasted with Paris and Helen. Aeschylus sets the yielding Oceanus against the stubborn Prometheus. Euripides also has scenes in which two characters are contrasted, e.g. the first scene between Jason and Medea. His *Hercules* ends with a scene between friends, where the sympathy of the minor character enables the major character to expand in

---

[1] *Appeal: Hec.* 787, cf. *Hel.* 894, *I.A.* 1146. *Persuasion: I.T.* 1152, cf. *Med.* 709, 869; *Hel.* 1193; *Bacch.* 787. *Debate: H.F.* 140, cf. *Andr.* 590 *Suppl.* 426. *Trial scene: Phoen.* 465, cf. *Heracl.* 134; *Hec.* 1129; *Tro.* 906

a genial atmosphere. In the dialogue between Heracles and Theseus we appreciate for the first time the greatness and the humanity of Heracles. But though Aeschylus and Euripides sometimes display their chief characters by contrasting them with other characters, the display of characters is not their chief concern and they do not develop the technique of foils so far as Sophocles.

Sophocles constructs his whole play of character contrasts. The contrast between the pairs of sisters, Ismene and Antigone, Chrysothemis and Electra, has long been appreciated and studied in detail.[1] But the technique of contrast is extended to many other characters. This can be most easily shown schematically.

AJAX

Ajax *v*. Odysseus = arrogance *v*. modesty.

Ajax *v*. Tecmessa = inflexibility *v*. entreaty (but also a co-operation of friends which produces the *sophrosyne* speech).

Teucer (Ajax) *v*. Menelaus = independence *v*. authority.

Teucer (Ajax) *v*. Agamemnon = valour *v*. official pride.

ANTIGONE

Antigone *v*. Ismene = idealism *v*. realism.

Creon *v*. guard = king *v*. subject.

Antigone *v*. Creon = duty to god *v*. duty to state.

Antigone *v*. Ismene = inflexibility *v*. entreaty.

Creon *v*. Ismene = duty to state *v*. duty to family.

Creon *v*. Haemon = prejudice *v*. reason.

Creon *v*. Tiresias = duty to state *v*. duty to god.

TRACHINIAE

Deianira *v*. nurse = anxiety *v*. action.

Deianira *v*. Lichas = timorousness *v*. confidence.

[1] Cf. Pohlenz, *Griechische Tragödie*, pp. 187, 334. For the whole technique of the *Antigone* see now Saunders, op. cit., p. 14 ff.; Croiset, op. cit., pp. 59–60, adds the contrast between Ajax and Tecmessa; Wilamowitz, *Hermes*, xxxiv, p. 63, notes the contrast between Creon and Oedipus, though he perhaps unfairly calls Creon a Pharisee; Reinhardt, op. cit., p. 26, notes the contrasts between Ajax and Odysseus, Creon and Oedipus.

Deianira *v.* Iole = sympathy *v.* reserve.
Deianira *v.* Lichas = frankness *v.* concealment.
(Deianira *v.* Heracles = loyalty *v.* faithlessness).
Deianira *v.* Hyllus = nobility *v.* suspicion.
Heracles *v.* Hyllus = prejudice *v.* reason.

TYRANNUS

Oedipus *v.* priest = king *v.* subject.
Oedipus *v.* Tiresias = human skill *v.* supernatural knowledge.
Oedipus *v.* Creon = prejudice *v.* reason.
Oedipus and Iocasta = sympathy of kinship.
Oedipus *v.* Theban herdsman = frankness *v.* concealment.

ELECTRA

Electra *v.* Chrysothemis = idealism *v.* realism.
Electra *v.* Clytemnestra = duty to kin *v.* physical affection.
Electra *v.* Orestes = emotion *v.* reason.

PHILOCTETES

Neoptolemus *v.* Odysseus = honour *v.* gain.
Philoctetes and Neoptolemus = sympathy of birth.
Philoctetes *v.* Odysseus = independence *v.* authority.
Philoctetes *v.* Neoptolemus = prejudice *v.* reason.

COLONEUS

Oedipus and Ismene = sympathy of kinship.
Oedipus and Theseus = sympathy of birth.
Oedipus *v.* Creon = frankness *v.* concealment.
Oedipus *v.* Polynices = duty to kin *v.* desire for gain.

The foregoing scheme only gives the broad outlines of these contrasts and sympathies; the details of the chief characters have already been described. But even so bald a statement will make two points clear. First, Sophocles uses his sympathies and contrasts more than once; they are part of his stock-in-trade. The sympathy between Oedipus and Theseus is like that between Philoctetes and Neoptolemus, and the contrast between Heracles and Hyllus is like that between Creon and Haemon. Secondly, these contrasts and sympathies illuminate the various aspects of the chief characters which we have described, their relations to sex, family, city, and gods, their reason and unreason, and their ideals.

The opposition of two characters is particularly clear when they use the same words in opposite senses. Reinhardt has noticed that in the *Antigone* Creon and Antigone use good, bad, friend, and foe in different senses; Creon and Tiresias use gain in different senses. In the same way Electra and Clytemnestra do not give the same meaning to justice, nor Electra and Chrysothemis to modesty.[1] The contrast is pointed by being focussed on single words.

The minor characters have passions and prejudices of their own, and to measure a major character against them can only be a relative measurement. The chorus, however, if they are, as I have tried to show, sane and independent spectators, do provide a fixed norm by which to measure the characters and are carefully chosen for that purpose.[2] Many of the choral odes serve this function; for instance, the ode on oracles in the *Tyrannus* shows that, for the moment at any rate, Oedipus and Iocasta are to be regarded as impious. And the chief function of the chorus when it comments on the longer speeches of the characters is to show the audience what view a sane man takes of such a speech. Thus when in the *Antigone* Creon has put forward his theory of fatherhood and government, the chorus agree that it is wisely spoken; Creon is to be accepted as a sound political theorist, but Haemon's more democratic pronouncements are also right; the two should be combined.

Besides using sympathies and contrasts Sophocles displays his characters by putting them into situations where

---

[1] Op. cit., p. 89, 99, 118, cf. Weinstock, op. cit., p. 103. *Ant.* 514 f., 1032 f.; *El.* 528 f., 365 f., cf. *O.T.* 360 f., truth and night; *Aj.* 480 and 524, nobility.　　　　　[2] Cf. Helmreich, op. cit., p. 30 f.

they must show their mettle. Euripides, as we have said, uses this method more than Sophocles, but two of Sophocles' favourite types of scene, the explanatory speech and the 'report to two', show the character's reaction to a situation rather than to a person. In all the plays the chief character makes his first speech to the chorus about a situation of which the audience have been told in the prologue, and explains his own position. Aeschylus similarly uses the explanatory speech after the *parados* to show the character of his protagonist in the *Prometheus* and the *Agamemnon*; the beacon speech shows the character of Clytemnestra as well as Aeschylus' knowledge of geography. While she is careful to characterize herself as a woman, the matter of her speech shows her manliness. It goes without saying that Euripides displays his characters in explanatory speeches, but only in the *Medea* and *Helen* does he use the characteristically Sophoclean position after the *parados*.

By 'report to two' I mean those scenes where news is brought which has opposite effects on the hero and a minor character. The emotion of the hero is thrown into strong relief by the opposite emotion of the minor character. In the *Electra*, Electra's despair, when she hears the report of Orestes' death, is made more obvious by Clytemnestra's joy.[1] Aeschylus, like Sophocles in his early days, did not use his three actors freely enough to exploit this type of scene to the full. The germ can be seen in the *Agamemnon*, where the report of the herald has different effects on Clytemnestra and the chorus. The earliest scene where the effect on two actors is contrasted and elaborated is the second act of the *Trachiniae*, where Lichas' speech rejoices Deianira but moves the messenger to indigna-

---

[1] Cf. the merchant's tale in the *Philoctetes* which has opposite effects on Philoctetes and Neoptolemus, and Polynices' appeal in the *Coloneus* which moves Oedipus to fury and Antigone to pity.

tion; but here Lichas is removed before the messenger
speaks. Euripides has one scene of this type which is
closely paralleled in Sophocles. In the *Hippolytus* the
nurse tells Hippolytus of Phaedra's love; Hippolytus
breaks into a tirade against women which shows his in-
ability to understand Phaedra; Phaedra decides that the
only course for her is suicide, and leaves the stage. In spite
of the differences of detail and the absence of tragic irony,
the main lines of the situation are strangely like the scene
in the *Tyrannus* where the story of the Corinthian messenger drives Iocasta to suicide and Oedipus to scorn and
elation. If the *Tyrannus* was in fact produced a year
before the *Hippolytus*, Euripides was presumably struck
by the effect of this scene and adapted it to his own ends.
In other plays he uses the 'report to two' for a different
purpose. News is brought to two listeners, the major
character rebels in agonized grief and the minor character chooses the part of heroic self-sacrifice.[1] We are not
asked to identify ourselves with the major character; his
grief is a foil to set off the heroism of the minor character
who may have been introduced into the play to secure
this single emotional effect.

In some situations silence is as significant as words.
This can only be fully appreciated on the stage. Some
instances, however, are fairly clear. Antigone never mentions Haemon, so completely is she absorbed in her duty
to her brother. Heracles says nothing of Deianira when
he learns her innocence, but cares only to provide for himself and Iole. The craven Aegisthus only cares for his own
safety when he sees the dead body of Clytemnestra. These
silences are all significant. In the last instance our interpretation is justified by the parallel in the *Choephori*,

[1] Polyxena in the *Hecuba*, Megara in the *Hercules*, Macaria in the
Heraclidae, Menoeceus in the *Phoenissae*, Menelaus, Achilles, and Iphigenia in turn in the *Iphigenia in Aulis*.

which Sophocles had in mind. When Clytemnestra sees the dead body of Aegisthus, she cries, before she turns to make her appeal to Orestes, 'Alas, you are dead, dearest Aegisthus'. Aeschylus' Clytemnestra may not be a sympathetic character, but she is not, like Sophocles' Aegisthus, a selfish coward.

So far we have only considered how Sophocles shows his characters in their breadth and manysidedness. The audience want further to be satisfied that these various qualities existed in the character before the play began. If the permanence of character is established, it is easier to recognize and appreciate any change that the characters may undergo in the course of the play. Sophocles has two chief methods of showing permanence—reference to a particular event outside the play which accounts for some trait in the character, and a more general reference to his past history.

The single event which has twisted the character may be recent or may have occurred in the more distant past. Ajax was always sensitive, but the decision to award Achilles' arms to Odysseus wounded his sensibility so deeply that his need to wipe off this stain became a consuming passion. Electra, on the other hand, owes her desire for vengeance, her emotionalism, and her fortitude to an event in the more distant past. Although she presumably possessed these qualities before Agamemnon was murdered, the horror of that night increased and intensified them so much that it can be held responsible for the present shape of her character.[1]

The permanence of a character may also be shown by a more general reference to past life. We are told of past

[1] Cf. the effect of exposure in Lemnos on Philoctetes, expulsion from Thebes on Oedipus in the *Coloneus*, the doubt thrown on his birth on Oedipus in the *Tyrannus*, the exposure of her child on Iocasta, the death of Iphigenia on Clytemnestra, and the wooing of Achelous on Deianira.

occasions where the character has shown the same qualities as he shows in the play. This method is particularly
valuable where the character only appears on the stage
for part of the play, or where the action on the stage tends
to overemphasize some one aspect. Ajax on the stage is
necessarily angry and revengeful. His heroism of which
he speaks himself is more fully explained by Teucer's
account of his past exploits. Philoctetes is a combination
of fury and nobility. We expect him to be furious because
Odysseus has told us that his groans and cries made it
impossible for the Greeks to sacrifice. Except in occasional
remarks to Neoptolemus and in his account of his fortitude on Lemnos, he does not give so much evidence of his
nobility, but we understand this better when he asks
Neoptolemus of his friends and enemies; his friends in the
Greek army were the noble characters Achilles, Ajax, &c.,
and his enemies the base characters Odysseus, Diomede,
and Thersites.[1]

With this knowledge of a character in its width and
permanence the spectator can understand any change that
the character may undergo in the course of the play. It
is often said that there is no development of character in
Greek tragedy. But if development means an important
change during the play, this would be hard to maintain.
When a character expresses views or adopts a course of
action which we should not have expected from our first
estimate of him, it is justifiable to speak of development
of character. We can find such changes as early as
Aeschylus. Eteocles in the *Septem* changes from the
prudent ruler to the reckless son of Oedipus, who cannot
be restrained from meeting Polynices. The change occurs
suddenly and unexpectedly during the last of the messenger's seven speeches, and the chorus, when Eteocles

[1] Cf. Creon's remark about Antigone, 'she was mad from birth' (562);
Oedipus tells us that he smote Laius' charioteer in wrath (*O.T.* 807).

leaves the stage, sing of the agency of the Curse. This change is credible to the audience because they know the story, and in so far as they allow with Aeschylus that a curse may enter a man's life and change his character. Aeschylus is more interested in the intervention of the curse than in the change of character in Eteocles.

Euripides has similar abrupt changes. Aristotle[1] complains that in the *Iphigenia in Aulis* the character of Iphigenia is inconsistent; her supplication to Agamemnon is in no way like her later heroism. But Euripides has represented, however abruptly, a credible change of outlook, to which Polyxena in the *Hecuba* provides a parallel. His object is not so much the representation of character as the dramatic situation, the heroic self-sacrifice of Polyxena and Iphigenia.

Sophocles more than either Aeschylus or Euripides is interested in change of character for its own sake, and in all the surviving plays one character or another changes his outlook. But the handling of the change is not always equally clear and intelligible. No one can doubt the change in Neoptolemus. Neoptolemus shows in the prologue that he dislikes the part which he is given to play. In the course of the first act his friendship and sympathy with Philoctetes can be seen increasing, and he fails to make profitable use of the merchant's tale. Philoctetes' spasm of sickness brings about the crisis, in which he abandons the desire for glory which has allowed him to play a false part and returns to the heroic ideal of justice and truth. Neoptolemus abandons a true for a false position and later swings back again to his true position, and the whole course of the change is perfectly clear.[2]

---

[1] *Poetics*, 1454ª31. See now the admirable treatment by Page, *Actor Interpolations in Greek Tragedy*, p. 208.

[2] Neoptolemus' change is also prepared by l. 431, where he had said from his heart 'Even clever plans are often thwarted.' (Cf. Johnson, *C.R.*

But there are three important changes which happen suddenly and with little preparation. All three are in early plays, and it would seem that Sophocles has not yet advanced far enough beyond the technique of Aeschylus to achieve the explicit representation of change which he has reached in the *Philoctetes*.

Ajax in his monologue says that he is going to purify himself to escape the dire wrath of the goddess. 'Henceforward we shall know to yield to the gods and we shall learn to revere the Atridae.' Ajax then leaves the stage and when next we see him he has already planted his sword in the ground, and when he has prayed for vengeance on the sons of Atreus he falls on it. Is his earlier speech an elaborate lie? If it is a lie, it is out of character; but perhaps, as the *Ajax* is an early play, too much weight cannot be placed on this argument. Certainly, the chorus and Tecmessa misunderstand the speech. But if Ajax' only object was deception, he did not need such an elaborate lie to escape from his obedient sailors.

If the speech is not a lie, it is yet out of keeping with the scene before, where Ajax swore undying hatred against the sons of Atreus and called Tecmessa a fool for trying to school him, and out of keeping with the suicide speech. The critics have proposed various solutions to this problem.[1] After much hesitation I have finally come to believe that he has repented and does not mean to die, but that

1928, p. 209 f.; I disagree completely with T. von Wilamowitz' treatment, op. cit., pp. 279, 290 f.; Weinstock's account of the whole problem is admirable, op. cit., p. 79 f.) Orestes' break-down in the *Electra* is prepared by his hesitation in the prologue, Ismene's change by her obvious affection for Antigone.

[1] T. von Wilamowitz, op. cit., p. 65, and Reinhardt, op. cit., p. 33, apparently regard the speech as an elaborate lie. Jebb in his edition and Schadewaldt, *Aias und Antigone*, p. 74 f., are extremely good on the development of Ajax' character. Weinstock, op. cit., p. 49 f., is over-subtle. Cf. also von Fritz, *Rh. Mus.* 1934, p. 113 f.; Kamerbeek, op. cit., p. 116 f.

when he is alone again with his sword by the sea-shore the old passion wells up and he commits suicide. Nothing that he says in either speech is inconsistent with this. 'I will go whither I must go' means one thing for Ajax and Tecmessa and another for the audience. The possibility of a sudden change of outlook is given by the change in Eteocles of which we have spoken. Something of Ajax' altered frame of mind remains in his last speech when he pictures his mother's grief and then checks himself; the mood of the monologue is incompatible with suicide and must be suppressed. It is noticeable also that he says nothing of Odysseus in his last speech: 'the foe is to be hated but as likely to become a friend'. The change would have been easier to understand if the monologue had come immediately after Tecmessa's appeal. But Sophocles does not write such long scenes at this period, and a swift repentance would have detracted from the picture of Ajax' stubborn immobility. The moral of the play is that the gods love the modest. That Ajax should, if only during one speech, yet during the central and most splendid speech of the play, show himself modest is a step towards the reconstitution of his character which takes place in the second part of the play. The strongest evidence for this interpretation of the two speeches is the parallel from the *Trachiniae*, which must now be examined.

Deianira extracts the truth from Lichas by telling him that Heracles has married many other women and never yet has any one of them been reproached by her. She apparently acquiesces in Heracles' love for Iole and leads Lichas into the house where she will prepare gifts to send back to Heracles. Then after the *stasimon* she comes out of the house again 'to tell what she has done and to ask for pity in her sufferings'. She cannot endure her position and she has determined to use the charm which Nessus has given her. For the moment, in spite of her protestations, she is a daring woman, and we wonder whether the *sophrosyne* of her speech to Lichas was a mask to conceal her already formed design to send the drugged robe to Heracles.[1] But her *sophrosyne* there accords with all that we have learnt about her in the prologue and first act, and when she discovers the true nature of the charm she decides that death is the only course to redeem her honour. The speech to Lichas expresses her real intentions. But when she is alone in the house, her misery becomes intolerable and she decides to try the love charm on the new robe which she had always intended to send to the victorious Heracles. When she finds out the truth, her daring leaves her and she returns to her original position. For the space of her speech to the chorus she is a daring woman. We do not see her change either from *sophrosyne* to daring or from daring to *sophrosyne*, because she changes, like Ajax, while she is off the stage and alone.

Antigone in her last speech passes through a series of moods not unlike those of Ajax between Tecmessa's appeal and his death. He started in stubborn hatred, then repented and became 'modest', and finally returned to his stubborn hatred. Antigone undergoes a similar change when, in her last speech, she leaves her warm and confident idealism and justifies her position by cold logic to return at the end to an imprecation on Creon. All of the last twenty-eight lines of Antigone's final speech have been condemned by one critic or another.[2] The chief charge is that their writer borrowed a story from Hero-

---

[1] Reinhardt, op. cit., p. 56, interprets as deception: so also T. von Wilamowitz, op. cit., p. 154. I agree with the account of Weinstock, op. cit., p. 131. Cf. also *Greek Poetry and Life*, p. 170.

[2] See also ch. ii, p. 53. Schadewaldt, op. cit., p. 82 f., is in the main right. In his *Actor Interpolations*, p. 86 f., Page seems to me to overrate both the verbal correspondence with Herodotus and the slight difficulties of translation in 909 and 910.

dotus. But as the lines are quoted by Aristotle there is a strong presumption that they are genuine. Up to this time Antigone has felt no need to defend herself. Here she appeals to the judgement of the wise. The brother of an orphan is irreplaceable, and therefore must be buried, even against the will of the citizens. This is a duty which cannot be avoided since it cannot be replaced by another equal duty. But since the state is under the protection of the gods, the transgression of the state's law even in such a case involves the transgressor in impiety. The change here is that Antigone for the first time recognizes that there is another point of view. It does not alter her position, but she finds it necessary to define her act as a special and justifiable exception to the citizen's obedience. In this central section of her speech she achieves modesty, like Ajax in his monologue. Like Ajax again, she still hates those who are the cause of her misfortunes, and her hatred wells up in a conclusion which is parallel to Ajax' last speech, 'But if they err, may they not suffer more evil than they do unjustly to me'. 'Not more than' means 'as much as' to a Greek. On these last lines the chorus rightly comment, 'The same blasts of the same winds still hold her soul'.

Deianira's change from *sophrosyne* to rashness and then back to *sophrosyne*, is parallel to the change in Neoptolemus which has already been described. There the change is clear and no one can be deceived. Deianira's speech to Lichas gives no indication that she will repent of her acquiescence. The suddenness of the change surprises us. This is the difficulty with Ajax and Antigone also. It is explained by the fact that Sophocles is still working in an Aeschylean technique which he has abandoned by the time of the *Philoctetes*.

Sophocles can represent a character in its width and depth and in its permanence and change. He also has, as we have seen, certain types of character which he likes to represent and he carefully notes their deviations from the standards which he requires. The conjunction of these two qualities, the power to represent characters in detail and the desire to represent ideal characters, won for him in antiquity the title of 'good draughtsman of character'.

V. Plot Construction

Reading and acting—plays of action and suffering—the diptych form—preparation—recurrent ideas—pattern of the play—shape of the play; prologue to *exodos*—sequence of emotions—dramatic irony—scenic problems—spectacle—actors—realistic representation.

WE have considered Sophocles' plays from two aspects. We have used them as evidence for his thought, and we have described his characters and character-drawing and have thereby learnt how he treated the traditional story. We have now to examine his plays as literature and as drama. The method of joining scenes, the pattern and rhythm of the whole play, and the sequence of emotions stirred in the reader or spectator are literary problems. Spectacle, action, and realistic representation concern the theatre alone. Sophocles must have considered his reading public, as well as his audience at the Dionysia. The Greek dramatist could only be certain of a single presentation of his tragedy on the stage, and therefore we may presume that he took steps to have his play published soon after its performance and to write a play which could be appreciated by readers, as well as spectators. When Dionysus was sent abroad on military service, he took Euripides' *Andromeda* to read on the boat.[1] And if the Athenians neither read tragedy nor knew their tragedy, plays like the *Frogs* would have fallen flat; only a small proportion of the audience can have seen the dozen or so plays of Aeschylus which Aristophanes quotes, since Aeschylus had been dead fifty years and it is hardly likely that all these plays had been revived.[2] The Greek poet

---

[1] *Frogs*, 52; cf. also the evidence of Aristotle, *Poetics*, 1453^{b}6, 1462^{a}12, *Rhetoric*, 1413^{b}12. See Page, *Actor Interpolations*, p. 1.

[2] See Note K, at end, p. 183.

constructed his play to be an 'everlasting possession, not a prize composition which is heard and forgotten'.

Sophocles' plays can be divided into tragedies of action and tragedies of suffering. In the *Ajax*, *Antigone*, and *Trachiniae* the act which causes the disaster is done during the course of the play. In the other four plays the fatal act is done before the play begins. The *Tyrannus* is in a middle position, because although Oedipus committed his crimes before the play began, he does not discover them until it is well advanced. In the last three plays the chief character is not responsible for the deed which sets the play in motion. Electra did not cause the murder of Agamemnon nor Oedipus his expulsion by the Thebans. These last plays are almost tragedies of suffering, and the scenes are constructed so that the characters may pass through a long series of emotions. But the three early plays are tragedies of action where the disaster is due to the *hybris* of the chief character or characters, as in the *Agamemnon*.

They are also like the *Agamemnon* in that the chief character dies rather more than half-way through the play and a second action begins. The second action is carefully prepared by an overlapping scene, and the overlap is greater in the *Trachiniae* than in the *Ajax* or *Antigone*. The second part of the *Ajax* is dominated by Teucer, and its main problem is Ajax' burial. It begins with the arrival of Teucer's messenger,[1] who starts the chorus and Tecmessa on their search for Ajax and tells them that Teucer himself will shortly arrive. After this scene the first part

---

[1] It is part of the tragic convention that the messenger should come before Teucer himself; in the *Agamemnon* the herald arrives before Agamemnon and in the *Trachiniae* the messenger precedes Lichas.

De Falco, *Osservazioni sulla struttura delle tragedie di Eschilo e di Sofocle*, p. 18, notes the general correspondence between the *Ajax* and the *Agamemnon*.

of the play ends with the suicide of Ajax. Similarly in the *Antigone* the Haemon scene, which begins Creon's discomfiture, is inserted before Antigone's death. In the *Trachiniae* the report of Heracles' agony is the first scene of the Heracles tragedy, but this scene is more organically connected with the first part of the play than the other two. Hyllus' report is the direct cause of Deianira's death, and Hyllus has been sent out in the prologue and is therefore expected to return; in addition, Heracles' arrival is felt to be certain from the time that the messenger first announces his safety. In the two earliest plays Sophocles is still working in the Aeschylean tradition. Aeschylus wrote the Cassandra scene of the *Agamemnon* to prepare his audience for the end of the play and for the next play; Cassandra for the first time tells the story of Atreus, Thyestes, and Aegisthus, and prophesies the vengeance of Orestes. When Cassandra has entered the house, the first part of the *Agamemnon* ends with the death of the king.

We have no evidence that Sophocles used the diptych form after the time of the *Trachiniae*. Presumably he found the single action more effective for the display of his hero's character. Euripides had other purposes, and therefore his plays have more variety. He uses the single action for his plays of intrigue.[1] The *Alcestis* and *Hippolytus* are diptych. The *Andromache* and *Hercules* are triptych. In the other plays the single action is broken by a scene but slightly connected with it, such as the trial of Helen in the *Troades* and the several scenes of heroism.

Inside its general outline the play is held together by preparation for the entry of new characters and the recurrence of important ideas. Sophocles prepares his entries with extreme care. Aeschylus' preparation is simpler because he has fewer entries to prepare. Euripides' tech-

[1] *Medea, Iphigenia in Tauris, Helen, Orestes, Bacchae.*

nique is different, as I have tried to show elsewhere.[1] He likes to surprise his audience by the arrival of a new character and then make that character give good reasons for coming. Aegeus arrives unexpectedly in the *Medea*, and then explains that Corinth lay on his route from Delphi to Troezen. Sophocles' technique is the opposite of this. Two instances will illustrate his method. Teucer dominates the second half of the *Ajax* and he is to appear as soon as Ajax has committed suicide. His arrival is carefully prepared in the first act where Ajax is heard calling for him, in the next scene, in the monologue, by the arrival of his messenger, in Ajax' last speech, and finally by Tecmessa, who cries, when she finds Ajax' body, 'Where is Teucer?' Aegisthus arrives in the last scene of the *Electra* and the audience must be prepared for his coming. In the first act the chorus ask Electra of his whereabouts and she answers that he is 'on the estate'. He is not so near that his arrival need be expected immediately, but he will probably arrive before the end of the play. Chrysothemis and Clytemnestra evidently expect him. During the murder of Clytemnestra Electra is sent outside to watch for him, presumably because the pedagogue has told her that Clytemnestra has had him summoned.[2]

— The songs of the chorus are also used to prepare the audience for what is going to happen. The preparation is simplest when the last verse of the song contains a direct reference to the beginning of the next scene. At the end of the *parodos* the chorus of the *Antigone* sing, 'Here is the king of the land, Creon', and thus make the connexion with the next scene.[3] Sometimes the forward reference is

[1] Cf. *C.R.* 1933, p. 117. On preparation in Sophocles cf. also Ackermann, *Über das* πίθανον *bei Sophocles.*

[2] Cf. 310, 386, 627, 1402 (cf. 1370, 1443). We are not meant to ask who told Aegisthus of Orestes' death.

[3] 155. Cf. *Aj.* 192; *Trach.* 222, 962; *Phil.* 201 f.

vaguer. When the chorus of the *Antigone* sing of the light over the last root in the house of Oedipus, they are pointing forward to Antigone's death.[1] A considerable number of these forward references are ominous words later fulfilled in a sense different from that in which they were spoken. The dramatic irony is clearest in the cheerful choruses which precede the catastrophe in the *Ajax*, *Antigone*, *Trachiniae*, and *Tyrannus*.[2]

But in other songs also a general reflection on what has passed is for the audience also a preparation for what is to come. The technique is the same as in the cheerful choruses, and can be shown in three typical instances, from the *Antigone*, *Electra*, and *Philoctetes*.[3] In the *Antigone* the chorus sing, 'In the contriving of his art he has a skill beyond all hope; sometimes he turns to the good and at others to the bad.' These words are a reflection on Creon's speech about the transgressor of his decree;[4] the audience know that the transgressor is in fact Antigone and that the words are much more applicable to Creon himself. But in the mouth of the Theban elders they are simply a comment on Creon's speech and the report of the guard. Only the audience can give them their further application to Antigone and Creon. Similarly at the end of the first *stasimon* of the *Electra*, when the chorus trace the troubles of the Pelopids back to the chariot race of Pelops, they are making a natural reflection, but their words have a further significance for the audience who remember the

[1] *Ant.* 599; cf. *Aj.* 945 to arrival of Menelaus. Sometimes words of the song suggest the possibility of something happening which later happens; in the *parodos* of the *Trachiniae* (96) the chorus pray to the sun to 'herald' the fate of Heracles, and soon afterwards Heracles' herald arrives.

[2] See Note L, at end, p. 184.

[3] See Note M, at end, p. 184.

[4] It follows that I disagree with Kranz (*Stasimon*, p. 219) who finds the reference to Antigone 'nur hineingedeutet um den Chor zu einer einheitlich denkenden Person zu machen'.

prologue. There they have seen Orestes instructing the
pedagogue to report his death in the chariot race, and
know that the pedagogue must soon arrive to make his
report.[1] Thirdly, at the end of the only *stasimon* in the
Philoctetes the chorus sing, 'Now he shall be happy and
great . . . Neoptolemus in the fullness of many months is
taking him home . . : where the bronze-shielded warrior
came to the gods'. In the scene before Neoptolemus has
expressed his willingness to take Philoctetes home, and the
chorus, taking their cue from him, naturally think of
Heracles; but the mention of Heracles prepares the audience for his arrival at the end of the play, and when they
hear 'Now he shall be happy and great', they perceive
the further sense that Philoctetes shall be healed and capture Troy.[2] I have discussed these choruses at length
because their technique is peculiar to Sophocles and
parallel to his use of dramatic irony in the dialogue and
in the plot.

Sophocles differs from the other two tragedians in making his intrigues a method of preparing the audience in
the prologue for the course which the play is going to take.
In the *Choephori* Orestes makes a plan to murder Aegisthus and Clytemnestra, and this plan which is made before
the eyes of the audience is balanced by its immediate
execution. In all the Euripidean plays of intrigue, as in
the *Choephori*, execution immediately follows and balances
plan. The *Trachiniae* is of the same type, although Deianira's discovery of her mistake fills an interval between her
plan and the report of its execution, and the plan is not
carried out before the eyes of the audience. But in the
Electra and *Philoctetes* Sophocles uses the intrigue in a new

[1] So Errandonèa, *Mnemosyne*, li, p. 310.
[2] Contrast Kranz (op. cit., p. 221). Helmreich (*Der Chor nach seinem
ἦθος*, p. 15) thinks that Philoctetes is already within earshot when the last
verse is sung; but there is no evidence of this.

way. The plan is made in the prologue and its execution forms the framework of the whole play.

In the prologue of the *Philoctetes* Odysseus tells Neoptolemus to persuade Philoctetes to come with him by saying that he is sailing home because he has been grossly wronged by Odysseus. If Neoptolemus seems to Odysseus to be taking too long, he will send the sailor, disguised as a merchant, with a further false story. Thus we are prepared for the tale of Neoptolemus and for the arrival of the merchant. We are also prepared for the return of Odysseus, since, if after the departure of the merchant Neoptolemus still delays, Odysseus will presumably have to intervene himself. As in the prologue of the *Electra*, the audience are told exactly what will happen. But, whereas in the *Electra* Orestes' later failure to execute his plan is only prepared by his momentary hesitation in the prologue, here Neoptolemus' break-down is prepared by his open opposition to Odysseus.

Certain ideas run through the plays like coloured threads and hold them together.[1] Of most of these little need be said but to some Sophocles gives particular prominence. We have already noticed the importance of the oracles in the *Trachiniae, Tyrannus, Electra, Philoctetes,* and *Coloneus.* The Laius theme in the *Tyrannus* is an excellent example of the gradual development of a motive. It plays the same part as the slaughter of the cattle in the *Ajax,*[2] but here the unfolding of the truth is slower and more complicated; in the prologue Creon says that Laius was

---

[1] See Note N, at end, p. 184.

[2] In the *Ajax* the actual events which are seen and related in the prologue are referred to by the chorus in the *parodos*, explained at length by Tecmessa, and by Ajax himself, and mentioned again later by Menelaus. The *Agamemnon* provides a close parallel; the beacon fire is seen by the watchman and gradually explained by Clytemnestra and the herald. On this gradual exposition see Kamerbeek, op. cit., p. 109.

murdered by robbers and that one of his party survived, the Theban herdsman who will later be summoned. In the first act the chorus attribute the murder to wayfarers. Tiresias declares that Oedipus is the murderer, but is not believed by Oedipus or the chorus. Iocasta enlarges on the story of robbers. When the Theban herdsman arrives, the whole story could be made clear, but is in fact forgotten in the search for Oedipus' father. Thus it is a recurrent theme for two-thirds of the play.

Ideas are echoed from song to dialogue and from dialogue to song. When a *kommos* is followed by a long iambic speech, the iambic speech takes up and develops the motives of the preceding lyric dialogue. The prototype is the iambic speech in the *Agamemnon*, where Cassandra explains her lyric prophecies. The *parados* of the *Electra* illustrates the type; Electra states the themes in her opening monody—her ceaseless lamentation, the murder of Agamemnon, the life of Clytemnestra and Aegisthus, the absence of Orestes—they are repeated through the lyric dialogue of the *parodos*, and are finally taken up by Electra again in her opening speech to the chorus.[1] Sometimes, however, the reference is not taken up immediately, but only after an interval. In the third *stasimon* of the *Tyrannus* the motive of 'the great haven the same for child and father' is taken up in Oedipus' speech when he reappears. The first *stasimon* of the *Ajax*[2] is unique in introducing three motives which recur in the third *stasimon*—Salamis, the horrors of Troy, and the

---

[1] Other instances are the lyric dialogues with Tecmessa and Ajax in the *Ajax*, the *kommos* with Antigone in the *Antigone*, the lyric dialogue with the nurse and the *kommos* with Heracles in the *Trachiniae*, the *kommos* in the *Tyrannus*, the *parodoi* of the *Philoctetes* and the *Coloneus*; the motives of all these are taken up by the succeeding speeches.

[2] *O.T.* 1207 points forward to 1403 f.; *Aj.* 596 to 1217, 600 to 1185, 609 to 1211; cf. also *O.C.* 510 f. which anticipates 960 f.

change in Ajax' fortunes. The origin may again be found in Aeschylus. In the *Agamemnon* themes from the *parodos* are repeated in the three *stasima*; the choruses stand, as it were, outside the play, have their own system of cross references, and form their own pattern.

The motives of the dialogue are often taken up by the song which follows the scene and then this commentary is the song's chief theme, although, as we have said, it may also prepare the audience for what is going to happen later. The first *stasimon* of the *Ajax* will again serve as an example. Tecmessa's appeal and Ajax' first speech provide the matter. The contrast between past and present and the reference to Ajax' father and mother are suggested by Tecmessa's appeal; Ajax' first speech is echoed when the chorus sing of his madness, his prowess, the ingratitude of the Atridae, and the impossibility of life in misery.[1]

The repetition of ideas in chorus and dialogue gives the play a pattern. When an idea is specially connected with a particular person, his entries form another such pattern. Odysseus in the *Ajax* and Creon in the *Tyrannus* are personifications of modesty. Each appears in the prologue and again in the last scene of his play, so that the plays begin and end with the theme of modesty. Sophocles loves to build up his play so that entry corresponds with entry, speech with speech, and song with song. We can show this in the *Antigone*. The Ismene scene in the prologue corresponds with the later Ismene scene. The two speeches of the Guard balance each other and are balanced by the later narratives of Tiresias and the messenger. Antigone's last speech is a centre piece to the *kommos* and the song of consolation. The Tiresias scene is parallel and opposite to the Haemon scene; young man

---

[1] *Aj.* 596 f. recalls in turn 485 f., 430 f., 506, 470 f.; cf. the excellent analysis of de Falco, *Tecnica Corale*, p. 62. Other songs of the same type are *Trach.* 821, *O.T.* 463, *El.* 472, 1058, *Phil.* 676.

has given place to old man, lover to seer. There are two debates, two *kommoi*, two long generalizing choruses (first and second *stasima*) and two cheerful choruses (*parodos* and fifth *stasimon*). This balanced composition can be traced back to Homer, and parallels can be found in Aeschylus and Euripides. The balance is perhaps more elaborate in Sophocles, but his use of it is not original; rather it is one form of the balance and antithesis which was so dear to the Greek genius.[1]

The recurrent motives and balancing scenes and speeches are like the patterns in a carpet. But the play also has a shape, a beginning, a middle, and an end, as Aristotle puts it. It begins with the prologue. Sophocles' prologues are all dialogues and the minor persons are never lay figures like many in the prologues of Euripides. Most of them make significant reappearances; even the priest in the *Tyrannus* and the Athenian in the *Coloneus* have successors in the chorus who carry on their parts.[2] Two prologues are often said to show the influence of Euripides, but we have not enough evidence to confirm this. Deianira's first speech is perfectly adapted to her character—her opening is as characteristic as Antigone's—and is answered by the nurse. Its resemblance to the Euripidean programme speeches is superficial. Electra's monody has no parallel in Sophocles, but we have only seven plays to compare.[3]

---

[1] For Homer, cf. J. L. Myres, *J.H.S.* 1932, p. 265 f. In Aeschylus note the Hermes and Oceanus scene in the *Prometheus*, &c.; in Euripides' *Ion* narrative prologue balances narrative epilogue, there are two revelations by Creusa and two recognitions; the scene between Xuthus and Ion is balanced by the scene between Creusa and the old man. For another Sophoclean example see *Greek Poetry and Life*, p. 180.

[2] Odysseus in the *Ajax*, Ismene in the *Antigone*, nurse and Hyllus in the *Trachiniae*, Creon in the *Tyrannus*, Orestes, Pylades, and the old man in the *Electra*, Odysseus and spy in the *Philoctetes*. On all formal questions connected with the prologue, see Nestle, *Struktur des Eingangs*.

[3] See Note O, at end, p. 186.

The exposition is shared between the characters, and themes are stated which will later be of importance. The seven plays are distinguished from one another by the amount of preparation in the prologue. In the first two plays we cannot foretell from the prologue either the discomfiture of Creon or the suicide and subsequent burial of Ajax. The oracles which are announced in the prologues of the *Trachiniae* and *Tyrannus* indicate the scope of the play. In the last three plays the course of the action is still more clearly defined.

After the prologue the chorus enter and sing the *parodos*. In the *Ajax* and *Antigone* the *parodos* still contains anapaests recited by the *koryphaios*. The *parodos* of the *Ajax* has a long anapaestic prologue like the *Agamemnon*. The *parodoi* of the *Trachiniae* and *Tyrannus* are *stasima* in form. In the last three plays the *parodos* is a lyric dialogue, in the *Philoctetes* and *Coloneus* accompanied by violent action. The lyric dialogue is more dramatic and realistic than the set song, and this change in technique is in keeping with the general trend towards realism in the late fifth century.

The sequence of scenes in the earlier part of the play has common features in all Sophocles' plays except the early *Ajax* and the late *Philoctetes*. In the *Ajax* the first act is divided into two by the second *kommos* and the second act is very short. In the *Philoctetes* the first two acts are run together and the intervening chorus reduced to a divided strophe and antistrophe. In the other five plays it is possible to speak of a normal structure. After the *parodos* the statement, development, and explanation of ideas from the prologue, and sometimes also from the *parodos*, forms the content of the first speech of the chief character. A new character then arrives and gives the action a new turn. This is the normal shape of the first act. It is noticeable that, although Aeschylus constructs his first act like this in the *Supplices*, *Persae*, and *Prometheus*, Euripides uses this form only in the *Medea*. This first act is followed by the central scene of the play, a long scene of several parts where the chief character goes through a long series of emotions. In the *Antigone*, for instance, the second act is in four parts—report of the Guard, accusation and defence of Antigone, Ismene's appeal to Antigone, and Ismene's appeal to Creon.[1] Aeschylus makes the second act the central scene in the *Prometheus*, *Septem*, and *Choephori*. But neither the tale of Io's wanderings nor the seven messenger speeches nor the *kommos* are designed to identify our feelings with those of the hero, but rather to sweep us away by a terrifying spectacle—the usual Aeschylean aim of *ekplexis*. In Euripides, as has been said, the form of the play and therefore the sequence of scenes is more varied. Where, as in his *Electra*, he has a long and complicated scene after the first *stasimon*, although the chief character may pass through a considerable series of emotions, the emphasis is rather on the deeds than the doers.[2]

The second act of the *Tyrannus* is a good example of Sophocles' developed technique. It has three parts: a debate between Oedipus and Creon, a scene of persuasion between Oedipus, Creon, and Iocasta, and a dialogue between Oedipus and Iocasta. The debate between Oedipus and Creon is stopped by the arrival of Iocasta. Then Creon swears an oath that he has not plotted against Oedipus. The central scene of persuasion culminates in a short lyric dialogue, which both marks the emotional high point of the act and takes the place of a *stasimon*, so that Sophocles can build a long act of several parts without

---

[1] See Note P, at end, p. 187.

[2] Cf. *Iphigenia in Tauris*, *Helen*, and *Orestes*. The *Orestes* is nearest to Sophocles but it turns into a play of intrigue. On Euripides' emotional sequences, cf. Solmsen, *Hermes*, 1934, p. 405.

an intervening chorus. When Creon has gone, Iocasta inquires the cause of the quarrel. She then tries to pacify Oedipus by quoting the oracle given to Laius. Laius was to have been killed by his son, but in fact was killed at a cross-roads. This mention of the cross-roads starts a new train of thought in Oedipus. He recalls how he once killed a man at the cross roads and that man may have been Laius.

The twist in the action when Iocasta, trying to comfort Oedipus by demonstrating the fallibility of oracles, starts him on a new fear, grows naturally out of the situation. Similarly in the next act the Corinthian messenger tries to dispel Oedipus' fear that he may yet marry his mother by telling him that he is not the son of Polybus and Merope, and thereby starts him on the discovery of his origin. This method of transition from one part of a scene to the next, where a remark of one character starts another character on a new chain of thought, first occurs in the last scene of the *Trachiniae*; Hyllus mentions Nessus, and Heracles, who till then has been thinking only of his vengeance on Deianira, realizes the coincidence of the oracles and, for-getting Deianira, prepares for his own end. Sophocles uses this technique again in the later plays.[1] The nearest parallel in Euripides to the Sophoclean twist is the read-ing of the letter which leads to the recognition scene in the *Iphigenia in Tauris*. Elsewhere he usually alters the course of the action inside the scene by the arrival of a new charac-ter. The new-comer may be unexpected, but his arrival is fully motived, e.g. Orestes in the *Andromache*. Partly for this reason Euripides has more entrances per play than Sophocles.

After the second act the scenes are shorter until the climax. Every play has a *kommos* after the climax, and most a messenger speech. In the *Tyrannus* the climax is reached

[1] Further instances: *El.* 404, 630; *Phil.* 320, 460; *O.C.* 461, 1150. Cf. Reinhardt, op. cit., pp. 72, 129, 184.

when Oedipus discovers his origin. When the truth has come out, Oedipus rushes into the house, crying 'O Light, may I see you now for the last time'. The chorus contrast his former glory with his present plight. The messenger announces the suicide of Iocasta and the self-blinding of Oedipus. Then Oedipus comes out blind and sings a long *kommos* with the chorus. After Oedipus' speech explaining the *kommos* Creon arrives. Oedipus' passion turns to shame before the man whom he has wronged; then he appeals to Creon and asks for his children. His two little daughters are led on to the stage. Oedipus laments their fate and prays for their future. This last scene has the same kind of emotional sequence as the last scene of the *Trachiniae;* it begins with physical agony and ends with something like acquiescence. The last scene in both is a gradual quietening after the passion of messenger speech and *kommos*. In all the plays the last scene restores a balance and brings a conclusion to the strife. The discomfiture of Creon is also the vindication of Antigone. The murder of Aegisthus brings freedom to Electra.

The reader's emotions are lulled to rest by the last scene just as they are aroused by the prologue. In the course of the dialogue he identifies himself with the chief character; when Electra holds the urn, he sinks to the depth of despair to rise again to the heights of joy when Orestes discloses himself. We have said something of these emotional sequences in discussing character-drawing. Sophocles likes sharp contrasts of emotion. He uses many of his choral odes to achieve them. Sometimes the song itself makes the contrast; sometimes the song repeats in an intensified form the emotion of the preceding scene and makes a contrast with the next scene.

The generalizing songs[1] belong to the first class; they

[1] The origin of the generalizing recapitulation is to be found in Aeschylus—the appeal from the particular instance to the general law behind

break the tension of the dialogue by their calmer and more reflective tone. After the passion of the Haemon scene the little hymn to Love[1] makes a calm interlude before the *kommos* with Antigone. In this song the chorus sing in the antistrophe, 'You stirred up this quarrel of kinsmen too', and even where the connexion with the preceding scene is not so obvious and the chorus take a wider sweep in their generalization, they often return to the particular instance at the end.[2] In the second *stasimon* of the *Tyrannus*[3] after the passion of the debate with Creon and the horror of Oedipus' recital about his crime on the road, the chorus sing first quite generally about the laws of Zeus and the dangers of the tyrant; in the second strophe and antistrophe they particularize, 'Why should I dance? . . . if *this* is not clear to see'.[4]

Some of the *parodoi* make the same kind of contrast with the prologue.[5] In the *Tyrannus* the anxiety of the chorus' prayer contrasts with the hopefulness of Oedipus at the end of the prologue. Similarly the triumph song in the *Antigone* makes a bright patch between the gloom and agitation of the prologue and first act. The sane common sense of the Trachinian women contrasts with Deianira's timorousness, but this *parodos* is not so bright as the *parodos* of the *Antigone*, because the high light is to be reserved

it—but Kranz (op. cit., p. 195 f.) regards the Sophoclean form as characteristic of the classical as distinct from the archaic chorus. He compares *Cho.* 585, *Ant.* 332, and *Hipp.* 525.

[1] *Ant.* 781; the theme arises naturally from the preceding scene; cf. *Aj.* 1185, the evils of war; *O.T.* 1186, human frailty; *O.C.* 1211, the miseries of old age. [2] Cf. Kranz, op. cit., pp. 121, 204, 207.

[3] 863; cf. Kranz, op. cit., pp. 195, 218. Other examples are *Ant.* 332, 944. [4] See Note Q, at end, p. 187.

[5] The *parodos* of the *Ajax* expresses the agitation and incredulity of the chorus at the news brought to them by Odysseus and contrasts with the calm of Athena's closing words, and the *parodos* of the *Electra* is a song of consolation, contrasting with the despair of Electra's monody.

for the next song. After the *parodos* Deianira again explains her troubles and fears; as she ends, the aged messenger arrives to say that Heracles is victorious and Deianira calls on the chorus to sing for joy. It is interesting to compare the *parados* and first act of the *Persae*; Aeschylus has used the same sequence of chorus, queen, and messenger, but, instead of the swift variation from calm through anxiety to excessive joy, the emotional change is slighter, from vague anxiety to certain distress.

The joyful song of the Trachinian women does not, like the *parodos*, make a break with the emotion of the preceding scene, but underlines it, so that the change in the next scene may be more obvious. It is in fact like the later cheerful song which the chorus sing when Deianira sends Lichas away with the drugged robe, and which contrasts sharply with her despair when she returns to tell the effects of the drug. The *Ajax*, *Antigone*, and *Tyrannus* have similar songs whose gaiety contrasts with the coming agony.[1]

These songs stand apart from the dialogue after them, just as the generalizing songs and the *parodoi* of which we have spoken contrast with the preceding dialogue. Their lyrical emotion is an intensification of the emotion of the scene before. This is the function of the chorus in the laments, whether they come after a messenger speech or arise directly from an event on the stage such as the discovery of Ajax' body. It is also their function in the strophes and antistrophes which divide the sections of long scenes.[2] When Neoptolemus' sailors call upon Cybele to

---

[1] *Aj.* 693, *Ant.* 1115, *Trach.* 205, 633, *O.T.* 1086 are high points of joy before a low point of despair. *El.* 823 is a low point of despair before a more cheerful scene. (Chrysothemis rouses Electra to purposeful planning.)

[2] *Phil.* 391, 507; cf. also *O.T.* 649, 678, *O.C.* 833, 876; de Falco (*Tecnica corale*, p. 127 f.) compares the divided syzygies in the *Hippolytus* and *Orestes* of Euripides. The same function is performed by the following lyric dialogues *El.* 1232, 1398; *Phil.* 827; *O.C.* 510, 1447.

witness the villainy of the Atridae and when later they beg
Neoptolemus to take Philoctetes home, they are under-
lining the two high points of the act. In such songs they are
not calm spectators, but prejudiced actors, whether they
perform any action, such as their search for Oedipus in the
parodos of the *Coloneus*[1], or merely heighten the suspense, as
when they pray that his passing may be peaceful.[2]

— Dramatic irony is another means of stirring the emotions
of the audience. It depends on a contrast of knowledge
and opinion, thought and feeling. In Clytemnestra's
speech to the herald in the *Agamemnon* the irony is of the
simplest kind. Clytemnestra says one thing and we know
that she means another. We can compare to this Electra's
reception of Aegisthus in Sophocles' *Electra* and Hecuba's
reception of Polymestor in Euripides' *Hecuba*. In the
early plays of Sophocles we find already a more advanced
form of irony. For instance, when Ajax pronounces his
monologue, the audience know that he is going to commit
suicide, and this knowledge is in opposition to their feeling
that he has repented and all is well. This feeling is carried
further by the lively song and dance of the chorus, 'Ajax
has forgotten his troubles again'.[3]

The most developed form of dramatic irony is found in
the *Tyrannus*, *Electra*, and *Philoctetes*. Oedipus' first
speech to the chorus in the *Tyrannus* is an amplification
of his last speech in the prologue and like that, is full of
dramatic irony. Oedipus says that he is a stranger to the
murder and that he will fight for Laius as if he were his

[1] Cf. *Aj.* 866 f., the *parodoi* of the *Ichneutae* and *Philoctetes*. De Falco
(*Epiparodos*, p. 60) compares the *epiparodos* of Aeschylus' *Eumenides*, Kranz
(op. cit., p. 208) the *parodoi* of Euripides' *Hercules* and *Ion*.
[2] *O.C.* 1556, cf. 1044, *El.* 1384.
[3] Oedipus' last speech before the arrival of the Theban herdsman (*O.T.*
1076 f.) has dramatic irony of the same kind but stronger because the
sympathy of the audience has been more carefully prepared.

own father, but the audience know that when Oedipus curses the murderer he is calling down curses on himself. At the end of the scene Sophocles subtly plays on this irony. The audience know that Tiresias prophesies true, and that his allusions to Cithaeron, blindness, exile, and the murder of Laius must be a preparation for a revelation of the truth in the later scenes of the play. Yet that knowledge is outweighed by their sympathy with Oedipus in his obvious desire to help Thebes, the plausibility of his suspicions, and the apparently unreasoning fury of Tiresias. Knowledge yields to feeling and the spectator identifies himself with Oedipus.

The plan which Orestes unfolds in the prologue of the *Electra* is a foundation for dramatic irony on a large scale. The first and second acts are so contrived that the spectator identifies himself with Electra. Therefore in spite of the knowledge with which he has been so carefully provided in the prologue, he believes the report that Orestes is dead, disbelieves the evidence of Chrysothemis, and shares both Electra's grief when she holds the urn and her joy when she finds that Orestes is at her side.[1] The audience know the truth, but they have so identified themselves with the chief character that their sympathy leads them to disbelieve what they know to be true.

This developed form does not occur in Euripides. Indeed, he seems careful to avoid it by reminding us of the truth so recently that we cannot forget it in our sympathy with the character. In the *Hippolytus* our memory of the prologue is too recent to make us hope with Phaedra for success from the love charm and our knowledge of Hippolytus is too recent to let us sympathize with the wrath of Theseus. Similarly in the *Ion* there is tragic irony in Creusa's lamentation for her lost son and her plot to kill

---

[1] So too in the *Philoctetes* the reader hears Neoptolemus' lies and the tale of the merchant with Philoctetes' ears.

Ion, but we have no chance of forgetting that Ion is her son because of the prologue and first act, which are recalled by her monody and the subsequent explanation.[1] The audience is prepared for the end, although it may not be the end which the character expects or intends. This is a development of the tragic irony of the *Ajax*; it has nothing to do with the Tiresias scene of the *Tyrannus* or the messenger speech of the *Electra*.

We can now turn to the dramatic as distinct from the literary side of plot-construction. Here particularly we are hampered by the absence of stage directions and the paucity of our material. But it is probably not pure chance that the earliest play demands a change of scene and that the two latest have a more elaborate setting than the canonical palace-front. The *Ajax* is more reminiscent of Aeschylus than any other play, and Sophocles' desire to outdo Aeschylus by making Ajax commit suicide on the stage has involved him in technical difficulties. The actor who has played Ajax comes on again as Teucer, and Ajax' body is discovered in the bushes and carried into the sight of the audience. If the *eccyclema* was not used,[2] bush and dummy body of Ajax could have been arranged behind the central doors as soon as Tecmessa left the hut to speak to the messenger, and the doors thrown open to disclose the bush when the chorus had left the orchestra. The next stage direction would read, 'Ajax discovered in a lonely place on the sea shore, planting his sword behind a bush'. But, since we are readers rather than spectators, we need not go too deeply into these technicalities of production.

The last two plays belong to the same period as Euripides' most spectacular plays, *Troades*, *Phaethon*, *Orestes*,

[1] Cf. the recognition scenes of the *Electra* and *Iphigenia in Tauris* where we are in no danger of forgetting the identity of Orestes.

[2] On the *eccyclema* see Bethe, *Rh. Mus.* 1934, p. 21. Cf. Groh, *Mélanges Navarre*, p. 245.

and *Bacchae*. In the *Philoctetes* the scene is set outside
Philoctetes' cave in Lemnos. The actual arrangement of
the stage is not quite clear, but probably a ramp leading
into the central doors forms one of the two entrances to
the cave, and an opening corresponding to them which
can be vaguely seen at the back of the stage buildings forms
the other entrance.[1] The plays between the *Ajax* and the
Philoctetes raise no such scenic problems.

We can trace the same development in the use of spectacle, as distinct from scenery. The *Ajax* with its three
kommoi and its suicide can truly be called Aeschylean.
The realistic *parodoi* of the *Philoctetes* and *Coloneus* may
owe something to the Euripidean melodrama (in the
proper sense of that word). So much can be said for
development. On the whole, Sophocles uses spectacles less
than the other two tragedians and only to achieve a particular effect at a particular moment. The last scene of the
Ajax is a tableau. The body is in the middle with Tecmessa and Eurysaces crouching beside it. On one side
stands Teucer with his guards, on the other Agamemnon,
Menelaus, and their heralds. Odysseus comes and stands
by the side of Teucer. Then Agamemnon and Menelaus
depart, then Odysseus. The chorus file out, some to one
side to prepare the grave, some to the other to heat water
for washing the body. Some of Teucer's soldiers go to
Ajax' tent to fetch his armour. Teucer, Tecmessa, and
Eurysaces move off in procession with the body. The play
ends in spectacle as it begins.[2] The two processions of the

---

[1] See on the scenery of the *Philoctetes*, Woodhouse, *J.H.S.* 1912, p. 239,
Errandonea, *Mnemosyne*, lii, p. 39 f. Both go further than the evidence
warrants.

[2] At the end of the *Antigone* Creon stands between the body of his son
and the body of his wife. His soldiers are grouped round Haemon's body
and her servants round Eurydice's. The *Tyrannus* begins, and the *Electra*
ends, with a tableau.

Antigone, the first when Antigone is led to death, the second when Creon returns with Haemon's body, are also spectacular.[1] In the *Coloneus* Oedipus, whose blindness and infirmity have been carefully emphasized through the play and finally described by Polynices, rises and leads his children, Theseus, and the Athenian soldiers off the stage; this too is spectacle, although it stirs a different emotion from the processions of the *Antigone*. The hurried exits of Eurydice, Deianira, and Iocasta are scenic rather than literary effects. The suicide of Ajax has lineal descendants in the agonies of Heracles, the blinded Oedipus, and Philoctetes. With these the list of Sophoclean spectacles is complete, since he uses spectacle sparingly. His spectacle is never an end in itself but always related to the chief character. When Eurydice rushes from the stage, we think of Creon and we see the procession of Heracles' captives with the eyes of Deianira.

In the later fifth-century Greek literature, like Greek art and music, moves towards realism. Sophocles' technique is effected in various ways. He uses his actors with greater freedom in the later plays and the use of the third actor is a criterion of date. He always manages his actors and mutes[2] skilfully; when an actor has to leave the stage in order to return in another part, his departure is dramatically justifiable; in the *Coloneus* the actor who takes the part of Ismene has to return as Theseus, and therefore Ismene is sent to perform Oedipus' sacrifice and to be captured by Creon. But the early plays have fewer scenes with three actors, and the three actors never speak together. In the *Antigone* the three actors only appear

---

[1] Cf. the procession of captive women and the procession with Heracles in the *Trachiniae*.

[2] Cf. Richter, *De mutis personis*. (He does not observe the mute return of Menelaus for the Agamemnon debate of the *Ajax*; but it is assured by ll. 1115, 1319.)

together in the second act; in the *Coloneus* the third actor is on the stage for practically the whole play.[1]

Besides the increase in the number of scenes in which the three actors appear together, Sophocles alters his method of using them. In the three early plays two characters speak and the third stands silent; they never hold a trio conversation. In the last scene of the *Ajax* Teucer does not speak after the arrival of Odysseus until Agamemnon has finished his dialogue with Odysseus. The absence of trio conversation in the *Trachiniae* is strong evidence for its early date; later Sophocles might well have made the messenger interrupt Lichas and Lichas would not have needed to leave the stage and return again. But in the *Tyrannus* when Iocasta persuades Oedipus to pardon Creon, Sophocles uses his three actors with complete freedom. The later plays all have successful trio conversation, and the poet is conscious of the separate identity of each of the three people who are facing the same situation.[2]

The growth of realism can be seen in a number of ways, particularly in the treatment of time and space. Sophocles seems to have become more conscious of the need of relating the apparent and actual time of action, although here again our lack of material makes a safe conclusion impossible. In the *Ajax* Sophocles is still working in the tradition of the *Agamemnon*. There the watchman leaves the stage at the end of the prologue to tell Clytemnestra of the beacon; then the elders of the chorus enter; they come because they have seen the altars blazing with the thank-offerings which Clytemnestra has sacrificed in gratitude for the watchman's news, but for the audience no gap separates the departure of the watchman from the arrival of the chorus. Similarly in the *Ajax* the chorus arrive

---

[1] See Note R, at end, p. 187.

[2] Cf. particularly the *Electra* after the messenger speech, the *Philoctetes* before the merchant's tale.

as soon as Odysseus has departed, but they come because
Odysseus has spread the news of Ajax' onslaught in the
Greek camp.[1] In the *Coloneus*, however, the stranger goes
off to summon the chorus thirty-seven lines before they
arrive; before Theseus arrives from Athens in answer to the
same summons, another considerable period elapses during
which Oedipus inquires carefully whether Theseus can be
expected to come. The time taken by the battle between
the Thebans and Athenians is an apparent exception to
this realism, but the interval is filled by an imaginary
description of the battle so that the spectator may not be
conscious of this unreal lapse of time.[2]

In the three last plays the action off the stage takes place
for the most part at some definite place which is known to
be near, the tomb of Agamemnon, the ship of Neoptolemus, the grove of the Eumenides, and the altar of
Poseidon.[3] The scene of the action—the palace of Atreus,
the sights of Mycenae, the cave of Philoctetes, and the
grove of the Eumenides with the towers of Athens in the
background—is described in the prologue. The action
itself is more violent and realistic in the later plays than
in the earlier. If the very special instance of the suicide
of Ajax be excepted, and it should rather be classed as
emotional spectacle in the Aeschylean tradition, there is
no action even in the *Tyrannus* to compare with the

---

[1] So in the *Antigone* the chorus enter at dawn but the second act takes
place after midday. In the *Trachiniae* between ll. 632 and 731 Lichas
crosses from Trachis to Euboea, Heracles puts on the fatal robe and Hyllus
returns from Euboea to Trachis with the news of his agony.

[2] *O.C.* 1044, cf. 1556 when the chorus pray that Oedipus' passing may
be peaceful, and *El.* 1384 where the chorus picture what is happening in
the house. Kranz (op. cit., p. 209) compares with the *Electra* chorus
Aeschylus, *Cho.* 783, and Euripides, *Med.* 1251, *H.F.* 875.

[3] Cf. Friedländer, *Die Antike*, 1925, p. 301. References for *Coloneus*:
in the grove of the Eumenides, mixing bowl; 472, 1593, brazen threshold;
57, 1590; altar of Poseidon; 55, 888, 1158, 1494.

parodos and last scenes of the *Philoctetes* or with the *parodos* and second act of the *Coloneus*. In the *Tyrannus* there is a flash of dramatic action when the Theban herdsman raises his stick against the Corinthian and when a few lines later Oedipus has the Theban seized. But the second act of the *Coloneus* is full of action. Creon arrives with his guards and appeals to Oedipus to come back to Thebes. Oedipus refuses, and discloses Creon's real intentions. Creon instructs his guards to seize Antigone. The chorus and Oedipus protest and the climax is marked by a short strophe of lyric dialogue. Antigone is carried off by the Theban guards and Oedipus curses Creon. Creon then tries to seize Oedipus. The antistrophe of the lyric dialogue marks the climax of the struggle. Theseus, hearing the noise from where he is sacrificing, arrives with his guards. He sends one of them to summon the Athenians from the altar of Poseidon. There is a last clash between Creon and Oedipus. Then Theseus carries Creon off to guide him to Oedipus' children. The scenes which we have mentioned in the two last plays demand more or less violent action on the stage and the words bear testimony to this action. The earlier plays may have more action than we suspect, but in the late plays the action is underlined by the words.

This realism in the later plays does not alter Sophocles' purpose. If we may sum up briefly the difference in technique of plot construction between the three tragedians, the difference is ultimately one of ends. Aeschylus' story is represented as an exemplification of the divine law, which is gorgeously enunciated in the choruses and its majesty sustained by music and spectacle. Euripides, in his later plays at least, shows the unpredictable workings of chance, and is always more interested in the elaboration of the particular scene, whether lyrical, emotional, or rhetorical, than in the structure of the play as a whole. Sophocles'

careful craftsmanship, his choice of scenes, his construction of the plot, his use of music, spectacle, and
dramatic irony are primarily directed to the presentation
of character and the identification of the audience with
the characters thus presented.

VI. Song

NO song in Sophocles is merely an interlude which could be transferred to another place or another play. Some of Euripides' choruses have but a slight connexion with the scenes on either side of them, and Aristotle notes that Agathon introduced the practice of singing 'interludes', which had no connexion with the action of the play.[1] The unconnected song was a development of the late fifth century, in part due to the increasing emphasis on music at the expense of words. But Sophocles was the pupil of Lamprus and not the friend of Timotheus, and his sober music is adapted to the needs of the play. Our survey of plot-construction has shown us Sophocles' chief types of song besides showing us their function in the play. In emotion the songs range from the quiet generalizations to the agitated laments. They take their emotional tone from what has passed and set the emotional tone for what is to come; their function in the play is to put the audience into a certain frame of mind after one scene and before the next. This means that different songs have to evoke different kinds of emotion in the audience. The generalizations and simple recapitulations should be quieter than the emotional recapitulations and the songs which accompany action.

Something is known of two traditional forms of Greek music, the prayer or hymn and the lament. Each had its own shape and its own type of music. The form of the Greek prayer or hymn can be traced back through Sappho to the Homeric hymns and Homer.[2] The lament already

---

[1] *Poetics*, 1456ᵃ 25 f.   [2] Cf. Ax, *Hermes*, 1932, p. 413.

had a definite shape when 'they set singers to lead the
lament, who in their wailing song lamented and the women
wailed thereto'.[1] Many of Sophocles' songs fall under one
or the other heading and his prayers and laments can be
used as a starting-point for examining the form, thought,
and rhythm of his songs.

The longest and most elaborate prayer in Sophocles is
the *parodos* of the *Tyrannus*.[2] Its general shape is that of the
traditional prayer — invocation, grounding, prayer. The
first strophe and antistrophe contain the invocation, the
second strophe and antistrophe contain the grounding,
the third strophe and antistrophe repeat the invocation
and give the substance of the prayer.

We must now look at the song in detail and consider in
turn the connexion between the verses, the movement of
thought inside the verses, and the correspondence of
rhythm and sense. The question in the strophe is separated from the invocation in the antistrophe by a clear
break. The second strophe follows naturally on the
antistrophe and gives the ground for the invocation. The
second antistrophe is joined to its strophe by the relative
pronoun 'of whom', which takes up the 'one after another'
of the strophe. This antistrophe ends with a repetition
of the invocation which the third strophe continues, 'and
(grant) that . . .', the third antistrophe further continues
the invocation, 'and thy arrows, Lycaean lord'.

After the first strophe the rest of the song forms a
closely interconnected whole with verse linked to verse
by simple and explicit connexions. This movement is
normal in the quieter songs. The connexion of thought
may be of various kinds—a continuation of the narrative,

---

[1] ω 720; cf. Pickard-Cambridge, *Dithyramb*, p. 123 f. Page, *Greek
Poetry and Life*, p. 220.

[2] Cf. Ax, loc. cit.; de Falco, *Tecnica Corale*, p. 44; Kranz, *Stasimon*,
pp. 134, 179, 185, 189, 193, 209; Wilamowitz, *Verskunst*, p. 354.

an answer to a question, an added example, an alternative, a denial, a consequence or a reason.[1] For instance, the *parodos* of the *Trachiniae*[2] starts with a prayer for news; the antistrophe, joined to the strophe by 'for', gives the reason for the prayer, Deianira's misery; the second strophe, also joined by 'for', gives the reason for Deianira's misery; the second antistrophe is joined to its strophe by a relative pronoun, and states the chorus' answer to Deianira; the epode, joined by 'for', justifies the answer.[3]

In the *parodos* of the *Tyrannus* the first strophe is separated from the rest of the song. Breaks are a sign of emotion; they are more frequent in laments than in ordinary songs. Only one of the generalizing choruses has such a break, the third *stasimon* of the *Ajax*; here, as in the prayer in the *Tyrannus*, the first verse is an outburst of emotion, 'What will be the end of my time in Troy?' and then the chorus settle down to their connected song. There are a few instances in the simple recapitulations;[4] in the first *stasimon* of the *Electra* the epode is unconnected and deals with a new subject at a different emotional level; in the first two verses the chorus are confident, in the epode they are dejected. Here the break marks a change of emotion. Such breaks are more common in the emotional choruses,[5] and we shall find the same use of asyndeton in the laments and the more emotional speeches.

---

[1] e.g. the song of consolation in the *Antigone* (944) advances from one example of suffering to another; the verses are joined by narrative δέ. Cf. *O.C.* 668, *Trach.* 497.   [2] Cf. Kranz, op. cit., pp. 193, 198, 209.

[3] Cf. the progression of thought in the second *stasimon* of the *Tyrannus* (863).

[4] *Generalizing: Aj.* 1185. *Simple recapitulations: El.* 472, *Aj.* 596 after first antistrophe, *El.* 1058 after second strophe, *Trach.* 821 after second strophe.

[5] e.g. the unconnected wishes or prayers at the end of the following songs: *Ant.* 1146, *Trach.* 655, *O.C.* 1085; cf. the breaks in the cheerful choruses of the *Ajax* and *Tyrannus*, and the prayer for the passing of Oedipus (*O.C.* 1556).

If we now look further into the movement of the thought in the *parodos* of the *Tyrannus*, we find that certain ideas and certain words are repeated. The thought of the first line of the first strophe, 'Sweet-spoken voice of Zeus' is repeated in its last line, 'immortal rumour'. The thought at the beginning of the first antistrophe, 'daughter of Zeus . . . appear', is repeated at the end, 'Come now,' and again at the end of the second antistrophe, 'Daughter of Zeus, send smiling help.' The thought of the beginning of the third strophe, 'and (grant) that fierce Ares may go', is repeated at the end of the third antistrophe, 'against the god dishonoured of gods'. Besides these repetitions of thought, key words,[1] such as 'Zeus, i-e, paean, daughter of Zeus, Artemis', and 'countless', are repeated. The song has one notable correspondence of sense and rhythm; in the second strophe and antistrophe corresponding lines end with ἀνέχουσι γυναῖκες and ἐπιστενάχουσι.

In the *parodos* of the *Tyrannus*, as in earlier prayers, the invocation at the beginning of each section is repeated at the end, so that the prayer is circular in shape. Other Sophoclean prayers and hymns have the same form; the hymn to love in the *Antigone*[2] begins 'Eros invincible in battle', and ends, 'for Aphrodite sports invincible'. Its use is extended to ordinary songs. The *parodos* of the *Trachiniae* is an intermediate stage. The first verse is a prayer to the sun, but the rest an ordinary song. The prayer has the circular form, 'I pray the sun . . . speak, lord of vision'; but the opening words, 'Whom starry night', and the idea of change are also echoed by the first words of the epode, 'But neither starry night abides'.[3] Sophocles

---

[1] See Sheppard's commentary.

[2] *Ant.* 781, cf. the prayers *Ant.* 1115, *Phil.* 391, *O.T.* 1085, *O.C.* 1556, which all start and end with invocations.

[3] See Note S, at end, p. 188.

also casts some of the speeches in his earlier plays into the circular form. He is using the old ritual form to organize his thought.[1]

In other choruses the thought progresses simply through three or four ideas and their variations, until the conclusion is reached in the last verse. In the first *stasimon* of the *Antigone*, for instance, the second antistrophe gives the conclusion to which the description of man's development has been tending, 'This devising skill is sometimes good and sometimes bad. May I have no company with the bad.'[2]

Key words in songs, as in speeches,[3] emphasize the structure and leading ideas. In the *parodos* of the *Tyrannus* Sophocles wants to stress the amount of suffering, and therefore he repeats 'countless' at the same place in the first line of strophe and antistrophe. The key words are very effective in some of the generalizing choruses. In the second *stasimon* of the *Antigone* 'god' and 'infatuation' are keywords which occur in the first *strophe* and again in the second strophe and antistrophe. The key word is yet more emphatic when not only the word, but also the rhythmical phrase is repeated. In the song quoted from the *Antigone* the key word (ἄτας) marks the end of a rhythmical phrase, and is repeated in the same place in the antistrophe; its sense is reinforced by the rhythm. The repetition of the same words in the same place impresses them on the mind of the audience and heightens their emotional effect.

The effect depends on the unity of sense and rhythm

---

[1] See Note T, at end, p. 188.

[2] Cf. *parodos* of *Antigone*, *stasimon* of *Philoctetes*.

[3] *Key words in Speeches*; e.g. in Oedipus' first speech to the chorus in the *Tyrannus*. *Key words in song.* *Ant.* 582 f. 'god' and 'infatuation'; *Trach.* 94 f., 'hope', 'sleep', 'wheeling'; *Aj.* 1185 f. 'joy'. In the *Ajax* as in the *Antigone* sense and rhythm correspond in 1204, 1216.

repeated from strophe to antistrophe. Even where there
is no repetition of words the mere recurrence of units of
rhythm which are also units of sense is effective in itself.
To put this more simply, the correspondence of metrical
endings and sense endings in strophe and antistrophe has
in itself an emotional effect. One instance has already
been quoted from the *parodos* of the *Tyrannus*. In the
third *stasimon* of the *Trachiniae* the last line of the second
strophe, 'The coming fate portends a treacherous and
mighty ruin' (ἁ Δ' ἐρχομένα μοῖρα προφαίνει Δολίαν καὶ
μεγάλαν ἄταν), form a whole of rhythm and meaning which
stands apart from the rest of the verse. This gives an
added force to the last line of the antistrophe which forms
a similar significant conclusion, 'and ministering Cypris,
silent but too plain, is proved the author of these deeds'[1]
(ἁ Δ' ἀμφίπολος Κύπρις ἄναυΔος φανερὰ τῶνΔ' ἐφάνη πρά-
κτωρ).

The coincidence of rhythm and sense by itself heightens
the emotional effect, even where not reinforced by repetition from strophe to antistrophe. In the lyric dialogue,
which is sung while Clytemnestra is being murdered, the
chorus end with four lines consisting of iambic *metron*,
three cretics, and two trimeters (the second with suppressions); in the strophe the divisions in sense correspond
to these divisions in metre and the correspondence gives
these four lines a kind of ghoulish elation; 'The curses are
working (iambic *metron*, τελοῦσ' ἀραί). Those beneath the
earth are alive (cretics, ζῶσιν οἱ γᾶς ὑπαὶ κείμενοι). The
dead are draining the blood of the living (trimeters).' In
the antistrophe the whole four lines are used for a single
quiet period. This emotive use of rhythm is more characteristic of the lament than of the quieter choruses.

We must now compare the laments with the prayer
choruses, treating them from the same three aspects—

[1] See Note U, at end, p. 188.

junction of parts, movement of thought, and correspondence of words with rhythm. In laments we shall include
all forms of song in which not only the chorus but one or
more of the actors participate. If we understand lament
in this extended sense, we can distinguish three main
forms. Perhaps the original is the form which we shall
call the iambic commentary. Here the actor sings and
the chorus comment at the end of each verse with one or
two trimeters. This form can be traced back through the
Cassandra scene of the *Agamemnon* to the lament for Hector, when 'the singers began the wailing song and the
women wailed thereto'. It is used by Sophocles for the
second *kommos* of the *Ajax* and the *kommos* of the *Tyrannus*. In the recognition scene of the *Electra*, Electra sings,
Orestes speaks iambics both in the middle and at the end
of her song.

Secondly, there is the epirrhematic lament where the
verse sung by actor or chorus is taken up by a verse sung
or recited by chorus or actor. In the first *kommos* of the
Ajax each verse of the chorus is taken up by anapaests
from Tecmessa.[1] This too can be paralleled in the Cassandra scene of the *Agamemnon*; as the chorus become
more excited they abandon their iambic commentary for
lyrics. The most elaborate variation of the epirrhematic
form is in the long lament in the *Trachiniae* when Heracles
is brought on to the stage. The lament opens with an
anapaestic dialogue between Hyllus, the old man, and
Heracles. Heracles then sings a short strophe (*a*), followed
by another short strophe (*b*); he then recites (or sings) five
hexameters, the first *epirrhema* (*A*). After this he sings

---

[1] There is a variant in the *parodos* of the *Antigone* where the chorus sing
the strophe and the *koryphaios* recites the anapaests. In the first *kommos*
of the *Antigone* Antigone sings the strophe and the *koryphaios* anapaests,
and then, as the chorus are more moved by her second strophe, they sing
lyrics. In the *parodos* of the *Electra* both chorus and Electra sing lyrics.

the first antistrophe (a') which is followed by the second
epirrhema (A') of five hexameters, sung or recited by the
old man and Hyllus. Heracles sings a third short strophe
(c), followed by the second antistrophe (b'), the third
epirrhema (A'') and the third antistrophe (c'). The shape
of the whole is: $a.b.A.a'.A'.c.b'.A''.c'$—three *epirrhemata*
with three strophes and antistrophes woven round them.[1]

We noticed that in the Cassandra scene of the *Agamemnon*, as the chorus became more excited, the form of the
lament changed from the iambic commentary to the epirrhematic. In the final *kommos* of the *Persae* the epirrhematic form changes to the lyric dialogue. This is the
third form of lament. In the *kommos* of the *Philoctetes* the
first two pairs of strophe and antistrophe are epirrhematic
and the epode is a lyric dialogue.[2] The Sophoclean lyric
dialogue is more realistic than the Aeschylean. In the
Aeschylean form each singer sings a complete metrical
unit inside the verse. In Sophocles each metrical system
is shared between the singers in such a way that not only
the line, but even the *metron* may be divided between two
singers. This advanced form is not found until the lyric
interlude in the second act of the *Tyrannus*.[3]

These are the three chief forms of lament. We can now
examine the junction of the verses. The songs which
accompany action or mark a turning-point in the dialogue
are very much akin to the ordinary choral songs. For
instance, when in the *Coloneus* the chorus question Oedipus of his past crimes,[4] the first strophe ends with the
demand of the chorus, 'Obey. For I obeyed all your
desires'. Oedipus then begins the antistrophe 'Well then,
I suffered misery'. He ends the antistrophe, 'They grew

---

[1] See Note V, at end, p. 188.
[2] *Phil.* 1081, cf. the *parodos* of the *Coloneus*.
[3] *O.T.* 649. Further examples: *Electra* 823, *O.C.* 510, 833, 1724.
[4] *O.C.* 510, cf. *O.T.* 649, *Phil.* 135, *O.C.* 117.

from the womb of our common mother'. The chorus begin the second strophe, 'They are then your children'. Oedipus ends it, 'I received a gift which I never should have received'. The chorus begin, 'What, unhappy man?'. Here part is joined to part clearly and explicitly and there is no technical difference from the choral songs. In the pure laments, however, the parts are sharply separated from one another. In the *kommos* of the *Tyrannus*[1] Oedipus at the beginning of the second strophe answers a question put by the chorus at the end of the first antistrophe, but neither strophe is connected with its antistrophe. Asyndeton is a means of producing emotional effect, as we noticed before when we compared the emotional songs with the generalizing songs.

Asyndeton is partly due to the movement of the thought. In laments the thought does not return full circle as in the prayer choruses or, as in the generalizing choruses, proceed to a conclusion, but various motives are picked up and cast out at random, particularly in the last antistrophe. In the *kommos* of the *Philoctetes* Philoctetes' hatred of Troy, his desire for suicide, and his loyalty to his father are all, so far as the *kommos* is concerned, new motives first introduced in the epode.

The correspondence of words and rhythms must necessarily be close in the strophes and antistrophes of lyric dialogues, since the division between speakers is always the same in both. It is also close in the iambic commentary, since the iambics divide the lyrics into fairly short sections. In the second *kommos* of the *Ajax* the correspondence goes farther; the first and last strophes and antistrophes all start with the same exclamation; in the first pair a pause in sense corresponds to the rhythmical pause at the end of the dochmiacs; in the last pair of verses the pauses in

---

[1] Cf. second *kommos* of the *Ajax*, second *kommos* of the *Antigone*, *kommoi* of the *Philoctetes* and *Coloneus*.

sense and rhythm coincide at the end of the dochmiacs
and again at the end of the iambics.[1] The *kommos* of the
Tyrannus has the same sort of correspondence, and the
sense is punctuated by recurrent exclamations like the recurrent invocations of Oedipus' subsequent speech. The
high points of emotion are accented by the pattern of the
lament.

The characteristics of the prayer are the ring form and
the key word, the characteristics of the lament are asyndeton and correspondence of sense and rhythm. These are
the two poles between which the Sophoclean chorus moves
and the two forms act upon one another. The more agitated songs are nearer the lament than the prayer, the
quieter lyric dialogues are nearer the prayer than the
lament. Both forms are probably sacral in origin, but
Sophocles adapts the original forms to his own ends.

We can now leave the forms and thought of the Sophoclean choruses and turn to a consideration of his metre.
We cannot say anything of his music, but we may be able
to tell what rhythms he chose to express different emotions.
The words guide us in our interpretation of the rhythms;
the pure lament is undoubtedly sorrowful and the cheerful
chorus must be cheerful. Before examining the individual
metres and their uses, we shall first look at two choruses
of the *Tyrannus* where the corresponding changes of
emotion and rhythm are easily observed. The three pairs
of strophe and antistrophe in the *parodos* contain question
and invocation, grounding of invocation, and prayer. The
rhythm changes with the subject.[2] The agitated question-
ing of the first strophe is chiefly dactylic, the sorrowful
description of the plague is introduced in resolved iambics,
the excited prayer of the third *strophe* is in iambics with
many resolutions and suppressions. The three chief

[1] 350 and 358; 395 and 413; 400 and 417.
[2] Cf. Kranz, op. cit., p. 186.

rhythms are fast and agitated dactyls, sorrowful iambics, and excited iambics. The relation of rhythm to emotion is even clearer in the first *stasimon* of the *Tyrannus*.[1] The first strophe starts with the question, 'Who is the murderer?' in excited iambics; then follows the description of his flight in fast glyconics, and then the pursuit of Apollo—and something of the remorselessness of this pursuit is expressed by the marching anapaests. The clausula is glyconic. In the second strophe the chorus are calmer and reflect on Tiresias' statement that Oedipus is the murderer. Here the metre is first choriambic and then ionic; both are quieter than the metres of the first strophe. These two choruses give us some idea of Sophocles' use of metre to express emotion and of changes of metre to express changes of emotion. We can now discuss the individual metres from this point of view.

Dactyls are a favourite metre with Sophocles, as with Aeschylus before him. We have already spoken of the fast and excited dactyls in the *parodos* of the *Tyrannus*. The *parodoi* of the *Ajax* and *Trachiniae* also begin with excited questions; they too are largely dactylic. Pure dactyls are used for the *epirrhemata* in the second *kommos* of the *Trachiniae* and in the sleep chorus of the *Philoctetes*. In the latter it has been said that Neoptolemus speaks in dactyls because the oracle spoke in dactyls. But both here and in the *Trachiniae* it is more natural to suppose that the poet wanted a more exciting rhythm than iambics, and that he wanted a falling rather than a rising rhythm and therefore could not use anapaests. Actors and chorus sing long runs of dactyls in the *parodoi* of the *Electra* and *Coloneus* and in the *kommos* of the *Philoctetes*; the singer is swept into a long flowing metre by his excitement. Dactyls can also be used with other metres. When they are used to introduce other metres, they give a swift beginning

[1] See Note W, at end, p. 189.

to the verse.[1] For the same reason they can be inserted in the middle of the most lively metres.[2] Dactyls whether alone or in runs are always a quick and excited metre.

Iambics can be used for most purposes. Three main classes may be distinguished; calm, excited, and lamenting. All three are already found in Aeschylus,[3] but the Aeschylean iambics have more suppressions than the Sophoclean, and Aeschylus has more runs of cretics and bacchiacs. Sophocles uses calm iambics after faster metres to slow up the rhythm, as in the epode of the *parodos* in the *Trachiniae* after dactyls and choriambs.[4] In the generalizing second *stasimon* of the *Tyrannus* the iambic trimeter with suppressions and resolutions is the dominant rhythm. Excited iambics are used with other metres, e.g. to form a *pnigos* after antispasts in the fourth *stasimon* of the *Trachiniae*, or by themselves with many suppressions and resolutions, as in the cheerful chorus of the *Antigone* and the paean of the *Trachiniae*. Excited iambics are the dominant rhythm in the strophe and antistrophe of the first *stasimon* of the *Electra*, where the chorus are excited by the report of Clytemnestra's dream and hope for vengeance. In the epode the mood changes and the iambics take the curious form, $-\cup\cup\cup-/--$, i.e. iambic *metron* followed by a second iambic *metron* with both shorts suppressed, a creepy rhythm which is akin to the dochmiac. In the third *stasimon* of the *Trachiniae*,[5] where the chorus are lamenting the news

[1] e.g. *Ant.* 134, cf. 582, 966, which should probably also be scanned as dactyls.

[2] With glyconics, *Ant.* 339, *O.C.* 676; with excited iambics, *Trach.* 212, *O.C.* 540; with dochmiacs, *Aj.* 881; with trochaics *Ant.* 879, *O.T.* 1088, 1091, 1094.

[3] e.g. calm, *Ag.* 367; excited, *Suppl.* 776; lamenting, *Pers.* 548.

[4] Cf. *El.* 1083 after glyconics and choriambs, *Trach.* 953 after lamenting iambics.

[5] In *Trach.* 827–8 follows the lamenting iambics 824–7 (cf. 947). Cf. *Electra* 160–1, *Aj.* 198, *Phil.* 835–6. Cf. Denniston, *Greek Poetry and Life*, p. 125.

which Hyllus has just brought it is joined to lamenting iambics. Therefore in the *Electra* too the epode must be classed as lamenting iambics, though the strophe and antistrophe are in excited iambics. We have already spoken of the lamenting iambics in the *parodos* of the *Tyrannus*. They occur again in the fourth *stasimon*, where the jerkier iambics follow the quieter glyconics of the first two verses and themselves change to another weeping rhythm, $-\cup-\cup-$,[1] which, like that just noticed in the *Electra*, is akin to the dochmiac. In the second *kommos* of the *Ajax* and the *parodos* of the *Electra*, this rhythm is associated with dochmiacs as well as iambics. Thus the various forms of iambic can be made to express any emotion.

The four metres which we have next to examine, glyconics,[2] choriambs, ionics, and antispasts, occur frequently with each other and in combination with other metres. Glyconics, like iambics, can be used to express a variety of emotions, excitement, joy, or sorrow. Sad glyconics can be inserted in stanzas of other metres,[3] or they can be used to build longer systems as in the fourth *stasimon* of the *Tyrannus*, where the first strophe is purely glyconic.[4] With this lamenting glyconic we can contrast the joyful movement of the *parodos* of the *Antigone*; here the first strophe is glyconic with choriambic clausula and the second dactylic with glyconics and choriambs. In the first *stasimon* of the *Antigone*[5] the first strophe is glyconic with iambic-dactylic clausula. Here the glyconic is quieter but can still be classed as

[1] *O.T.* 1208, cf. *Aj.* 401, *El.* 246–7.
[2] I am using this name to cover also pherecratean, telesillean, &c.
[3] In iambics, *O.C.* 1242; in mixed iambics and dochmiacs, *Ant.* 841.
[4] Cf. *Phil.* 169 f., *Phil. kommos*, *O.C.* 1211 f., cf. *Suppl.* 955, *Cho.* 321.
[5] Cf. Friedländer, *Hermes*, 1934, p. 56 f. Compare *O.C.* 668 f. and the cheerful glyconics of Euripides, *H.F.* 781.

cheerful. This cheerful or lively glyconic can also be used with other metres.[1]

Some uses of the choriamb we have noticed already, particularly its very close connexion with the glyconic. Trochaic or iambic metron with choriamb are the metrical equivalent of glyconics and can be used with them without breaking the rhythm.[2] Pure choriambs are, however, a slower rhythm and can suitably be used to end a glyconic stanza, as in the *parodos* of the *Antigone*. For the same reason choriambs and ionics follow the excited metres of the first strophe in the first *stasimon* of the *Tyrannus*. Similarly in the third *stasimon* of the *Electra* the beginning and the end of the first strophe are mostly in choriambic dimeters, the middle section which contains the oath is in glyconics.

Ionics are a metre of the same kind and value as choriambs. The ionic *a maiore* and trochaic *metron* is frequently used with glyconics and other metres. The pure ionic is not so common in Sophocles as in Aeschylus and Euripides. There are, however, long stretches in the *Tyrannus* after the choriambs which open the second strophe of the first *stasimon*, and in the *parodos* of the *Coloneus* after glyconics and iambics and leading on to anapaests and dactyls.

Stretches of ionics are often said to exist in the first *stasimon* of the *Coloneus* and the second *stasimon* of the *Electra*, but in both cases the lines should probably be scanned as antispasts, since otherwise it is difficult to account for their beginnings and ends. In the *Coloneus* the first strophe is glyconic, and this metre is echoed in the second antispastic strophe; in the *Electra* the antispasts follow choriambs. Antispasts can also be used as a long slow line in a glyconic stanza, as an introduction to a

[1] With iambics, *Aj*. 696; with mixed iambics and dactyls, *Phil*. 136, 856; between iambics and anapaests, *O.T.* 467.

[2] So also Aeschylus, *Cho*. 322, &c., Euripides, *H.F.* 784, &c.

glyconic stanza, or to form the body of a slower stanza after a fast stanza which is echoed by a glyconic clausula. They can be used with iambics, either as an introduction to an iambic run, or as a clausula to lamenting iambics.[1]

Trochaics and anapaests are perhaps the least common of the Sophoclean metres, and both are used less by him than by the other two tragedians. Trochaics of course occur in the construction of glyconics and dactylo-epitrites. Schroeder finds also a run of trochaics in the epode to the *parodos* of the *Trachiniae*, but Pearson is right in regarding them as iambics with the first short of the first *metron* suppressed. Trochaics are certainly used in the recognition scene of the *Electra* and in the second strophe of the second *stasimon* of the *Coloneus*. In both they are a faster and more exciting rhythm than the iambics. In the cheerful chorus of the *Tyrannus* the predominant rhythm is trochaic.

Anapaests also are a rare metre. Short sections of anapaests rounding off the end of a scene or introducing a new character are only found in the *Ajax* and *Antigone*. The long anapaestic prelude to the *parodos* in the *Ajax* is a mark of early date and similar to the preludes in the *Supplices*, *Persae*, and *Agamemnon*. In the Sophoclean preludes[2] the anapaests are used as an excited metre which makes a transition from the iambic dialogue to the lyric of the song proper. In the *Electra* alone they are sung by the actor instead of being recited. Used with other metres in a song[3] anapaests are of much the same value as dactyls except that they are a rising instead of a falling rhythm.

---

[1] Antispasts: *El.* 832, *O.C.* 694. In glyconics, *Aj.* 629; before glyconics, *O.C.* 178; as a slow verse, *Phil.* 707; introduction to iambics, *Ant.* 944; clausula, *Trach.* 849.

[2] First *kommos* of *Ajax*, both *kommoi* of *Antigone*, second *kommos* of *Trachiniae*, *kommos* of *Tyrannus*, *parodos* of *Electra*.

[3] See Note X, at end, p. 189.

The last metre which we have to examine is the dochmiac. It is used in much the same way by all three tragedians and is always an excited rhythm. It is used in three
of the prayers, as an exciting clausula to the iambic prayer
to Cybele and the dactylic prayer to Sleep in the *Philoctetes*, and all through the prayer to Death in the *Coloneus*
though with iambic insertions. Single lines or groups of
two lines in dochmiacs mark the high points of emotion in
the lyric dialogue of the *Tyrannus* and the recognition
scene of the *Electra*; in these dochmiacs are inserted in
iambics. Dochmiacs are inserted in glyconics in the first
stasimon of the *Ajax* and in the lament of the *Philoctetes*.[1]
The dochmiac is particularly the metre of the lament, and
is used with iambics in both the laments of the *Ajax*, in
the second lament of the *Antigone* and the lament of the
Tyrannus. It is noticeable that Creon's wild lament in
the *Antigone* is almost pure dochmiacs and therefore contrasts with Antigone's more sober lament of which the
predominant metre is iambic and glyconic with only occasional dochmiacs.

The results of our examination of the metres of Sophocles' songs may be summed up briefly. Dactyls and anapaests are always fast metres, dochmiacs are always excited.
But the other important metres, particularly glyconic and
iambic, can be used to express any emotion, and the emotion which they express is determined not by the kind of
metre, but by its juxtaposition with other metres and by
subtle variations inside the metre itself, such as suppres-
sion, resolution, and the like, but above all by the words.
If more were known, it might be shown that many of the
metres had sacral origins.[2] As it is, perhaps all that can be
safely asserted is that the dochmiac was probably a common metre for the *threnos*.

[1] *O.T.* 656, *El.* 1233, cf. 1387, *O.C.* 1449. Dochmiacs in glyconics, *Aj.* 627,
Phil. 1092, 1096.   [2] See particularly Ax (*Hermes*, 1932, p. 426 f.).

There is a final problem of which a word must be said. Is there any trace of special rhythms running through all or most of the songs of a play? It has been maintained that the creepy rhythm in the epode of the first *stasimon* of the *Electra* is reminiscent of the *parodos*.[1] We must admit the possibility in the case of such a rare rhythm. But the majority of the rhythms are so common and are used so frequently that it does not seem possible to make out a case for significant recurrence. Rhythms recur, as we have seen, inside individual songs, and ideas are echoed from song to song. There may be a reminiscence of tunes from song to song but that we have no evidence to decide.

[1] Thomson, *Greek Lyric Metre*, pp. 137–9.

VII. Style

Early and late vocabulary—early and late style; type of argument—
method of argument—versification—speech division—word pattern—sound pattern.

DISCUSSION of Sophocles' style must start from his
own account of its development.[1] 'Sophocles used
to say that after he had fought his way through the pomp
of Aeschylus and later the unpleasantness and artificiality
of his own style, he then changed to his third manner,
which was the best and had the most *ethos*.' Even if the
words are a paraphrase by Plutarch, which is very possible,
we can hardly doubt that Plutarch knew a genuine saying
of Sophocles, which presumably came from his book, *On
the chorus*.

Sophocles recognized three stages in his own style, the
first Aeschylean and pompous, the second unpleasant and
artificial,[2] the third the best and most 'ethical' (in the
Aristotelian sense of 'adapted to the temper of the particular speech'). We shall speak of these stages as Aeschylean, early and late, since we are accustomed to speak of
the *Antigone* as an early play and it is hardly likely that
Sophocles in his forties was still in his full Aeschylean
period.

Great obstacles stand in the way of demonstrating the
truth of Sophocles' saying from the surviving plays and
fragments. In the first place, if we possessed all the plays
of Sophocles, we should not be able to arrange them neatly
into three classes, since the classes would inevitably overlap. Secondly, our evidence is confined to seven plays and

[1] Plutarch, *De prof. in virt.*, p. 79ᵇ. I accept Διαπεπαλαιχώς for Διαπε-
παιχώς. κατασκευή and κατάτεχνος seem to be words of the Roman period.

[2] 'Unpleasant'. πικρός here is the opposite of βέλτιστος and is not used
in any technical sense.

a great many undated fragments out of a total of some hundred and twenty. Thirdly, our knowledge of Aeschylus, Euripides, and the rest of fifth-century literature is itself so fragmentary that we cannot say for certain what is purely Sophoclean and what he has borrowed and what are the sources of his borrowing.

Nevertheless it may be possible to give a rough interpretation of this saying in terms of Sophocles' practice. We know that the *Triptolemus* was produced in 468 and the *Thamyras* not long after, that the *Antigone* was produced in 443 or 441, the *Philoctetes* in 409, and the *Coloneus* after the death of Sophocles. Further, we can justifiably associate the *Ajax* and the *Trachiniae* with the *Antigone* as early plays and the *Electra* with the *Philoctetes* as late, while the *Tyrannus* can be dated between the *Trachiniae* and the *Electra*. We may then have specimens of all three periods, although the certain evidence for the first is confined to a few dated fragments. At least we can attempt to distinguish these three periods by an examination of vocabulary and style.

Unfortunately few fragments remain of Sophocles' earliest play, the *Triptolemus*, which should provide the best evidence for the Aeschylean period. But two lines have the heavy rhythm which we associate particularly with Aeschylus; one recalls the Aeschylean metaphor of the tablets of the mind and, if three fragments which have reasonably been assigned to this play are added, we gain one reminiscence and three Aeschylean words.[1] The foreign words which occur in the fragments of the *Thamyras* may also be due to the influence of Aeschylus.[2] Thus

---

[1] *Rhythm*: fr. 596, 611. *Metaphor*: 597 (see Pohlenz, *Gr. Tr.* ii, p. 25). *Reminiscence*: 754 with Aesch. fr. 300. *Words*: 837 Δερχθέντες, 844 χειρῶναξ and γοργῶπις (cf. Reinhardt, op. cit., p. 17 f.).

[2] Frs. 238, 243 (cf. Kranz, *Stasimon*, ch. 3, on foreign elements in Aeschylus).

even from our fragmentary evidence we can understand what Sophocles means by his Aeschylean period.

For the early and late periods we have the evidence of the surviving plays, and we shall examine first vocabulary[1] and then style. A large number of Aeschylean words[2] may be expected in the early plays as a survival from the Aeschylean period, and this expectation is justified by such words as ἀσφάλαστος, ἀείμνηστος, λευκόπωλος, and ὀπτήρ in the *Ajax*, Δυσβουλία, μόρσιμος, ὁμόσπλαγχνος in the *Antigone*, ἀμφίβληστρον, ἀρτίκολλος, and ἱπποβάμων in the *Trachiniae*. All these words occur in the dialogue, ἀκάρπωτος and ἀγχίαλος in the choruses of the *Ajax*.

Besides Aeschylus, Sophocles could draw on the vocabulary of Homer and the lyric poets. Many of these Homeric and lyric words, which are not found in Aeschylus, occur chiefly in Sophocles' early plays; many of them are used later by Euripides but not, so far as we know, by Sophocles himself in his later period. It is natural that Sophocles, the most Homeric of the tragedians, should also borrow from Homer's vocabulary, and we find αἰπύς, ἀμενηνός, and τανύπους in the *Ajax*, ἔναντα in the *Antigone*, ἀλινός, ἀγακλειτός, and ναύλοχος in the *Trachiniae*. Of the words found in the lyric poets it will be sufficient to quote εὐνομία from the *Ajax*, Δεννάζειν from the *Antigone*, and ἀγνωμοσύνη from the *Trachiniae*. Neither class of words is confined to either dialogue or songs.

So far we have noticed the elements in Sophocles' early vocabulary which can definitely be assigned to the influence of earlier poetry. Now we have to look at words whose poetic origin we cannot trace. Some of the words which are first found in Sophocles' early vocabulary

[1] The following discussion of Sophocles' vocabulary is based on a list of rather over five hundred words which belong exclusively either to the early or the late period.

[2] Cf. Schmid-Stählin, p. 290, n. 7.

assuredly come from poetry (e.g. ἀλίκτυπος, ἀπολωβᾶν in
the *Ajax*, βαθύρριζος in the *Trachiniae*). ἀλίκτυπος occurs
again in the *Hippolytus* and other words such as λάλημα
and τύμβευμα (*Antigone*), ἐμπόλημα and ὑπαγκάλισμα (*Trachiniae*), though not found later in Sophocles, are used
again by Euripides. Other words undoubtedly come from
everyday speech whether they are quoted from prose or
only from early Sophocles. To this class I should assign
ἀνταμύνεσθαι, κομψεύειν, σκαιότης in the *Antigone*, ἀναζεῖν
and ζήτησις in the *Trachiniae*.[1]
If we review Sophocles' early vocabulary as a whole, certain classes of words stand out as distinctive. First, he likes
privative adjectives and compounds; ἀμέριμνος, ἄσπλαγχνος,
ἀγωνάρχης, ψηφοποιός from the *Ajax*, ἀκτέριστος, ἀείφρουρος, λιθοσπαδής from the *Antigone*, ἀξύμβλητος, ἀνάνδρωτος,
ἐξόμιλος, θυμοφθορεῖν from the *Trachiniae* will illustrate
the class. Most of the verbs compounded with ἐπεκ- and
ἐπεν- are early. Secondly, he likes agents and abstracts
(particularly the neuter verbal form and often in a concrete sense), e.g. ἄλημα, ἄμυγμα, ὀφειλέτης from the *Ajax*,
κοίμημα, ἁμιλλητήρ from the *Antigone*, στέργημα and ἐνλυτήρ
from the *Trachiniae*. Thirdly, the non-adjectival adverbs
are common, e.g. ἐγερτί, ἀνάμιγδα, ἀνοιμωκτί. Lastly, some
words are variations from the normal form, made to fit
the particular needs of the line, e.g. ἀσεπτεῖν, εὐσκευεῖν,
τανταλοῦν.

In the later plays Sophocles is still borrowing from
Aeschylus, but the borrowing is much reduced; however,
ἀγλάϊσμα and αἰκεία in the *Electra*, ἀμαυρός and ὀμματοστερής
in the *Coloneus* are new Aeschylean words. A considerable
number of the distinctive words of this period are also

[1] A small group of words are common to the early plays and Herodotus.
It is not easy to say which writer is the source. But Sophocles may well
have borrowed λόκησις, ἐπανάστασις, ζήτησις, σκαιότης, and ἐθελοντής
from the historian.

found in Euripides and may therefore have been borrowed from him, e.g. λυπηρός, μηκύνειν, τητᾶσθαι, εὐλάβεια, ἱππεία in the *Electra*. Words like Δυσχέρεια (*Philoctetes*), ὑπηρετεῖν, εὐημερεῖν (*Electra*), συνταλαιπωρεῖν, ἐνθύμημα (*O.C.*) are also found in prose. The most notable additions to the vocabulary are the abstracts in -ις such as ἄμβασις, ἀνάλυσις, ἄρκεσις, ἐνθάκησις, ἐπίκτησις, κερτόμησις, ὠφέλησις. The beginning of this development can be seen in the *Tyrannus* where we have ἀνακίνησις, ἀνακούφισις and φρόνησις. The late plays have fewer privatives and the compound words are restricted to highly coloured passages, e.g. ποικιλόστολος in Neoptolemus' fictitious narrative and πυκνόπτερος in Antigone's romantic description of the scene at the beginning of the *Coloneus*.

From this mass of detailed evidence the following picture can be constructed. The earliest plays were probably far more Aeschylean in vocabulary than any of the plays which have come down to us. But from the first Sophocles extended the vocabulary of both his lyrics and his dialogue by words borrowed from Homer[1] and the lyric poets, and by words taken from contemporary prose and from everyday speech.[2] He particularly liked certain classes of words of which the privative adjectives (often long and prefixed by a negative),[3] the neuter verbal form, and the non-adjectival adverbs are typical examples.[4] He also, not unlike Homer, used words of a form which varies slightly from the normal so as to be more easily accommodated in his verse. These variant forms and the negatived

---

[1] θαιρός (fr. 596) is Homeric, *Triptolemus*.

[2] ταριχηρός (fr. 606) is a word of the market, *Triptolemus*.

[3] ἀπυνδάκωτος (fr. 611). Demetrius quotes the line from the *Triptolemus* as an example of frigidity. A line from the *Laconian Women* (fr. 367) well illustrates the use στενήν Δ' ἔδυμεν ψαλίδα κοὐκ ἀβόρβορον. We can understand the later Sophocles calling this 'unpleasant and artificial'.

[4] Cf. fr. 596 ἀμφιπλίξ, *Triptolemus*.

privatives produce a smooth but slightly artificial style highly coloured by the compound words and the words borrowed from Aeschylus and Homer.

In the later plays the Homeric and Aeschylean colouring is much reduced; the old privatives are gone and the new privatives are shorter and simpler; compound words are fewer; the agents, adverbs, and variations of form are gone. On the other hand, the number of abstract words has increased. The new abstracts mostly end in -ις, instead of the neuter verbal noun of the earlier period. The abstract words are the last remnant of artificiality' and make the necessary differences from the language of everyday life. Otherwise the language is adapted to the purpose of the speakers; though not the smooth colourful language of early Sophocles, it is yet the most 'ethical'.

So far we have only interpreted Sophocles' account of his diction in terms of his vocabulary. We have now to consider style. To this end we shall compare the early debate in the *Antigone* with the late debate in the *Electra*. The situations are roughly parallel. Creon is the father of Haemon, and Clytemnestra the mother of Electra; the subjects are the death of Antigone and the death of Agamemnon. A summary analysis of the four speeches will facilitate reference to them.

CREON *to* HAEMON

639–40.	General reflection on obedience.
641–4.	Reason; four-line period balanced by
645–7.	three-line period.
648–54.	Command to let Antigone die.
649–52.	Reason put between the two halves of the command.
655–9.	Statement of intention to put Antigone to death.
659–62.	Justification of action, balanced by
663–5.	Condemnation of Antigone, both in general terms.
666–71.	The good citizen, balanced by

672–6.   Anarchy.

677–80. Conclusion; we must not yield to a woman.

HAEMON *to* CREON

683–4.   General reflection on wisdom.

685–7.   Expression of obedience; application of 'wisdom'.

688–91.   Creon's position.

692–700. The views of the city (N.B. hyperbole and metaphor).

701–9.   Expression of obedience; application of 'wisdom'.

710–18.   Restatement, ending in appeal to yield.

719–23.   Conclusion; it is good to learn.

CLYTEMNESTRA *to* ELECTRA

516–27.   Prologue; abuse of Electra, self-defence, admission of
          particular charge—murder of Agamemnon.

528–33.   Narration; facts of murder. Agamemnon had killed
          Iphigenia, which was criminal.

534, 537, 539, 542, 544. Questions to prove the murder of
          genia unjustifiable.

546–8.   Conclusion to questions.

549–51.   Conclusion to speech, with self-justification and abuse
          of Electra.

ELECTRA *to* CLYTEMNESTRA

558–62.   Prologue; Clytemnestra's plea dishonourable, whether
          (1) unjust or (2) just, (3) her real reason.

563–76.   1. First argument; Agamemnon justified.

573–6.   Conclusion to first argument.

577–83.   2. Second argument; further consequence of retribu-
          tive justice, if Clytemnestra's premise is granted.

584–94.   3. Third argument; Clytemnestra still lives with
          Aegisthus.

593–4.   Conclusion of third argument.

595–609. Conclusion of speech; abuse of Clytemnestra; justi-
          fication of Electra's own position.

The movement of Creon's thought is simple and is nowhere stressed, 'You must obey your father; let Antigone
go; I shall kill her; we must not yield to a woman'. He

supports each step by appeal to general principles. At one point[1] he makes a difficult transition from family life to city life. 'The man who can behave in the family will also behave in the city. The man who transgresses the laws, I cannot approve.' The argument only becomes clear when it is remembered that the first is Creon and the second Antigone; in its general form it is obscure. Then he develops the contrast between the obedient citizen and anarchy. We shall find other blurred transitions in the early speeches, and there is no need to alter the text. The thought of Haemon's speech is equally simple, 'You cannot see everything; do not think that you alone are right; yield from your anger'. The reasoning is general and Haemon returns in the middle and at the end of his speech to his opening gnome, 'wisdom is best'. The whole movement of the thought is circular, like the thought of a prayer chorus. In both speeches the versification is smooth; all the major and most of the minor sections end at the end of a line. Only two lines[2] are jerky and realistic. Creon stresses his high points by irony and anaphora.[3] Haemon is more colourful with his 'dark rumour', the men who are 'opened and found to be empty', and the images of the trees and the ship.

In the later debate Clytemnestra's speech, except for the prologue, the narrative, and the three-line conclusion, is constructed on the question, 'Why did he kill her?' and the alternative possibilities. It is not a simple unstressed movement, but a complicated piece of argument with the structure clearly defined. The reasons are not general principles, but either particular arguments for this case or else attacks on the other party. 'You speak ill of me; you ought to help justice, if you are sane . . . get you just thoughts before you blame your neighbours.' The main sections of the speech are clearly marked.

[1] 661 f.   [2] 658, 659.   [3] 654, 673 f.

Electra's speech again is a careful and relevant piece of argument. The prologue states the divisions of the speech —justly, unjustly, Aegisthus. The first argument starts after a clear break and has its own four-line conclusion. The second argument is introduced by 2' οὖν. A single line introduces the third argument which again has its clear conclusion. Finally, the argument *ad hominem* is developed. In both speeches the versification is speeded by the questions, by pauses within the line, and by overlaps of sense from one line to the next.

The two debates are quite distinct in style. In the earlier the versification is smooth, in the later it is jerky and realistic. In the earlier the thought is simple and the reasoning general; in the later, although the whole speech is constructed on a clear scheme, the movement of thought is more complicated, the reasoning is particular and *ad hominem*, and the images and gnomes have given place to force and pungency of argument. It is a parallel development in style to the development from the artificial to the ethic vocabulary. It remains to be seen whether the distinction can be substantiated by an examination of other speeches. Otherwise it may be said that the difference between the *Antigone* and *Electra* is due solely to the situations and the characters.

The *Ajax* is an early play, perhaps earlier than the *Antigone*. The pair of debates at the end may be compared with the debate of Haemon and Creon. The movement of thought is like that in the *Antigone* debate. The speakers begin without explicit statement of the lines on which the speech is going to proceed. Menelaus starts with reasons for his proclamation, then enlarges on the proclamation itself, then with no real connexion continues his general reasons. The conclusion gives the proclamation again, swinging back to the beginning like Haemon's speech in the *Antigone*. Teucer begins his answer to

Menelaus with four lines of general argument on the in-
compatibility of birth and character, and his last words
echo the opening gnome. In Agamemnon's speech again
the conclusion echoes the beginning. Teucer's answer to
him starts with a general prologue on gratitude.

These four speeches are more particular and personal
than the debate speeches of the *Antigone*, but the reasoning
is general, and three of the four speeches have the circular
form of Haemon's speech. Menelaus and Agamemnon
enforce their arguments with images—the city, the strong
man, the ship of state, the broad-backed man, the great
ox. Teucer makes his descriptions pictorial—Hector leap-
ing over the trenches, the lots in the helmet, Aerope cast
to the mute fish. Reinhardt well speaks of 'the sound and
imagery of the knightly world' in connexion with this
play.[1] This imagery has already been noticed in the
Antigone debate.

The use of imagery for argument has a long history
before Sophocles, a history which stretches back through
Pindar, Aeschylus, and Simonides to the personification of
prayers in the ninth book of the *Iliad*. In the fifth century
Pericles himself was famous for his metaphors and similes,
and Herodotus uses imagery very like Haemon's in his
speech to Artabanus.[2] With the rise of the professional
rhetorician the particular superseded the general argument, and Sophocles also felt this influence. It is therefore
not unexpected that the figures for Sophocles' images
(taken from the list in Schmid-Stählin) show a marked
difference between the earlier and the later plays. They
are as follows: *Ajax* 47, *Antigone* 62, *Trachiniae* 44,
Tyrannus 37, *Electra* 29, *Philoctetes* 22, *Coloneus* 30. These

---

[1] Reinhardt, op. cit., p. 27 f. I have not been able to consult Terzaghi,
Stud. it. di fil. class. xiv, pp. 415 ff. Another clear example of this rich
imagery is Ajax' monologue (646 f.).

[2] Cf. ch. ii, p. 53.

figures are significant of the difference in style between the two groups, but even in the early plays the images are ornaments which Sophocles applies sparingly for his particular purposes; he does not continually think in pictures like Aeschylus and Pindar.

In the late plays, as Navarre long ago saw,[1] Sophocles is influenced by contemporary rhetoric. This does not mean that the late speeches are rhetorical exercises, but that Sophocles' characters inevitably express themselves in the forms used by the contemporary speaker, because these forms were the most expressive of character. The *Electra* is in this respect nearer to the *Medea* and *Troades* than to the *Antigone*. A last analysis may make this change clearer. When Creon appeals to Oedipus to come home,[2] he does not start with general reasoning, but designs his prologue, like an orator, to win the goodwill of his audience, the chorus. 'You are afraid of me, but I am old and Athens is strong.' Then he states his purpose, to bring back Oedipus. 'I am sent by the whole city, because I am Oedipus' nearest relative.' This gives the main lines of the speech which he then proceeds to work out. He appeals to Oedipus on behalf of the whole city, but particularly on his own behalf, because he sees Oedipus' misery. Then the appeal is repeated at the end, 'Come home, having well bespoken Athens, for she deserves it. But Thebes would more justly have your reverence'. The three points of the speech are given at the beginning and then worked out in detail. The speaker is conscious of the Athenian elders, and begins and ends with words calculated to gain their approval. He speaks in long periods which befit the old king. This is the ethic style.[3]

---

[1] *Essai sur la rhétorique grecque avant Aristote*, p. 72 f.

[2] *O.C.* 728.

[3] Compare *Phil.* 1314, *O.C.* 258, 1181, 1284, and see Radermacher's analysis in his edition.

The early style differs from the later in method as well
as type of reasoning. The beginning of Tecmessa's appeal
to Ajax[1] is a good instance of the early method. The
speaker starts to explain one thing, and then by a curious
blurred transition ends in saying something else. Tecmessa
says, 'There is no greater evil for men than the lot given
by necessity. I was born of a free father and now I am a
slave. For that was the will of the gods and chiefly of your
hand. Therefore, since I am come to your bed, I wish you
well and I beg you. . . .' The link is not a logical link, but the
purely external link from *your* hand to *your* bed and *your*
good fortune. The logical link would be: 'the lot appointed by destiny is hard, but I have borne it and therefore you can bear it, and I ask you since I am your wife. . . .'
Creon's first speech in the *Antigone*[2] is similarly argued.
Logically Creon should say, 'I sent for you because I knew
that you were faithful. Therefore I felt it advisable to
explain and justify my policy to you'. But he actually says,
'I sent for you knowing that you were faithful to Laius,
Oedipus and his sons. Therefore, now that they are dead
I have the power. But it is impossible to know any man's
temper until he has been seen ruling.' We expect him to
end his first sentence 'knowing that now that they are dead
and I have the power you are likely to be faithful to me'.
Instead 'I have the power' becomes a main sentence. On
a smaller scale a sentence from Oedipus' first speech to the
chorus in the *Tyrannus* has a similar break in construction.
'But now, since it is both my lot to have the power which
he once had and to have his bed and wife, and common
children would have been born, had his offspring not been
unfortunate, but now fortune has leapt on his head.
Therefore I will fight.' If Sophocles had kept to the
logical structure of the sentence, 'now fortune . . .', would
have been a genitive absolute and 'therefore I will fight'

[1] *Aj.* 485 f.   [2] *Ant.* 164 f.

would have been the main sentence to the causal clause 'since it is my lot'.[1] Here, as in the *Ajax* and *Antigone*, a sentence starts in one form and ends in another. This blurring of transitions is not peculiar to Sophocles. It is found also in Aeschylus and Herodotus and can be traced further back to the lyric poets and Homer.[2] But in Sophocles it is more common in the earlier than in the later plays.

In his later plays he is a complete master of the periodic style. Here, again, it is legitimate to see the influence of contemporary prose. The first sentence of Neoptolemus' lying report to Philoctetes is typical.[3] 'For when fate ruled that Achilles should die, there came to fetch me in a gallant ship goodly Odysseus and the guardian of my father, saying whether truly or, it may be, falsely, that it was not right, now that my father was dead, for any other than me Troy to take.' This is a five-line period with a break between the second and third line bridged by the swing of the metre; 'came' demands a subject which is found in the next line; subject and verb together are complete, therefore the rest of the sentence is put between them. Similarly, in the second part of the sentence 'saying' demands an object clause, and therefore the 'whether ... or ...' is inserted before the object clause; 'it was not right' demands an infinitive and the subject and object of the infinitive are inserted before the infinitive itself. The sentence is a masterpiece of careful and logical construction and shows on a small scale the same method of skilled preparation which we have noticed in the whole construction of the later plays.

[1] *O.T.* 258 f. For simpler instances see Bruhn, *Anhang*, § 191; cf. also *Ant.* 661 (see above), *Aj.* 1085, 1255, 1288-90.

[2] Cf. H. Fränkel, *Göttinger Gelehrter Nachrichten*, 1924, pp. 72 ff. for lyric poetry; Aeschylus, *Ag.* 638 f., &c.; Hdt. i. 77. 1-3 &c.

[3] *Phil.* 343. The ἐπεί clause (331) should be added at the beginning.

The third distinction which we noticed between the *Antigone* and *Electra* lay in the treatment of the versification. The speeches in the *Antigone* are smoother than those in the *Electra*; sentence endings and line endings tend to coincide. It is true that lines can be found in the early plays where the jerky movement of the verse expresses the emotion of the speaker, but broken lines are more common in the later plays. There is no need to multiply examples, but perhaps the most striking are the broken-hearted short sentences in Electra's lament (a few lines later she speaks anapaests) and the despairing lines in Philoctetes' appeal to Neoptolemus.[1] These passages have an emotion and a realism which Sophocles would not have expressed in his earlier period. The emotional iambics of the late plays have a parallel in the development of the realistic lyric dialogue from the time of the *Tyrannus*.

The preservation of Sophocles' own assessment of his style has caused us to dwell at length on the contrast between the earlier and the later plays and possibly to exaggerate it.[2] The main differences are three; in the later style the versification is freer and the movement of thought more explicit; the earlier style is more picturesque in its argument and the later more personal.

We may now turn to the more general characteristics of Sophocles' style which can be found in all his plays. It is difficult to express in a word the common quality which the language of all shares. Perhaps 'pattern' is the best

[1] *El.* 1151 οἴχεται πατήρ· τέθνηκ' ἐγὼ σοι· φροῦδος αὐτὸς εἰ θανών. γελῶσι δ' ἐχθροί.

Phil. 949 νῦν δ' ἠπάτημαι δύσμορος· τί χρή με δρᾶν; ἀλλ' ἀπόδος. ἀλλὰ νῦν ἔτ' ἐν σαυτῷ γενοῦ.

τί φής; σιωπᾷς. οὐδέν εἰμ' ὁ δύσμορος.

See also Note Y, at end, p. 189.

[2] Reinhardt (op. cit., pp. 168, 184, 188) from the same point of view compares the laments in the *Ajax* and *Electra*, the appeals in the *Ajax* and *Philoctetes*, and the agonies in the *Trachiniae* and *Philoctetes*.

name. Just as the flowing trochee and the staccato
dochmiac can both be called rhythm, so the term 'pattern'
covers both tautology and asyndeton. But it must be
understood from the outset that 'pattern' is much more
than an artistic device for beautifying speeches; it is in
speeches, as in songs, a means of expressing the highest
emotion. In order to show that 'pattern' in this extended
sense is an essential element of Sophocles' style, we shall
examine his methods of joining sentence to sentence and
section to section, and then the various elements of pattern
inside the sentence or speech, such as repetition, antithesis,
alliteration, and assonance.

Some of Sophocles' transitions simply bridge a gap and
have no emotional significance. He sometimes completes
one subject with a μέν clause and begins the next with
a 2έ clause. This form of transition is very common
in Homer and in the narrative passages of Herodotus.
Sophocles uses it most in his early plays. Like Herodotus
again, he sometimes joins two sentences by picking up the
main verb of the first sentence with a participle at the
beginning of the second.[1] When in the middle of a speech
a quotation has been given in direct or indirect speech, the
conclusion of the quotation is marked by the phrase, 'so
he said', or the like. This phrase makes a transition of the
same kind as the μέν . . . 2έ transition of which we have
spoken. To take one of many examples, the nurse in the
Trachiniae, having quoted Deianira's words, continues,
'Having said this much she loosed her dress. . . .'[2] Apparently Aeschylus does not use this transition until the time
of the *Oresteia*, but it is very common in Homer.

Other methods of joining sentence to sentence and
paragraph to paragraph, such as enumeration, key words,

[1] For the μέν . . . 2έ transition, cf. *Aj.* 295, 823, 1021. For the main
verb picked up by participle, *O.T.* 1404; cf. Norden, *Agnostos Theos*, p. 367.
[2] *Trach.* 923, cf. Schmid-Stählin, op. cit., p. 493, n. 7.

and invocations, are not merely bridges, but have an emotional significance. We shall give one striking example of
each. The middle section of Electra's first iambic speech
is divided by enumeration; she begins with 'first', goes on
with 'then' and 'thereafter'; then the enumeration is
carried on by the repetition of verbs of seeing, 'I see . . .
and I see there . . . and I see . . . seeing'.[1] Here first the
enumeration and then the repetition is indignant and
emphatic. Numbers in themselves seem to have had some
kind of emotional significance for Sophocles. This at least
seems to be the only reasonable explanation of his numeral
antitheses such as 'when we two were robbed of two
brothers killed on a single day by a double hand'.

Oedipus' first speech to the chorus is divided by key
words, 'I proclaim . . . I forbid . . . I curse . . . I add the
prayer . . . I command . . . I pray'. These verbs in the
first person divide the speech into sections, but also give
the sections an added solemnity and emphasis.[2] Emotional
speeches are divided by invocations and, as Schadewaldt
has pointed out, each new invocation marks a new stage
in the speaker's emotion. The repeated invocations in
Philoctetes' appeal to Neoptolemus will serve as an
example;[3] 'O fire and foul monster . . . O harbours and
headlands . . . O two-gated shape of rock'. These three
methods of division, enumeration, key words, and invocations, all give a pattern to the speech and at the same time
heighten its emotional effect.

Inside the sentence or paragraph Sophocles uses pat-

[1] *El.* 261, 262, 266, 267, 268, 271, 282. Further examples of enumera-
tions; *Ant.* 165, *El.* 967. Numeral antithesis: *Ant.* 13, 170, *Trach.* 943,
O.T. 1280. See also Thackeray, 'Sophocles and the perfect number', *Pro-
ceedings of the British Academy*, xvi.

[2] *O.T.* 223, 236, 246, 249, 252, 269. Reinhardt (op. cit., p. 153) regards
this as archaic, quoting *Trach.* 534.

[3] *Phil.* 927, 936, 952; cf. Schadewaldt, *Monolog und Selbstgespräch*,
pp. 71 ff.

terns of a different kind. He has more repetitions than Aeschylus. When Odysseus says to Philoctetes, 'It is Zeus, that you may know, Zeus, the lord of this land, Zeus who has resolved on this', the triple Zeus is emphatic, but repetition can also be used to express scorn, anger, agony, or hope.[1] The figure called *anaphora*, which is also more common in Sophocles than in Aeschylus, is a variety of repetition, in which the same word begins successive clauses. Sometimes the word is repeated more than once as in Oedipus' appeal to Tiresias, 'Save yourself and the city, save me, save all that is polluted by the dead'.[2] In this figure the idea which is common to all the clauses is stressed as much as the ideas which are peculiar to each of them. Oedipus could have said 'Save yourself and etc.', but then the emphasis on the things saved would have been greater than the emphasis on the saving. The repetition of 'save' gives the whole appeal an additional emotional emphasis. This emphasis is achieved even where the repeated word itself is comparatively colourless, as in Electra's appeal to Chrysothemis, '*It is yours* (πάρεστι) to mourn, robbed of the possession of your father's wealth; *it is yours* to grieve, growing so old, unwedded and un-husbanded'.

In a more advanced form of *anaphora*, instead of simple repetition another word of like meaning but different form is used. In Antigone's last speech she says that she hopes that her coming will be *dear* to her father, *very dear* to her mother, and *dear* to her brother. The most advanced stage of this form of *anaphora* is in Electra's lament where she says, 'Like a whirlwind you are *gone*. Our father is *departed*. I am *dead* to you. You yourself are *lost* in

---

[1] *Phil.* 989, cf. *Trach.* 408; *Ant.* 441; *El.* 1445; *O.C.* 892–3; *El.* 459, cf. Schmid-Stählin, pp. 296, 489.

[2] *O.T.* 312–13, cf. Schmid-Stählin, p. 490, n. 2. Add *El.* 959, *Phil.* 482, 663.

death'.[1] All four verbs are different but their meaning, 'gone', is the same, and the figure can still be called *anaphora*.

Sophocles also repeats the same word in the same sentence but in a different case or form. The chorus of the *Ajax* say of their search, 'Toil adds toil to toil'; this shows how foreign simple repetition is to the Greek; an Englishman would inevitably say, 'Toil, toil, toil'. The correctness of Orestes' earlier driving is emphasized by the repetition of the idea 'upright' in the line, 'Upright he drove, upright in upright car'.[2] The form of *oxymoron* where the two juxtaposed words have the same root, although they are of opposite meaning, comes very near to this repetition.[3] *Oxymoron* is a form of antithesis, and Sophocles can use antithesis to express the heights of emotion, as two examples from Tecmessa's lament and Electra's lament will show. Tecmessa says, 'His death is bitter to me, as sweet to them, but joyful to him', and Electra ends her first lament, 'Thanks if he slays, grief if I live, for life no desire'.[4]

Oxymoron and antithesis gain their emotional force from their compression. Asyndeton has the same effect. The messenger speech in the *Tyrannus* ends with a string of four nouns in asyndeton, 'lamentation, ruin, death, shame'. At the other end of the scale is the fullness of expression which is so effective at the end of the priest's speech to Oedipus, 'For ship and wall are nothing, if empty with no men dwelling in them'.[5]

[1] *Ant.* 898; *El.* 1151. A middle stage is represented by *Aj.* 457. Cf. Bruhn, *Anhang*, § 218.

[2] *Aj.* 866; *El.* 742. Cf. *O.T.* 1250, *O.C.* 982–3. Cf. Bruhn, *Anhang*, § 223.

[3] e.g. *Phil.* 297 ἔφην' ἄφαντον φῶς.

[4] *Aj.* 966, *El.* 821, cf. *El.* 1128.

[5] *Asyndeton*: *O.T.* 1284, cf. *El.* 1151, *Aj.* 843, *Aj.* 314. *Fullness of expression*: *O.T.* 60.

So far we have only spoken of the word-pattern. We have said nothing of the sound-pattern, although repetition and *anaphora* contribute to the alliteration and assonance of the sentence. Sophocles uses alliteration more than Aeschylus, and uses it for particular effects. The *p*'s and *t*'s of Oedipus' rebuke to Tiresias emphasize his exasperation; the *l*'s of Clytemnestra's prayer are essentially soft and cringing; the sibilants of Creon's first speech in the *Antigone* echo the beating of the storm through which the city has passed.[1] Sophocles also uses associations of long vowels to achieve particular effects. In Teucer's lament the repeated long *o*'s, *a*'s, and *e*'s express the grief of the speaker. Sometimes he uses alliteration and assonance together. In the prologue of the *Ajax d, s,* and *th* with long vowels express Ajax' fiendish joy over his captives.[2]

These are all means which Sophocles uses, conscious means, and so far his language might be called artificial. But this is not the artificiality of which he himself speaks, because it occurs in all the plays and in some of its forms more pronouncedly in the later plays. The artificiality of which he himself speaks is rather a matter of vocabulary, movement of thought, type of argument, and versification. The earlier style is smoother and more colourful than the later, the later more passionate and realistic than the earlier. The change of style corresponds to a change of outlook in the author. The two stages can be called Aeschylean and Euripidean, if these two words do not express too great indebtedness. Although the freedom of

---

[1] *O.T.* 380, *El.* 655, *Ant.* 162–3, cf. *O.T.* 371, *Phil.* 927, fr. 63, 683. See Bruhn, *Anhang*, § 241. Riedel, *Alliteration*, notes that Sophocles uses alliteration more in dialogue and less in lyrics than Aeschylus, i.e. more for emotional effect and less for sound.

[2] *Assonance: Aj.* 992, cf. *Ant.* 891–4, *Phil.* 315. *Alliteration and assonance: Aj.* 105–6, *El.* 17–19, *Phil.* 760.

versification, emotion, and realism in the ethic style is far advanced beyond the earlier plays and still further beyond Aeschylus, Sophocles would never have written the loose iambics of late Euripides. His sense of the rhythm of an iambic line is always too strong. The same sense of rhythm and pattern causes him to express his high points of emotion by the figures of which we have been speaking rather than by the elaborate images of Aeschylus or the realistic detail of Euripides. All his figures, antithesis and repetition, just as much as alliteration and assonance, give the sentence or speech a certain shape with a rhythm or pattern running through it. The expression of emotion by rhythm and pattern can be misunderstood as cold, formal, and conceited. It would be more truly regarded as the sublimation of emotion in rhythm. In any case it is the essence of Sophocles' art.

VIII. Conclusion

SOPHOCLES, if not born an aristocrat, was in any case a member of Cimon's circle. Aristocratic Athenians shared the Dorian ideal of *arete* which Pindar sets before his athletic victors. They were also open to the artistic and intellectual influences of the islands and Ionia; Polygnotus and Ion were friends of Cimon, and Herodotus was the friend of Sophocles. But these intellectual and artistic forces were not in them, as in some Athenians, revolutionary or demoralizing; they were kept in check by the twin virtues of *sophrosyne* and *apragmosyne*. *Sophrosyne* is the lesson which the sculptural decoration of the Parthenon is designed to instil. Phidias and the craftsmen in his employ had every artistic device in their power, but used them not to play upon the lower emotions of the people like the artists in Plato's *Republic*, but to convey the same message as Sophocles' Athena in the *Ajax*. Many, when they saw the Parthenos with Gigantomachy and Amazonomachy on her shield and Centauromachy on her sandals, must have remembered the lines of the prologue.[1] 'Seeing these things, never yourself speak a boastful word to the gods, nor be puffed with pride, if your hand is heavier than another's or your coffers deeper. For in a single day all human things may set and rise again. The gods love the modest and hate the wicked.' The same spirit lies behind Aristophanes' attacks on Euripides and the sophists, and later it becomes magnificently articulate in Plato.

Aristocratic environment has two chief effects on Sophocles. First, he is ready to understand and use the intellectual ideas of his day. We have seen how greatly he is

[1] *Aj.* 127 f.

indebted to contemporary thinkers. His religion and his
political and moral ideas show their influence, and the
literary sophists provided the atmosphere in which he
could elaborate and expound his careful craft.

The second effect is even more important. He believes
in *physis* and all that the word implies for an aristocrat.
The belief in *physis* is part of the ideal which Pindar puts
before his athletes, and becomes the keystone of Plato's
thought. It is a belief in personality, which is often inherited from ancestors and which carries with it high
standards of conduct. Perhaps the clearest expression of
the ideal of *physis* is found in the words of Neoptolemus,[1]
'I was born to use no evil art, neither I, nor, as they say, he
who begat me'. Sophocles himself said that he drew the
sort of characters that ought to be drawn, and he designed
his plots to illuminate the personality of his chief characters. If we think of his plays as plays and not as poetry, we
remember them primarily as a collection of personalities.
Ajax, Antigone, Deianira, Oedipus, Electra, and Philoctetes, however different in detail, are alike in being great
personalities with high ideals. And we do not only remember the chief characters: Tecmessa, Iocasta, Clytemnestra,
and Neoptolemus are also unforgettable.

Character drawing is one side of Sophoclean tragedy.
Religion is another. We know that Sophocles was regarded
as 'one of the most religious men' in Athens and that
adherence to the traditional religion was characteristic of
the circle in which he moved. Again we think of Plato
and Aristophanes. Socrates died saying that he owed a
cock to Asclepius. The mockery of Dionysus in the *Frogs*
does not obscure the truly religious feeling of the chorus
of initiates. The same contrast that we find between the
comic and serious passages of Aristophanes can be found
between the satyr plays and tragedies of Sophocles.

[1] *Phil.* 88 f.

The satyr plays reproduce the light-hearted gods of the Homeric hymns. The religion of the tragedies has little to do with the dark mysticism of Aeschylus or the intellectual criticism of Euripides; it is the traditional religion refined and purified. The myths are holy stories which must be treated with respect. If any part is objectionable, it need not be criticized, but can be suppressed or tacitly emended. But the story, as finally presented, must be acceptable to the believer, and even the greatest personality transgresses the laws of the gods at his peril.

Thirdly, Sophocles is an artist. For sheer dramatic effect the Tiresias scene of the *Tyrannus* and the recognition scene of the *Electra* fear no rivals. We have considered his character drawing and plot construction, his sense of spectacular effect, and his ability to play on the emotions of his audience. We have not been able to speak of his literary reminiscences, although in a few instances we can say that Sophocles means his audience to recall a passage in another author and skilfully uses their memories for his own artistic ends. When Anchises sees Aeneas in the underworld, he says 'quas ego te terras et quanta per aequora vectum accipio!'. The reader is meant to recall Catullus' address to his brother, and the scene wins an added pathos from the recollection. Similarly Sophocles' audience is meant to remember the scene between Andromache and Hector in the *Iliad*, when they hear Tecmessa's appeal, and therefore, when Ajax speaks to his son, to contrast Ajax' arrogance with Hector's humility.[1]

[1] Cf. the Iole scene in the *Trachiniae* contrasted with the Cassandra scene of the *Agamemnon*, the prologue and *parodos* of the *Tyrannus* with the prologue and *parodos* of the *Septem*. Reinhardt, op. cit., p. 207, has noticed that the form of the *Coloneus* can be traced back through Euripides' *Supplices* and *Heraclidae* to Aeschylus' *Supplices*. In all the three earlier plays suppliants are attacked by a herald. But Sophocles gives this part

The strongest evidence for his craftsmanship is his feeling for form. His plots have a definite shape and individual scenes correspond and contrast. The minor figures are created as foils to show up different sides of the hero so that the characters form a related pattern. Their speeches are a web of recurrent ideas. The emotional effect of the songs is heightened by the correspondence of sense and rhythm. This craftsmanship is extended to his language. His thought is cast in definite forms so that the result is not only beautiful as sound, but has the added beauty of restraint and pattern. His high points of emotion gain by their strict form. To quote one instance, the chorus of the *Coloneus* end their song of the evils of old age:

> Some from the setting of the sun,
> Some from his rising-place,
> Some from the noonday south,
> And some from Rhipae, mountains of the night.[1]

These qualities appear in all the plays; they form the *physis* of Sophocles. But, as Democritus says,[2] 'Learning gives a man a new rhythm, and by giving a new rhythm makes *physis*'. Although our material is scanty, it is possible to trace Sophocles' development. In his earliest period he was under the influence of Aeschylus, and if we discovered the earliest plays, they would undoubtedly be more Aeschylean than anything that we possess. Our knowledge depends on fragments, and on the *Ajax*, which comes at the very end of this phase. In Sophocles' earliest play Triptolemus probably appeared in the winged car which was to carry him over the earth, and his journey was described like the wanderings of Io in the *Prometheus*. In the *Polyxena* Achilles' ghost rose above his tomb like the

to Creon, the king of Thebes, and by so doing changes the scene into a clash of three characters, Oedipus, Creon, and Theseus.

[1] *O.C.* 1245 f., tr. Robert Willis.
[2] Fr. 33.

ghost of Darius. Headlam translates the opening of the
ghost's speech:[1]

> From those unanthem'd and abysmal shores
> I come, the birthless floods of Acheron,
> Still echoing to the sound of rending groans.

Words and spectacle might cause an Aeschylean *ekplexis*.
In the *Niobe* one of Niobe's daughters died on the stage.
The structure of the opening scenes of the *Ajax* has close
analogies with the *Agamemnon*, as we have seen. Its language and spectacular effects show his influence, and
Sophocles has not yet cut loose from the Aeschylean
tradition of short scenes. But the character drawing, the
contrast of characters, the diminution of the choric parts,
and most of the language are Sophoclean. The artificiality
of language of which Sophocles himself speaks can be
traced back beyond the *Ajax* to plays which for one reason
or another seem to belong to his earliest period.[2] The
other elements cannot usually be traced beyond the surviving plays, but probably, if we possessed the *Triptolemus*
itself, it would be clearly distinguished from Aeschylus by
the emphasis on the character of the hero.

The middle period is represented for us by the *Antigone*,
Trachiniae, and *Tyrannus*. Other plays can be associated
with these three, notably the *Tereus* and *Odysseus Acanthoplex* which must both have been very like the *Trachiniae*.
In these plays the Aeschylean colouring has faded much.
It can still be seen in some of the language and in reminiscences such as the Iole scene of the *Trachiniae*. The
dramatic technique is purely Sophoclean. These are the
most classical of the tragedies, if 'classical' implies clear
definition of parts with a careful contrast and balance
between them and rigid economy of emotional effects
such as music and spectacle. It is not purely fanciful to

---

[1] Fr. 523.   [2] See Appendix.

compare the spirit and the technique of these plays with contemporary white *lekythoi* and the Parthenon frieze. This group of plays greatly influenced Euripides, and their mark can be seen on the *Alcestis*, *Medea*, and *Hippolytus*.

The *Tyrannus* is the end and summit of this period. Here Sophocles has abandoned the diptych form which he inherited from Aeschylus, and makes free use of certain types of scene with which he had experimented in the *Trachiniae*, yet he does not sacrifice any of the formal beauty of lyric and language and arrangement which characterizes this group. Sometimes we can see the gradual development of Sophocles' art. The second act of the *Trachiniae*, where Lichas makes his report and fills Deianira with dismay and the messenger with indignation, is an experiment which bears fruit in the scene between the Corinthian messenger, Oedipus, and Iocasta. The last scene of the *Trachiniae*, where the word 'Nessus' makes Heracles forget his vengeance on Deianira and prepare for his own death, has the first of those naturalistic twists which occur in all Sophocles' later plays. We can trace his use of the sudden exit from Eurydice through Deianira to the most dramatic exit of Iocasta. At the beginning of the scene with the Corinthian messenger Iocasta comes out and prays to Apollo for relief. Her prayer appears to be answered immediately by the arrival of the Corinthian messenger, but the relief turns out to be fresh trouble. Sophocles has used this motive again in the *Electra*, but there he has developed the actual prayer so that Clytemnestra's appeal to Apollo is one of the most moving and terrible passages in the play. The germ of the scene in the *Tyrannus* is to be found in the *Antigone*. Eurydice was coming out to pray to Pallas when the messenger arrived. Eurydice's speech ends, 'I shall hear as one not unused to ill'. This sentiment occurs in Atossa's speech to the messenger in the *Persae*.[1] After the Salamis speeches Atossa prays to the gods for relief. We can see how Sophocles took this idea, reversed the order of events, and gradually developed his scene until he achieved its most dramatic form in the *Electra*.

The *Tyrannus* has already some of the marks of the last period, which is represented for us by the *Electra*, *Philoctetes*, and *Coloneus*. The full use of dramatic irony and the long scenes in which the hero passes through a long series of emotions recur in the latest group. But it would be incorrect to regard this last group simply as a development from the *Tyrannus*. In spite of many links which bind the two groups together, there is an essential difference between them. The new quality of these latest plays can be called realism, but it is something different from the realism of Euripides and probably owes little to him. The kind of realism which Aristophanes ridiculed in the *Acharnians* is not found in Sophocles; the pathological study of the mad Orestes and the portrayal of the old slave in the *Ion* are quite alien to his art. Nor do Electra and Neoptolemus owe much to Hippolytus and Medea. All that Sophocles meant by calling himself an idealist and Euripides a realist separates these two pairs. Hippolytus is a realist's portrait of Neoptolemus. Sophocles could never have made the Euripidean Medea a heroine.

Again, comparison with art illustrates the distinction between Sophocles' middle and late plays. The white *lekythoi* of the late fifth century, compared with those of the forties and thirties, show the same increase in emotion, the same subjection of story to character, the same blurring of the clear lines and contrasts, and the same realism of representation as the *Electra*, compared with the *Antigone*. In the *Tyrannus* the story is still important and exciting for itself; in the later plays the story only provides

[1] *Pers.* 290, 517 f.

a series of emotions through which the chief character passes. The recognition scene of the *Electra* has perhaps the subtlest emotional sequence in Sophocles. Orestes enters confidently to carry out his plan of gaining admission to the house. He is almost impatient with the cropped, tattered woman, who cries out when she sees the urn. Then he realizes that she must be a friend, if not a relative, and tells his servants to give her the urn. Electra's strength and determination is broken and she despairingly laments Orestes' death. 'Therefore receive me into this thy house, nothing to nothing, that I may dwell with thee below henceforward.' Orestes learns from the lament that she is his sister and from the chorus that she is Electra. The horror of this discovery shatters his resolution to enter the house without disclosing himself. His sympathy rouses Electra from her despair, and she asks if he is her kinsman. He takes the urn from her in spite of her protests and discloses his identity. For the moment both give way to an outburst of joy. Electra breaks into excited lyrics, but Orestes has mastered himself and speaks in calm iambics urging her to keep silence. To this emotional realism other kinds of realism are added—realism in style, realistic action, and realism of time and place.

The *Coloneus* has less dramatic irony than the other late plays but makes a fitting close to Sophocles' career. His belief in nobility finds expression in the characters of Oedipus and Theseus, his love for Athens in the Colonus ode, and his religion in the whole theme of the play. The plot is built on the lines of Oedipus' oracle; 'Here I should end my unhappy life, my residence a gain to my welcomers and ruin to my senders who drove me out. He warned me that signs of this would come, either earthquake or thunder or lightning of Zeus.'[1] The characters are grouped round Oedipus, three friends, and two foes. For beauty of lan-

---

[1] *O.C.* 91.

guage the Colonus ode and the messenger speech are un-
surpassed. Athenian, aristocrat, believer, dramatist, and
poet have united to produce a final perfect work.

Sophocles did not use his careful craftsmanship and
exquisite language to frighten his audience into accepting
a high mysticism, nor did he wish to reflect in his plays the
latest philosophical theories and the latest music and
rhetoric. He preserved the traditional religion, only
emending or suppressing where necessary to be consistent
with contemporary morality. His primary concern was to
show his Athenian public great personalities in surround-
ings where their greatness and their weakness could be
displayed. The nobility of Athens was not lacking in such
personalities, and Sophocles was 'like one of the Athenian
nobles'.

Appendix on the Chronology of the Fragments

SOME of the external evidence for the chronology of the fragments has already been given in the chapter on Sophocles' life. Several of the lost plays are quoted by Aristophanes (references can be found most easily in Pearson, *Fragments*, vol. i, p. xlvii); for these plays we have a *terminus post quem*, although we cannot assume that the date of production was near the *terminus* (thirteen years separate the *Acharnians* from the *Telephus*). Sophocles' surviving plays have few mythological references, and where they occur they may be references to his own earlier plays. Further, the main subject of an earlier play may become part of the background of a later play.

Otherwise we are dependent on internal evidence and must apply the criteria which we have learnt in our examination of the surviving plays. Tragedies of action are earlier than tragedies of suffering. The diptych form is earlier than the single action. Spectacle of the Aeschylean kind is early—spectacular choruses (the *Agamemnon* alone of Aeschylean plays has a chorus of ordinary citizens), stage machinery, long laments, spectacular descriptions. Anapaestic preludes to the *parodos* and anapaestic introductions are early. Style also helps, but must be used carefully, since many of the fragments are only quoted for their strange words.

In the following list I have confined myself to plays about which I feel some degree of certainty and which seem to me interesting. I have kept the order of the plays in Pearson's edition to facilitate reference.

AJAX OF LOCRI. The climax seems to have been the scene where Ajax swore that he had not raped Cassandra. This scene was painted by Polygnotus. In the *Tyrannus* Creon swears that he has not wronged Oedipus; the chief motive of the *Ajax of Locri* has become part of the background of the *Tyrannus*. Zielinsky (*Eos*, 1925, p. 38) convincingly identifies this play with the *Captive Women*. Perhaps the argument to the *Ajax* has preserved the names of the tetralogy; *Captive Women* (= *Ajax of Locri*), *Ante-*

noridae, *Memnon* (= *Ethiopians*), *Rape of Helen* (= *Helen's Marriage*). The *Memnon* had an Ethiopian chorus. Αίγλος, βωμιαῖος (*Captive Women*), ἐκβαβράζειν (*Antenoridae*) are early words. Probably the whole tetralogy belongs to the Aeschylean period.

ACRISIUS. Danae is the first of the parallels which the chorus adduce in the consolation song of the *Antigone* (944), and Sophocles may be referring to his own *Danae* with which the *Acrisius* should be identified. As we shall find other evidence that the *Andromeda* and *Larisaeans* were early plays, he probably wrote a Perseus trilogy in which the first play dealt with the birth of Perseus (*Danae-Acrisius*), the second with the release of Andromeda, and the third with the death of Acrisius. (Cf. Zielinsky, *Tragodoumenon*, p. 289: Schmid-Stählin, p. 435.) The chorus of the *Andromeda* was composed of Orientals, and the play was probably spectacular. The *Larisaeans* had descriptions of the games in which Perseus took part. Δαιμονίζειν (*Danae*), μάσθλης, σάρητον (*Andromeda*) are early words.

ALEADAE. We have discussed (p. 3) the evidence for a *Telepheia* containing the *Aleadae*, *Mysians*, and *Assembly of Achaeans*, written probably before 430 B.C. In the *Aleadae* the birth of Telephus was questioned, and the fragments show that a discussion of his legitimacy was an important part of the play. In the *Mysians* Telephus was to marry his mother Auge; on the wedding night she prepared to kill him; then the recognition took place. Illegitimacy and incest are part of the background of the *Tyrannus*. We may therefore conclude that these plays are earlier than the *Tyrannus*. The *Mysians* had a chorus of Orientals. The *Assembly of Achaeans* had the diptych form. The first part dealt with the recognition of Telephus and the second with his healing by Achilles. The papyrus fragment (fr. 142) preserves the join between the two. Achilles arrives and is met by Odysseus; the second part of the action will then start; he is to be persuaded by Odysseus to heal Telephus, who will guide the Greeks to Troy. Neither Achilles' arrival nor Odysseus' is announced by the chorus. Odysseus must have waited on the stage while they sang, just as Deianira waits for Lichas. It is therefore further probable that Achilles' coming had been already announced by a herald, and that, as in the *Ajax*, the scene with the herald linked the second part to the first. The choral fragment is predominantly glyconic, with insertions of other rhythms to make it excited. It is not unlike the cheerful choruses of the *Ajax* and *Antigone*. Κωπήρης, νωχελής, μέλλημα, ἐκκωπεύειν and πεμπτήρ are early words. All the evidence suggests that the *Telepheia* belongs near the *Antigone*.

EPIGONI. The chorus of the *Electra* (837) try to comfort Electra by the example of Amphiaraus 'who now rules under the earth . . . the murderess was tamed . . . there appeared one who paid heed to his lamentation'. This is the story of Amphiaraus, Eriphyle, and Alcmaeon. Sophocles' *Amphiaraus* was a satyr play and cannot have had this story. But the *Epigoni*, with which the *Eriphyle* should be identified, dealt with the murder of Eriphyle and some one, probably Alcmaeon himself, appealed to Amphiaraus, 'Do you hear this, Amphiaraus, hidden under the ground?' (fr. 186). This play was, on this evidence, earlier than the *Electra*. The first part contained the murder of Eriphyle and the second the madness of Alcmaeon. Alcmaeon, like Heracles in the *Trachiniae*, was carried on asleep after a bout of madness. Thus the play had the diptych form, and one scene very like a scene in the *Trachiniae*.

EURYPYLUS. This play with its Eastern setting and long lamentations cannot have been unlike the *Persae*. The papyrus fragment contains parts of two messenger speeches with a short section of *kommos* between them. It is probably a strophe which was followed by an antistrophe after the second speech. In this *kommos* Astyoche sings iambics or broken iambics and the chorus sing dochmiacs, iambics, and broken iambics. The nearest parallels for the metre are in the third *kommos* of the *Ajax* (891, cf. also *Trach.* 876), where strophe is followed by ten iambic lines and antistrophe by thirteen. The scene in the *Eurypylus* must have had the same general form. Φύρδαν, ἀσχημόνως, πλησιαίτατος, ἀλοιδόρητος, λάξοα are characteristic of Sophocles' early style and the play undoubtedly belongs to his Aeschylean period.

THAMYRAS. The external evidence for an early date and the language have already been discussed (ch. i, p. 3, ch. vii, p. 144). It was a play of action, and Thamyras was guilty of *hybris*. The chorus was composed of Thracians. Thamyras sang a monody in hexameters (fr. 242, cf. Wilamowitz, *Gr. Verskunst*, pp. 347 ff.). The *parodos* had a prologue in anapaests (fr. 237–8). One of the fragments is in a wild trochaic rhythm without parallel in Sophocles (fr. 240).

COLCHIAN WOMEN. This play, the *Scythians*, and the *Rhizotomi* are all early and probably formed a Medea trilogy. *Colchian Women* and *Scythians* must both have had a Scythian chorus. In the *Colchian Women* Medea described the trials of Jason beforehand (fr. 336) and the messenger described his success afterwards (fr. 341). The *parodos* of the *Rhizotomi* had an anapaestic prelude in which the chorus prayed to the sun and described Medea picking herbs (fr. 534–5). ἀνθυπουργεῖν, νεοσφάλαστος (*Colchian Women*) are words of the early style.

NAUSICAA. The external evidence for early dating has already been given (ch. i, p. 3). The plot must have followed the sixth book of the *Odyssey* closely. Nausicaa's game of ball with her maidens was spectacle of a pleasing kind. Athena probably appeared in the prologue as in the *Ajax*.

NIOBE. Quotation in Aristophanes dates this play before 422 in any case, but it is certainly much earlier. The *Antigone* (825) has a reference to Niobe, 'whom a rocky growth tamed . . . very like to her the god puts me to sleep'. In the *Electra* (150) Sophocles speaks of Niobe 'ever weeping in her rocky tomb'. In both he is probably recalling his own *Niobe*, which in that case will be earlier than the *Antigone*. The *Niobe* was a play of action and Niobe was guilty of *hybris*. The papyrus fragments show that one at least of the children of Niobe was shot down on the stage, a spectacle of the same kind as the suicide of Ajax. The question of the identification of the *Niobe* and the *Tantalus* must be left undecided (see, besides Pearson, Pickard-Cambridge, *New Chapters* 3, p. 85, *Greek Poetry and Life*, p. 119; Reinhardt, *Hermes*, 1934, p. 233 f.).

ODYSSEUS ACANTHOPLEX. This play should be identified with the *Niptra* (see Pearson; contrast Séchan, *Ét. sur la trag. gr.*, p. 173).

It had the diptych form. In the first part Odysseus returned from his wanderings and was recognized by Eurycleia, in the second he was wounded by Telegonus. He was carried on to the stage in agony and then recognized that his fate was in accordance with the oracle. This is so like the ending of the *Trachiniae* that it seems safe to argue for proximity in date (cf. Pohlenz, *Gr. Trag.*, p. 213).

OENOMAUS. The *Oenomaus* is quoted in the *Birds* and therefore must have been written before 414. The allusion to Herodotus (fr. 473) gives an upper limit of about 443. The choral fragment (476) has the same kind of metre as the *parodos* of the *Trachiniae*. The elaborate images of plumb-line and hen belong to the early style; ĭ and θηρατηρίος agree with this. The evidence suggests a date in the late forties or early thirties.

PELEUS. Aristophanes quoted this play, Aristotle's example of the 'ethic' tragedy, in 424. The line, 'Do not deceive me, Zeus, do not conquer me without a spear' (493), is most easily interpreted, if, as in the *Trachiniae*, a misunderstood oracle was one of the leading motives. The fragment in anapaests (492) must belong to the introduction of a new character. The choral fragments (489–91) suggest in metre and language the astrophic song of the *Trachiniae*. This play also probably belongs to the early thirties.

POLYXENA. The appearance of Achilles' ghost is said to have been one of Sophocles' most striking stage effects. Χιτὼν ἄπειρος is an Aeschylean phrase, and the play was probably early.

SCYRIANS. New knowledge is provided by the papyrus fragment (Pfeiffer, *Philol.*, 1933, p. 1). In the *Philoctetes* Neoptolemus says that Odysseus and Phoenix came to fetch him from Scyros after the death of Achilles; we now know for certain that this was the plot of the *Scyrians*, which must then have been produced either before or in the same year as the *Philoctetes*. A line of a connected speech in the papyrus begins εἶεν· τί 2[ῆτα?]; this transition is characteristic of the late style, and the Scyrians must have been a late play.

TEREUS. We have discussed (p. 4) the external evidence for dating the *Tereus* shortly before 431. It is quoted by Aristophanes in 414.

Tereus committed a sin of *hybris*, and Procne, the nightingale, is called in the *parodos* of the *Electra*, 'the messenger of Zeus'. The phrase is usually explained as 'harbinger of Zeus', but is surely a reference to the vengeance taken by Procne on Tereus who had sinned against Zeus by his treatment of Philomela. The *Tereus* had the diptych form. The first part dealt with the loneliness of Procne (frs. 583, 584; cf. *Trach.* 144 f., Eur. *Med.* 230 f.) and the return of Tereus from Athens. Tereus reported Philomela dead (585). A messenger brought the truth and supported it by the robe (588, 586, 595). Perhaps he met Tereus and Tereus tried to escape by a counter charge (587). The second part dealt with the vengeance taken by Procne and the transformations (589, 581).

TRIPTOLEMUS. Date and language have (pp. 2, 144) been considered. Further Aeschylean elements are Triptolemus' winged car and the spectacular descriptions (p. 166).

TYMPANISTAE, FIRST and SECOND PHINEUS. The last two verses of the Consolation in the *Antigone* (966) relate that the sons of Cleopatra and Phineus were blinded by Phineus' second wife. The scholiast refers to the *Tympanistae* of Sophocles; this must have been an earlier play in which Eidothea (or Idaea?) arrived with her priests of Cybele, married Phineus, and blinded his sons. The priests of Cybele formed a spectacular chorus. The *First Phineus* dealt with a later stage in the story, when Phineus was blinded and the sons recovered their sight. In the *Second Phineus* Phineus was delivered from the persecution of the Harpies. We have no indication of the date of the two Phineus plays except the Herodotean reference (fr. 712) in the *Second Phineus*. A trilogy is possible, but it seems more likely that the *Second Phineus* belongs to the class and period of the *Coloneus* and represents the sufferings and deliverance of an old man who has committed a crime in his earlier years (contrast, however, Herkenrath, *B.Ph.W.* 1930, p. 331).

SECOND TYRO. This play is quoted in the *Birds*. It was like the *Electra*. Tyro was persecuted by Sidero as Electra was persecuted by Clytemnestra. Like Electra, she had a chorus of women to comfort her (fr. 649. 26). Like Clytemnestra, Sidero had an ominous dream (frs. 649, 9, 37; 660, 661). As in the *Electra*, the recognition took place towards the end of the play (Schol. to Eur. *Or.* 1691); the twins were recognized by their *skaphe* and delivered their mother from persecution (fr. 657). On this evidence the play cannot have been produced long before 414.

These plays can tentatively be grouped round the surviving plays.

1. Before *Ajax* and *Antigone*:
    Triptolemus, *Thamyras*, *Nausicaa*, *Ajax of Locri*, *Niobe*, *Polyxena*, *Eurypylus*, *Medea* trilogy, *Tympanistae*, *Danae* trilogy.

2. Near *Antigone*:
    Telepheia, *Oenomaus*, *Peleus*.

3. Near *Trachiniae*:
    Tereus, *Odysseus Acanthoplex*, *Eriphyle*.

4. Not long before 414 and near *Electra*:
    Second Tyro.

5. Near *Electra*:
    Second Phineus, *Scyrians*.

Additional Notes

CHAPTER I

A. *De Mus.* 1142 b. Doubts have been raised as to the connexion of Lamprus with Sophocles. The chief argument against it is based on a passage in the *Menexenus* (236 a) where Socrates pairs Lamprus with Antiphon as good teachers; if Lamprus taught Sophocles, he must have been at least twenty years older than Antiphon and the pairing of the two is curious, though not impossible. Lamprus is also mentioned in a fragment of Phrynichus (*ap.* Ath. ii. 44 d), who draws him much as Aristophanes (*Ach.* 386, *Av.* 1372, fr. 149) draws the lyric poets Hieronymus and Cinesias: 'In which Lamprus often died away, a water drinker, shrill hypersophist, skeleton of the muses, ague of the nightingales, hymn of Hades'. We learn nothing about the chronology of Lamprus from this fragment, since the words do not show whether he is alive or dead, and in any case we do not know whether the fragment comes from the *Muses* of Phrynichus (produced in 405) or from some earlier play.

B. See for the number of plays Pearson, *Sophocles' Fragments*, i, pp. xiii ff. It is possible that he produced proportionately more plays as he grew older. In the first argument of the *Antigone* that play is said to be his thirty-second. This number seems to refer to some chronological arrangement of his plays in the Alexandrian library. At first sight it appears that Sophocles' rate of production must have increased greatly in his later years. But Pearson (p. xvi f.) gives reasons for thinking that about thirteen of the plays had already been lost in Alexandrian times, and if, as is probable, this loss was chiefly among the earlier plays, the discrepancy is not so great. If, for instance, the *Antigone* was really his forty-first play and the first of the trilogy, Sophocles wrote forty-four plays in his first twenty-five years and seventy-nine in the remaining thirty-eight years.

C. Recently discussed by Pickard-Cambridge, *New Chapters in Greek Lit.*, Third Series, p. 69; see also Fromhold-Treu, *Hermes*, 1934, p. 324; Mazon, *Mélanges Navarre*, p. 297. The inscription records that two men, Epichares and Thrasybulus, each won a choregic victory; Epichares won his victory with the *Pirae* (perhaps *Spirae*) of Ecphantides and the *Telepheia* of Sophocles. As a first production at Aexone is unlikely, and as we know that Ecphantides won no victory at the Lenaea, the inscription must refer to the Great Dionysia. As Ecphantides did not compete at the Lenaean contests, which were instituted about 442, he probably ceased to write about 442. The upper and lower dates

of Epichares' comic victory are fixed at 457 and 442. It is probable that
the two occasions on which Epichares acted as *choregos* were not very far
apart. We should expect the *Telepheia* to be nearer to the *Antigone* than
to the *Tyrannus*.

The natural interpretation of *Telepheia* is a trilogy about Telephus. It
is true that Aristophanes once appears to use the *-eia* form when referring
to a single play and not to a trilogy. Euripides asks Aeschylus in the *Frogs*
to read him the prologue from the *Oresteia*, and Aeschylus then quotes not
the *Agamemnon* but the *Choephori*. It is therefore assumed that *Oresteia*
means 'a play about Orestes'. But Aristophanes may equally well mean 'the
famous prologue from the trilogy', i.e. the prologue which the sophists discuss. And before the relevance of this passage to our inscription can be
admitted, it must be proved that 'a play about Telephus' would ever be
called *Telepheia* in a semi-official inscription.

Such a trilogy might well have been composed of the *Aleadae*, *Mysians*,
and *Assembly of Achaeans*. The satyr play is uncertain. It may have been
the *Telephus*, but the existence of this play depends on a doubtful Rhodian
inscription, and in any case it may not have been the satyr play of this
trilogy (see Pearson). The Aexone inscription gives us two points, first a
date before 430 for the *Aleadae*, *Mysians*, and *Assembly of Achaeans*, and
secondly the knowledge that Sophocles wrote connected trilogies.

D. The *Ajax* has two possible references to external events. In the anapaestic part of the *parodos* (156 f.; cf. 964) the chorus sing that it is impossible to teach fools the need for co-operation between great and small in
the state. Their jealousy will not leave the great man alone. Sophocles may
be referring to some great man who has suffered from the jealousy of
foolish small men. He may be thinking of the ostracism of Thucydides, son
of Melesias, in 443. Secondly, the scene with Menelaus has been thought to
show that the play was written at a time when relations between Athens
and Sparta were bad. The time before the thirty years peace has been
suggested, but on the same premises the play might have been written during the Archidamian war, when it would be parallel to Euripides' *Andromache*. In truth there is no evidence of hostility to Sparta; the relations
between Ajax and the Atridae were given by the story, and the poet has
made the Atridae mean and small, because in the second part of his play
he wanted to show the greatness of Ajax. See Reinhardt, *Sophokles*, p. 245.

E. Aristophanes, *Kts.* 591–4 with *parodos* of *O.T.*; 1240 with *O.T.* 738;
Ach. 27 with *O.T.* 629. Bates's attempt to connect *Ach.* 1174 f. with *O.T.*
1223 f. seems to me unsuccessful (*A.J.P.* 1933, p. 166).

The Callias story: Athenaeus, vii. 276 a; x. 453 c. See also Körte, *R. E.*,
Kallias. In the second and more detailed account Athenaeus says that Callias

wrote a little before Strattis. The detailed interpretation of this obscure story does not concern us here; it is enough to note that after the *parodos* of the alphabetic tragedy came a speech constructed of vowels, and that in the line and a half from the first act of the *Tyrannus* (332-3) which Athenaeus quotes seven out of ten words begin with vowels. The explanation of the story may be this: Callias, who, if he is the poet of the old comedy, won his first victory in 446, wrote his alphabetic tragedy soon after the production of the *Medea* and *Tyrannus* and caricatured the alliterations and assonances in those plays; later Strattis, who produced plays at any rate from 409 to 375, said in one of his comedies that Euripides and Sophocles plagiarized Callias. This would not seem plausible unless *Medea*, *Tyrannus*, and alphabetic tragedy were produced about the same time. If it is allowed that this story places the *Tyrannus* near the *Medea*, it is slight confirmatory evidence for dating the *Tyrannus* to 429.

F. His edition of the *Electra*, p. 30 f. T. von Wilamowitz (*Dramatische Technik*, p. 230 f.) never counters this argument. He has two reasons for believing the Sophoclean play to be the earlier. He first argues that Sophocles took the sequence of false messenger speech and recognition scene from Euripides' *Cresphontes*. Euripides left the false messenger speech, which he uses later in the *Helen* and *Iphigenia in Tauris*, out of his *Electra*, because Sophocles had already used it in a play on the same subject. It is in any case rash to argue from a lost play, but in fact the *Cresphontes* seems to have been more like the *Ion* than Sophocles' *Electra*. The messenger speech inspired Merope's attempt to murder Cresphontes and then the recognition was brought about by an old man. The connexion with Sophocles' play is not obvious. As for Euripides' own *Electra*, here he had sufficient reason for abandoning the false messenger speech in that he wanted to report Aegisthus' death at length in a true messenger speech. The necessity of shortening the earlier part of the play to make room for both the intrigue and the report of Aegisthus' death also has a bearing on T. von Wilamowitz's second argument. In Sophocles' *Electra* and in the *Iphigenia in Tauris*, *Ion*, and *Hypsipyle* the recognition is immediately followed by a short lyric dialogue; this lyric dialogue is absent from Euripides' *Electra*. The argument is the same; Euripides did not want to reproduce a form which Sophocles had already used for the same story. Again the need for shortening the recognition scene explains the absence of the lyric dialogue.

On the two *Electras* see, besides Jebb and Bruhn, Schmid-Stählin, p. 388 f. (with literature). On the date of Sophocles' *Electra* see now Owen, *Greek Poetry and Life*, p. 145.

G. It will be well to state the evidence for the rest of Sophocles' military service. The 'Life' says (1) that he was considered worthy to serve as general with Pericles and Thucydides, the first men of the city, and that he served on state business and embassies, (9) that when he was sixty-nine years of age the Athenians chose him as general in the war against the Anaeans seven years before the Peloponnesian war. Secondly, Plutarch (*Nicias*, 15) tells a story of Sophocles and Nicias serving together as generals; Nicias asked Sophocles to give his opinion first. 'I', replied Sophocles, 'am the older, but you are the senior.' Thirdly, Aristophanes in the *Peace* (695 f.), which was produced in 421, says that Sophocles has grown so old and sordid that he would put to sea on a sieve for money, and the scholiast explains that he got money from his generalship in Samos.

H. We can carry our interpretation a little further if we consider the parallel of Cratinus' *Pytine*, produced two years before the *Phratores*. There Cratinus represented the contest between his wife Comedy and his mistress Drunkenness. If we suppose that Theoris and Nicostrate have become transposed in our sources, we can imagine that Leucon constructed his play on the same lines as Cratinus. Then Theoris is the mother of Iophon. She is not only the Sicyonian *hetaira*, but also the 'Spectator' of Sophocles' tragedies; her name arose from a line in one of the tragedies, just as Euripides' greengrocer mother arose from a line in the *Melanippe* (Sophocles, fr.765; see also Maas, *Philol.*1921, pp. 18 ff. For Euripides see Murray, *Euripides and His Age*, p. 26 f.). Nicostrate, 'victorious in battle', is the mother of Ariston, 'champion', and represents Sophocles' military career; in the same year as Leucon's *Phratores* Aristophanes produced his *Peace* in which he said that Sophocles was willing to sail on a sieve for money. If this transposition is correct, Iophon accused Sophocles of deserting his true wife Theoris (Art) for Nicostrate (War), just as Cratinus deserted Comedy for Drunkenness.

CHAPTER II

I. Cf. Jebb's introductions and Schmid-Stählin, p. 98, for other instances. The following innovations are characteristic. In the *Ajax*, Ajax conceives the murder in sanity; it is an act of his free will. The chorus are free Salaminians, so that they may be able to speak freely to and of him. In the *Trachiniae* the most important innovation is the transference of Heracles' marriage with Deianira to an early period of his life; this transference makes the conception of Deianira as the faithful and now middle-aged wife possible. In the *Tyrannus* the setting of the murder of Laius in Daulia and the invention of the plague (cf. Nestle, *Griechische Religiosität*, ii. p. 96) emphasize the importance of Apollo. In the *Philoctetes*, where we have evidence in Dio Chrysostom (*Or.* lii) for the other two tragedians, two innovations are important. Sophocles isolates Philoctetes (as he isolates Electra), by making the chorus sailors of Neoptolemus instead of Lemnians, and he introduces Neoptolemus who is the only kind of character that could bring out the best side of Philoctetes. In the *Coloneus* Oedipus' curse is not the result of some trivial wrong in Thebes, but the final expression of Oedipus' indignation at the treatment which he has received from his sons. It is perhaps not insignificant that, while Aeschylus and Euripides dramatized the epic contest between Eteocles and Polynices, Sophocles chooses the moment before in the *Coloneus* and the moment after in the *Antigone*, because he is primarily interested in the characters of Oedipus and Antigone.

J. Aeschylus, *Eum.* 48 f.; Soph. *Aj.* 835, *El.* 112, 489; Heraclitus, fr. 94. In several other passages of Sophocles the personification is vaguer and Fury means little more than spirit of evil, e.g. *Ant.* 603, fr. 577. With the Furies it is convenient to consider three other personifications. These are Nemesis, the wrath of the gods, Aidos, the reverent spirit of the good man, and Justice. All can be traced back to Hesiod, and all are personified by other writers. It is, however, worth noticing that in Sophocles Justice is not the daughter of Zeus, as in Aeschylus and Hesiod, but she sits on the throne of Zeus, she is the ally of the gods, she dwells with the gods below, and she has a golden eye. These three personifications, like Time, are poetical symbols.

Nemesis: *El.* 792, *Phil.* 518, 602; Hesiod, *Op.* 200; Pindar, *O.* viii. 112, *P.* x. 69; Hdt. i. 34. See Schmid, *B. Ph. W.* 1933, p. 739.

Aidos: *O.C.* 1267; Hesiod, *Op.* 200; Schmid-Stählin, p. 461, suggests that Sophocles' immediate source is Protagoras.

Justice: *Ant.* 451, *O.T.* 274, *El.* 476, 528, *O.C.* 1381, fr. 12; Hesiod, *Op.* 256; Solon, iii. 15; Bacchylides, xiv. 53; Aesch. *Septem,* 662, &c.; Parmenides, fr. i. 14.

CHAPTER V

K. This evidence seems to me fatal to the theory of T. von Wilamowitz, who writes (*Dramatische Technik*, p. 39): 'For a dramatist who must have considered presentation on the stage as the only object of his plays, it is only natural that the dramatic effect of the single scene and of the single situation should be more important than the unity and coherence of the whole, that he therefore did not aim at a construction which should be organic and everywhere clear, but in fact, as Goethe said, sewed together single purple patches without being afraid of the thread sometimes remaining visible.' He goes on to say that Sophocles subordinates the words and actions of his characters to his immediate dramatic object. He rejects all psychological explanations and refers everything to the exigencies of the momentary scenic effect, whether he is interpreting the scepticism of Iocasta or the repentance of Neoptolemus. His explanation of the place of a given phrase or speech in the scene is often right, but the phrase may also be in keeping with the character and admit of a psychological as well as a dramatic explanation. Sophocles' use of dramatic irony proves that he can make one phrase serve two purposes at once. Detailed criticism of Wilamowitz' treatment of the *Philoctetes* and *Electra* will be found in Kamerbeek's *Studiën over Sophocles*.

L. In the *Trachiniae* Heracles comes in answer to the prayer of the chorus, and 'the persuasion of the centaur' has 'wasted him away' (662), but his body, not his mind, has been changed. The 'pessimistic' chorus of the *Coloneus* (1211) can be joined to the cheerful choruses; it is an inverse preparation for the passing of Oedipus just as the cheerful choruses are an inverse preparation for the catastrophe. The chorus sing of the miseries of old age when Oedipus is about to throw off his infirmities and lead the way to the place of his passing. On the cheerful choruses see De Falco, *Tecnica Corale*, p. 148. In his *Osservazioni* (p. 2) he notes the likeness between these choruses and the hymn to Argos in Aeschylus, *Suppl.* 625.

M. *Ant.* 365; *El.* 504; *Phil.* 719. The second *stasimon* of the *Antigone* (particularly l. 622), though in the mouth of the chorus a reflection on the fate of Antigone, contains for the audience a warning to Creon. The *parodos* of the *Trachiniae* ends with the words (139), 'For who saw Zeus so empty of counsel towards his children?' The chorus mean that Heracles will come safe home, the audience are meant to remember that the fulfilment of Zeus' counsel includes the poisoned robe and the burning pyre, as the chorus recognize in the end when they say, 'There is none of these things that is not Zeus.' In the *Tyrannus* both the first and the second *stasimon* contain references of this kind; in the first the chorus describe the life of the murderer in his attempt to frustrate the oracle, particularly 477 f.; this is, as the next scene shows and as the audience knows, an accurate description of the life of Oedipus; in the second *stasimon* the chorus pray for the punishment of impiety and the justification of oracles (863 f.), not realizing that this involves the suicide of Iocasta and the self-blinding of Oedipus (this is well explained by Sheppard in his edition, pp. xli ff.). In the *Electra* the lyric dialogue after the messenger speech (823) and the second *stasimon* (1058) point forward to the end of the play.

N. For Aeschylus, cf. Winnington-Ingram, *C.R.* 1933, p. 99. on the *Oresteia*.

For Euripides, cf. Sheppard, *C.Q.* 1916, p. 72, on the *Hercules*.
The chief motives in the surviving plays of Sophocles are:

AJAX.

Athena and Ajax: prologue, cf. also 401, 457, 656, 952.
Arms of Achilles: 41, 442, 572, 933, 1135, 1239.
Hatred of sons of Atreus: 44, 390, 447, 718, 837, 930, 1055, 1390.
Hatred of Odysseus: 101, 149, 380, 954.
Greatness of Ajax: 119, 169, 205, 364, 439, 612, 1212, 1272, 1340.
Salamis and Telamon: 134, 462, 596, 849, 860, 1008, 1217.

ANTIGONE.

House of Labdacus: 2, 50, 471, 583, 856, 893.
Obedience: 67, 291, 370, 381, 676, 853.
Impiety: 77, 199, 284, 745, 921, 1020, 1349.
Piety: 74, 450, 924.
Good and bad counsel: 1050, 1242, 1269, 1348.
Friendship: 99, 182, 523, 658.
Hybris: 127, 473, 604, 711, 1028, 1350.
Tyranny: 213, 505, 666, 744.

TRACHINIAE.

Heracles' prophecy: 46, 78, 154, 821, 1164.
Changeableness of human fortunes: 1, 129, 296, 439, 945.
The wooing of Deianira: 9, 22 (= 526 with Wilamowitz' reading), 504.
The dangers of beauty: 25, 465.
Nobility: 61, 308, 721.
The gods: 139, 1266, 1278.
Heracles' greatness: 176, 244, 488, 644, 811, 1011, 1046.
Nessus: 558, 661, 680, 831, 1141.

TYRANNUS.

(see also Sheppard's edition).
Plague: 22, 168, 302, 635.
Sphinx: 35, 391, 507, 694, 1197, 1525.
Oedipus as king: 62, 408, 443, 509 (and particularly 50 = 1220).
Bribery and sedition: 124, 383, 515.
Oedipus' decree: 132, 223, 350, 744, 1290, 1380.
Apollo and his oracle: 70, 151, 242, 376, 463, 720, 788, 909, 994, 1175, 1329.
Murder of Laius: 112, 292, 362, 495, 733.

ELECTRA

Apollo and the gods: 32, 498, 637, 682, 1266, 1376, 1424.
Justice: 70, 338, 475, 528, 1041, 1440, 1505.

Furies: 112, 276, 490, 1386.

Agamemnon, Clytemnestra, and Aegisthus: 95, 125, 261, 439, 585, 957, 1101, 1154, 1402, 1473, 1495.

Niobe and immurement: 150, 380, 626, 1007. Antigone compared to Niobe, *Ant.* 823.

Modesty: 176, 219, 369, 610, 830, 990, 1171.

High birth: 145, 257, 307, 341, 616, 989.

Agamemnon's power in the underworld: 459, 837, 1068, 1417.

PHILOCTETES.

Philoctetes' cries: 11, 216, 873, 1032.

Philoctetes' noble birth: 5, 180, 263, 492, 1210.

Neoptolemus' noble birth: 79 (= 1228), 874, 902, 1310.

Neoptolemus, son of Achilles: 4, 260, 331f., 940 (= 1066).

Obedience: 6, 385, 925, 1143, 1243.

Tongue as leader: 99, 407, 1307, 1370.

The prophecy: 68, 196, 605, 839, 915, 989, 1055, 1337.

Misfortunes of a long life: 179, cf. 505.

The Gods: 192, cf. 839, 989, 1116, 1326.

Desire for vengeance: 315, 791, 1019, 1113, 1285.

COLONEUS.

Oracle: 91, 413, 603, 792, 1331, 1472.

Eumenides: 42, 127, 458, 864, 1010, 1391.

The blessing on Athens: 72, 287, 578, 1489 (cf. Aesch. *Eum.* 289).

Oedipus' blindness: *passim* (N.B. that there are more καὶ μήν preparations in this play than any other; see my article *C.R.* 1933, p. 120).

Nobility: 8, 569, 911, 1042, 1636.

Behaviour in a foreign town: 13, 171, 913.

Oedipus' innocence: 240, 270, 522, 964.

Oedipus' love for daughters: 327, 344, 1140, 1205, 1365, 1529, 1617; *hatred of sons*: 337, 427, 765; *curse*: 421, 1348.

O. An earlier parallel can be found in the *Prometheus*, where Prometheus' first speech in iambics and anapaests is practically a monody and is followed by a lyric dialogue between Prometheus and the chorus who, like the chorus of the *Electra*, are come to sympathize. It is of course true that Euripides had been using monodies in the prologue for many years, before the *Electra* was produced, but then we have no reason to assume that the *Electra* contains Sophocles' first monody. If Sophocles was influenced by Euripides, the end of the prologue, *parodos*, and beginning of the first act of the *Electra* are nearer to the *Medea* than to any of Euripides' surviving plays.

P. In the *Trachiniae*, as here, the central scene is the second act where Deianira is confronted with Lichas, the messenger, and Iole; it is in three parts, Deianira and Lichas, Deianira and the messenger, Deianira and Lichas. In the *Tyrannus* and *Electra* again the tripartite second act is the central scene; the three parts in the *Tyrannus* are Oedipus and Creon; Oedipus, Creon, and Iocasta; Oedipus and Iocasta: in the *Electra* the debate between Clytemnestra and Electra, Clytemnestra's prayer and the messenger speech, and Electra's lament form the three parts. In the *Philoctetes* first and second acts are run together into one long scene and the first *stasimon* is reduced to a strophe after Neoptolemus' speech and an antistrophe after Philoctetes' appeal; this long scene is in five parts, the exposition of Philoctetes' life (the normal content of a first act), the tale of Neoptolemus, Philoctetes' appeal, the tale of the spy, the departure of Philoctetes and Neoptolemus. In the *Coloneus*, although the first act is greatly extended, the central scene comes after the first *stasimon* and has three parts, the debate between Oedipus and Creon, the seizure of Antigone and Oedipus, the debate between Theseus and Creon.

Q. Twice, however, the procedure is reversed and the thought goes from the particular to the general. In the second *stasimon* of the *Antigone* (582) the chorus sing first of the Labdacids and Antigone and then proceed to a more general consideration of Ate; similarly in the first *stasimon* of the *Coloneus* (668) the chorus proceed from their address to Oedipus, 'Stranger, you are come,' to the more general praise of Athens.

The majority of these songs have some general theme which is suggested by the particular event and which probably has some future importance. Three songs, although like the rest they are an enlargement on something that has been said or done in the scene before, are of a different type. In the fourth *stasimon* of the *Antigone* (944) the chorus try to console Antigone by quoting mythological examples of suffering (so Headlam on *Ag.* 1040 (1024)). For this use of mythological examples, cf. lament of *Antigone*, *parodos* of *Electra*, *stasimon* of *Philoctetes*). The first *stasimon* of the *Trachiniae* (497) gives the narrative of Deianira's wooing as an example to prove the strength of Cypris, a theme suggested by the news of Heracles' love for Iole. The first *stasimon* of the *Coloneus* is an encomium of Athens which amplifies Oedipus' remark on her glory and fair fame.

R. In the *Ajax* the scenes with three actors are the prologue and the last scene; in the *Antigone* only the long scene, with first Creon, Guard, and Antigone, and then Creon, Ismene, and Antigone; in the *Trachiniae* only the prologue and the long scene with Deianira, Messenger, and Lichas; in the *Tyrannus* four scenes, the prologue, the scene with Oedipus, Iocasta, and Creon, the two scenes between Oedipus and the Corinthian messenger; in the *Electra* the prologue (if Electra's monody is included), the scene with the messenger speech, the scene when the Pedagogue re-appears, and the scene with Aegisthus; in the *Philoctetes* the scene with the Emporos and the two scenes with Odysseus at the end.

CHAPTER VI

S. There is a parallel to this in the fourth *stasimon* of the *Tyrannus* (1186), where lines of the first strophe, 'What man wins more of happiness than a semblance and after the semblance a setting ?' are echoed at the end of the second antistrophe by 'you gave me life and you have put me again to sleep'. Other songs with this circular form are the second *stasimon* of the *Antigone* (582), where the idea of Ate sent from god which comes in the first strophe is echoed by the same idea in the second antistrophe, and the fourth *stasimon* of the same play (944), where, 'Yet she was of high birth, my child, ... but the power of fate is hard,' is echoed in the second anti-strophe, 'Child of the gods. But on her too the long-lived fates were hard, my child.'

T. For circular form in speeches, cf. Haemon's speech in the *Antigone*. Another common element in the Greek prayer is the invocation of the god from the various sacred places where he lives. This again can be traced back to Homer (Kranz, op. cit., p. 188). The prayer to Dionysus in the *Antigone* (1115) contains a list of places where Dionysus may be found, such as Italy, Eleusis, and Delphi. This too Sophocles adapts to other choruses which are not prayers. It can still be seen in the list of alterna-tive places where the battle may be fought in the battle chorus of the *Coloneus* (1044), 'either by the Pythian or by the torchlit shores ... or in the west.' Cf. *Aj.* 172, 879.

U. *Trach.* 849 and 860. The final lines of both strophes and antistrophes are similarly emphasized in the second *stasimon* of the *Tyrannus* (863 f.). The fourth *stasimon* of the *Tyrannus* is an example of careful correspon-dence of sense and metre; in the first syzygy breaks in sense and metre at 1188 and 1192 correspond to breaks in sense and metre at 1198 and 1201; in the second syzygy the break at the end of 1206 corresponds to the break at the end of 1215. In the first *stasimon* of the *Antigone* παντόπορος· ἄπορος of the second strophe corresponds to ὑψίπολις· ἄπολις of the *antistrophe*. In the fourth *stasimon* of the *Trachiniae* the first antistrophe (950) echoes the first strophe line for line. See Dale, *Greek Poetry and Life*, p. 193 f.

V. Münscher (*Hermes*, 1927, p. 154 f.) compares the mesodic arrange-ment of the great *kommos* in the *Choephori*; for the dactyls cf. Wilamowitz, *Verskunst*, p. 348. The *Philoctetes* has two simpler variants of the epirrhematic form; the *parodos* has the form—*a.A.a'.A'.b.b'.A".c.c'*., where *A* is 6 anapaestic lines, *A'* is $1\frac{1}{2}+6\frac{1}{2}+1$, *A"* is 10; the 'sleep' song has a single *epirrhema* of four dactyls sung by Neoptolemus after the strophe. The second *kommos* of the *Antigone* is like the *parodos* of the *Philoctetes*, only more complicated. It has the form *a.A.a'.A'.b.A'.c.b'.A".c'*. In the middle of the first strophe and antistrophe the chorus have a line of iambic commentary.

W. *O.T.* 463. In the *parodos* of the *Trachiniae* there is a change from the excited dactyls of the opening question through quieter dactyls and choriambs in the second syzygy to the calm iambics of the epode. There is a similar change in the *parodos* of the *Ajax*, where the excited questions in dactyls change in the epode to command and reflection in iambics, and in the second *stasimon* of the *Antigone* where the excited commentary on the last scene is in dactyls and iambics, but the general reflections of the second syzygy are in quieter choriambs and ionics. In the first *stasimon* of the *Septem* Aeschylus has a similar change of rhythm; iambics for the fears of the chorus (288 f.), glyconics for the excited description (295 f.), and choriambic for the prayer (301 f.).

X. In the first lines of the first *stasimon* of the *Trachiniae* (497) μέγα τι σθένος ἁ Κύπρις ἐκφέρεται the anapaests seem to be the equivalent of the later dactyls; the single line in the second syzygy of the third *stasimon* of the *Trachiniae* (842), if it should be scanned as anapaests which is by no means certain, has the same value as the lone dactylic line among the glyconics in the first *stasimon* of the *Coloneus* (676); in the same way the long anapaestic lines (469) in the first *stasimon* of the *Tyrannus* are faster than the preceding glyconics.

CHAPTER VII

Y. Cf. *O.T.* 813 f., *El.* 711, 745, &c. Earlier broken lines in the *Ajax*, 466, 470, 1010. In the late plays the trimeter is more often divided between two or more speakers than in the early plays. The figures for this division are given differently in different authorities (Radermacher, *Trachiniae*, p. 39; Schmid-Stählin, p. 326 n. 3; Zielinsky, *Iresione*, i, p. 380). The following list excludes all broken trimeters in lyric dialogues. The figures are: *Ajax* 8 (in two runs of 4), *Antigone* 0, *Trachiniae* 2, *Tyrannus* 11 (including two runs of 4), *Electra* 15 (including two runs of 3), *Philoctetes* 30, *Coloneus* 44 (including runs of 7, 5, 3). The runs, in which each trimeter is divided at the same point between two speakers, are lyrical expressions of emotion and should be discounted as having nothing to do with realism. Then the increase is regular from the *Ajax* and *Antigone* (both 0) to the *Philoctetes* and *Coloneus* (30 and 29). Statistics for resolution, elision, and other metrical peculiarities do not give such clear results (see Siess, *Wiener Studien*, 1915, p. 244 f.; 1916, p. 27 f.), but in general it would certainly be justifiable to say that we can detect a freer versification from the *Tyrannus* onwards.

Addenda and Corrigenda
to First Edition

p. 2. Chronological table. See below on p. 6 for alterations.

p. 3. On the early plays see Appendix, p. 196. On recent unsuccessful attempts to date the *Ajax* see Holger Friis Johansen, op. cit., 171.

p. 4. Two recent articles, H. A. Pohlsander, *A.J.P.*, 84, 1963, 280ff., D. J. Raven, *A.J.P.*, 86, 1965, 225ff., date *Trach.* near *O.T.* on metrical grounds.

p. 5. I should have realised that Hippolytus' self-defence is probably modelled on the earlier Euripidean play, cf. my *Tragedies of Euripides*, 67.

p. 6. Now that the Euripidean *Electra* has been redated before 416, there is more room for the Sophoclean *Electra*, and 413, the year before the *Helen*, becomes likely (see A. M. Dale, *Euripides Helen*, x).

p. 6–7. Chronological table. Add 463(?), Sophocles second to Aeschylus' Danaid trilogy, *P. Oxy.* 2256, fr. 3. 447, Sophocles first with Herakleides as actor, see Appendix, p. 196. *Antigone* should probably be dated 442, as Euripides was victorious in 441. *Telepheia* is probably earlier than *Ajax*, see Appendix, p. 196. *Electra* should be dated 413(?).

p. 7ff. On the Company of the Educated and on the connection of Sophocles with Polygnotus see Appendix, p. 196.

p. 8. On the sayings of Sophocles see below on p. 143.

p. 10. On the connection with Ion of Chios see my article in *Hermes* 71, 1936, 263, and F. Jacoby, *C.Q.*, 41, 1947, I ff.

p. 11ff. On Sophocles' public life see V. Ehrenberg, *Sophocles and Pericles*, 1954, ch. 6.

p. 16. Texts of *Ichneutae* and *Inachus* are conveniently published by D. L. Page, *Greek Literary Papyri*, I, Loeb 1942, Nos. 6 and 7. For details of later discussions see Holger Friis Johansen, *op. cit.*, p. 276ff. Add for *Inachus* A. M. Dale, *C.R.*, 10, 1960, 194. The new papyrus of the *Inachus*, *P. Oxy.* 2360, gives Inachos describing the transformation of Io into a cow. It seems certain that Io subsequently appeared, and that the Aeschylean mask with horns on the forehead would not have been sufficient by itself. Miss Dale argues that she may have worn hoof-gauntlets, as she is described not as a total heifer but as a seated 'beast-woman'. This may very well be right, but on a South Italian vase, dated 440–30, Boston 00.366, Trendall, *Lucanian, Campanian, Sicilian Red-figure Vase-painting*, 16, No. 9, she does appear as a cow with a female head. The new papyrus also apparently describes 'the stranger skilled in drugs' as 'black'; one should perhaps remember Hermes with his face blacked with soot in Callimachus, *Hymn* III, 69.

Illustrations of satyr-plays, as well as tragedies, are listed in *Bulletin of the Institute of Classical Studies, London,* Supplement 20, 1967. *Amykos, Dionysiskos, Pandora* were all on this evidence early.

p. 25. 'But in the later plays of Euripides the force in the background is Chance.' This is an overstatement. See my *Tragedies of Euripides,* 287, n. 1.

p. 27ff. There is an excellent discussion of Sophocles' divine laws in V. Ehrenberg, *Sophocles and Pericles,* ch. 2.

p. 28, n. 2. The Pindar fragment has now been extended by *P. Oxy.* 2450, frg. 1. For interpretation see M. Ostwald, *H.S.C.P.,* 69, 1965, 109; but I should guess that after the burial of Amphitryon, Heracles' mortal father, the poem ended with the Apotheosis of Heracles, the 'justification' of his violence.

p. 34f. See Appendix, p. 196 on the Euripidean plays in which the passions are said to be stronger than the will, and on the corresponding Sophoclean plays in which the motive is distinguished from the act.

p. 47, n. 1. On the *nomos-physis* contrast see F. Heinimann, *Nomos and Physis,* Basel, 1945. The Antiphon fragment has been reinterpreted by J. S. Morrison, *Phronesis,* 8, 1963, 35.

p. 51. On Sophocles and Heraclitus, see J. C. Kamerbeek, *Studia Vollgraff,* 84.

p. 74. On Sophoclean women see A. M. Dale in *For Service to Classical Studies,* Melbourne, 1966, 71ff. (to be reprinted in A. M. Dale, *Collected Papers,* Cambridge, 1968).

p. 87. On Euripides' scenes of sympathy and contrast see my *Tragedies of Euripides,* 288.

p. 96. On Ajax's speech see Holger Friis Johansen, *op. cit.,* 177.

p. 98. On Antigone's last speech see Holger Friis Johansen, *op. cit.,* 198.

p. 115. On the second stasimon of the *O.T.* see G. H. Gellie, *A.J.P.,* 85, 1964, 113; J. C. Kamerbeek, *Wiener Studien,* 79, 1966, 80.

p. 119. The *eccyclema* was, of course, used, cf. my *Greek Theatre Production,* 17f.

p. 120. On the staging of the *Philoctetes* see A. M. Dale, *Wiener Studien,* 69, 1956, 104f. (reprinted in *Collected Papers*).

p. 135ff. This passage was written before the publication of A. M. Dale, *Lyric Metres of Greek Drama,* Cambridge 1948 (the second edition, 1968, is quoted below as *LM.*). The main lines hold, but I should have distinguished between dactylic and dactylo-epitrite and between glyconic and other forms of aeolo-choriambic. I also, under Koerte's influence, adopted the antispast much too readily, on which see now *LM.*, 96.

p. 137, n. 5. On these lines see *LM.*, 85, 103, 117.

p. 138, n. 1. The 'weeping rhythm' is the hypodochmiac, cf. *LM.*, 114f.

p. 140, n. 1. These antispasts are better taken as aeolo-choriambic or ionic, cf. *LM.*, 96, 122, 140, 143–4, 155.

p. 141, n. 1. *Aj.* 627–639 could be either dochmiac or the aeolo-choriambic Dodrans A; in the context the latter is the better interpretation.

p. 143. Sophocles' account of his own development. C. M. Bowra, *A.J.P.*, 61, 1940, 385 (=*Problems in Greek Poetry*, 1953, 108) makes the *Ajax* representative of the second stage and the *Antigone* of the third. F. R. Earp, *Style of Sophocles*, 1944, makes the *Antigone* representative of the second stage. The problem is tied up with the date of the account itself; Bowra attributes it to the anecdotal *Epidemiae* of Ion of Chios, who was dead by 421. In favour of this is the fact that all the quotations of Sophocles are introduced as 'sayings' rather than 'writings'. With Bowra's interpretation the conversation could even have taken place in 440, the date of Ion's recorded meeting with Sophocles (cf. above, p. 10). But Ion was in Athens much later, certainly in 428, when he was third in the tragic competition; and one could much more easily see the *Oedipus Tyrannus* as the beginning of the third stage, as a recognisable first step in the development which leads on to the three late plays.

p. 145ff. The general case put forward here is argued with much more detail by F. R. Earp in *Style of Sophocles*.

p. 148. On Sophocles' use of abstracts see now in detail A. A. Long, *Language and Thought in Sophocles*, London, 1968. The debates in tragedy are analysed and discussed by J. Duchemin, *L'Agon dans la tragédie grecque*, 1945.

p. 151. Reduction of gnomes in late speeches, see H. Friis Johansen, *General Reflection in Tragic Rhesis*, Copenhagen, 1959.

p. 153. The imagery of the *Antigone* has been discussed in detail by R. F. Goheen, *Imagery of Sophocles' Antigone*, Princeton, 1951, and the chief images of the *O.T.* by H. Musurillo, *A.J.P.*, 78, 1957, 36.

p. 156. E. B. Ceadel, *C.Q.*, 35, 1941, 84ff., has counted the resolved feet in the iambic trimeters of Sophocles: his figures per 100 lines are *Aj.* 6,2; *Ant.* 3,9; *Trach.* 5,9; *O.T.* 6; *El.* 3,4; *Phil.* 9,1; *O.C.* 5,96. The figures exclude proper names, which would raise the percentages to 7,7; 5,2; 6,9; 7,5; 5; 10; 7,9. The variation shows nothing chrono-logically. I do not know any study of the location of resolutions in Sophocles' plays; it is startling to observe that the great angry speeches of Philoctetes, 740–819, 923–962, 1004–1044, show an average of 30 per

100 lines, the kind of percentage that Euripides shows overall in his latest plays (cf. my *Tragedies of Euripides*, 2ff.).

p. 161. Sound pattern. See now W. B. Stanford, *The Sound of Greek*, Berkeley, 1967.

p. 172ff. The fragments. Page, *Greek Literary Papyri*, I, gives the papyrus fragments. The early plays are discussed further in the following Appendix.

p. 175. COLCHIAN WOMEN. My guess about a Medea trilogy was unfortunate. Medea had a different mother and Apsyrtus was killed in different places in *Colchian Women* and *Scythians*, and nothing connects *Rhizotomi* with Pelias.

Appendix on the Early Plays of Sophocles and Euripides

In the later fifth century there are three occasions where we can see Sophocles and Euripides reacting to each other. The most obvious is the sequence of Electra plays: Aeschylus's *Choephoroi* must have been revived shortly before the second edition of Aristophanes' *Clouds*, and Euripides reacted with his highly original *Electra* about 419, which Sophocles answered in 413 with his combination of 'matricide and good spirits' and was answered in turn by Euripides in 408 with the *Orestes*, which asks how would a complete modern family behave if the son murdered the mother. Another such sequence can perhaps be seen for the Theban story. The easiest explanation of the present shape of Aeschylus' *Septem* is to suppose that the ending was added for a revival after the production of Sophocles' *Antigone* and to put this revival late in the fifth century to account for the references in Gorgias and the *Frogs*; then Euripides reacted with the *Phoenissae* in 410, which again switches the emphasis from the single figure of Eteokles to the whole family including Iokaste and Oedipus, who have lived on to see their sons kill each other. Probably in 408 Euripides produced his very original *Oedipus* in which Oedipus, young, intelligent and happy-go-lucky, allowed the jealous Kreon to hunt out the murderers of Laios and blind him and the queen of Corinth to reveal the secret of his birth; Iokaste seems to have remained loyal to him through all this. Sophocles reinstated the old determined and angry Oedipus in the *Oedipus Coloneus*.

The earliest sequence is in the late 30's and early 20's.[1] This sequence is Euripides' *First Hippolytus* in which Phaidra approached Hippolytus herself and then faked a scene of rape on Theseus's return to cause Theseus to curse Hippolytus; then Sophocles' *Phaidra*, in which Phaidra had the excuse that she believed that Theseus was dead and that Eros was a great and invincible god; she approached Hippolytus through her nurse

[1] Cf. my *Tragedies of Euripides*, 64 ff., particularly 75 f.

(perhaps by a letter?) and when Theseus returned she falsely accused Hippolytus to save her children. In the *Second Hippolytus* in 428 Euripides took over the indirect approach to Hippolytus and the motivation of the false accusation; but removed both the excuses. Theseus is not in Hades and Aphrodite is merely a hypostatisation of sex. His first Phaidra was just a bad woman, a 'prostitute' the comic poets called her; the new Phaidra of 428 knows what is right but under temptation yields to her passion, just as Medeia in 431 knows what is right but yields to her anger and kills her children. This Medeia also is a new Medeia: we have no evidence that Medeia in the *Peliades* in 455 or in the *Aigeus* soon after 450 was anything but a straight murderess.

Bruno Snell sees Euripides creating his new Medeia and Phaidra to conduct a sort of dialogue with Sokrates, who asserted that if you knew what was right you did it. Curiously he has failed to notice that in the late thirties and early twenties the comic poets were saying that Euripides' plays were put together by Sokrates. Whether we accept Snell's view or not, at least I think we must say that the relation of reason to emotion was very much a discussion topic in the late thirties and early twenties, and we can add that Sophocles takes quite a different line from Euripides in three plays that can reasonably be dated in this period: in the *Phaidra* Phaidra does not know that Theseus is coming back from Hades, in the *Trachiniae* Deianeira does not know that the love-charm is a poison, in the *Oedipus Tyrannus* Oedipus does not know his origin or the identity of the old man whom he murdered. We might say that Sophocles accepts the Socratic paradox and Euripides refutes it. My chief point, however, is that this is a new problem at that time to which both dramatists react in different ways.

The two earlier plays of Sophocles which survive, the *Antigone* dated in 442 and the *Ajax* probably not far distant in date, both deal with the problem of a great individualist clashing with the state and this, as far as I can see, is a problem which Euripides does not touch. Aeschylus had led the way in the *Prometheus Vinctus* at the very end of his life, and I cannot help thinking that the clashes of Kimon and his successors with the rising power of Perikles had something to do with these plays. Euripides' first picture of a self-seeking politician seems to have been Odysseus in the *Philoktetes* of 431; after that there are many, but the rebel perhaps only occurs in the *Bellerophon*, and he rebels against the gods rather than against the government.

We can make a good case for supposing that the formula which Euripides used for his productions in 438 and 431 was his normal formula in the early years: one play about a bad woman (Aerope in the *Kressai* in 438, Medeia in 431), one play about a woman in distress (Arsinoe in the *Alkmaion in Psophis* in 438, Danae in the *Diktys* in 431), and one other play (*Telephos* in 438, *Philoktetes* in 431), and each of the three plays is drawn from a different cycle of legend. I could make this case in detail, but I should prefer simply to look for a moment at the *Peliades* of 455, the first production, and ask how far Euripides is already Euripides.[1] The play was produced only three years after the *Oresteia* and it is a reasonable guess but probably an over-simplification to say that Euripides was fascinated by the Aeschylean Klytemnestra and divided her into a murderess and an adulteress: the murderess was the model for Medeia in the *Peliades* and *Aigeus* but was reshaped for the *Medeia* of 431; the adulteress was the model for Aerope, Stheneboia, the villainesses of the *Phoinix* and *Peleus*, and the first Phaidra, but was reshaped for the second Phaidra of 428.

But what he seems to have done is to strip Klytemnestra of all her Aeschylean splendour and ask what she would look like in the fifth century, though actually the fragments preserved from the *Peliades* belong to Pelias rather than to Medeia; Pelias is the fussy old king, who tells his daughter not to have more independent thoughts than a girl of her age should have and to leave the planning to men ($603N^2$), who complains of the difficulties of tyranny which is forced to kill its friends in fear ($605N^2$) and who preaches a sermon to the young to seek good companions ($609N^2$). He is the ancestor of Kreon in the *Medeia* and as helpless in Medeia's ruthless hands. Medeia may have been inspired by the Aeschylean Klytemnestra, and the Aeschylean *Danaides* may have suggested a chorus of daughters of Pelias with one recalcitrant daughter as a character, but the dialogue seems to have been

[1] Cf. my *Tragedies of Euripides*, 32 ff.

entirely modern. 'Men as they are', as Sophocles said of Euripidean characters.

Sophocles himself, on the other hand, admitted to an Aeschylean period, whatever the extremely difficult words of the judgment recorded by Plutarch (*Moralia* 79B) mean in detail. His first production in 468 B.C. included the *Triptolemos*. We cannot reconstruct this play[1], but the following facts are worth noting: (1) Kimon and his generals adjudged the victory to Sophocles over Aeschylus, which implies some kind of sympathy between Sophocles and Kimon, (2) Demeter sent Triptolemos out to give corn to the world in a chariot drawn by snakes (596P does not necessarily imply that the chariot was shown on the stage), (3) Demeter's phrase 'in the tablets of your mind' (597P), her geographic descriptions (598P), and the four-word lines of frs. 596P, 611P are all remarkably Aeschylean.

The next step is to examine the two plays, *Thamyras* and *Nausikaa*, in which Sophocles is said to have acted himself; they must be before the date when according to the *Life*: (4) he 'abolished acting by the poet' on account of his own lack of voice. If we can date this change, we have a bottom date for *Thamyras* and *Nausikaa*. No one has ever suggested that Euripides acted himself, so that the change was either before or not long after 455, his first production. We are, however, on firm ground when we find on the inscriptional records: (1) that Sophocles was victorious in 448–47 and Herakleides was his actor (*I.G.* ii², 2318), (2) that Herakleides was the first actor to win the actors' competition (*I.G.* ii², 2325). Once the competition was established there was no question of the poets' acting, unless he also won the competition, and on this evidence the competition would seem to have been established about 450. This gives a bottom date for the *Thamyras* and *Nausikaa*.

According to the *Life* (6) Sophocles, when he wrote, considered the nature of his actors and choruses and collected from the

---

[1] Pearson records guesses, to which add F. Brommer, *Philologus*, 94, 1941, 336, who on the strength of a vase at least 20 years later than the play guesses that it was a satyr-play. I have profited from discussions on this and other early plays with Mrs. Akiko Kiso of Kyoto University, who will, I hope, publish her interpretations.

educated a company in honour of the Muses. I used to think it
was a literary society, but I now wonder whether it was not a
dramatic school founded now. A further suggestion (already made
by Oehmichen in 1887)[1] is that the Suda's statement 'Sophocles
was the first to compete with play against play' should be connected with the institution of the actors' competition, and implies
that the festival was rearranged so that instead of each poet
producing his three tragedies together on one day, the poets now
spread their three tragedies over three days. Connected trilogies
were thereby made impossible until the rules were changed again,
and therefore if we find traces of a connected trilogy in Sophocles
we have to ask whether it was early. The only attested Sophoclean
trilogy is the *Telepheia* recorded on an inscription of about
380 B.C. from Halai Aixonides (C. J. Eliot, *Coastal Demes of Attika*,
26 f.). This deme has no theatre, and therefore the inscription
probably refers to a City victory. Epichares, as choregos of comedy,
won a victory with Ekphantides' *Peirai*; and, as choregos of
tragedy, with Sophocles' *Telepheia*. Ekphantides was certainly
producing in the 450's (and was apparently dead before the
institution of the Lenaia in 442) and therefore the *Telepheia* may
well also have been written in the 450's. The first two plays may
have been the *Aleadai*, in which Telephos, taunted with
illegitimacy, killed his uncles and was sent to Mysia to seek
purification and his mother, and the *Mysoi*, in which Teuthras
betrothed him to his mother Auge, and he was prevented by a
miracle from being murdered by her on the wedding-night. For
the third play we have a choice between the *Eurypylos* about
Telephos' son and the *Achaion Syllogos*. The latter was the obvious
choice when the Berlin papyrus with its reference to Telephos was
ascribed to it, but now the papyrus has been proved to belong to
Euripides' *Telephos* of 438 B.C.[2]; we may, however, still argue that
there Achilles' 'where is the assembly of friends?' is a back reference to Sophocles' play and Sophocles' play certainly contained a
reference to a night voyage (143P) and a muster of those who had
sworn to recover Helen (144P). If this was the third play, the

---

[1] Details in *Hermathena*, 100, 1965, 21 ff.

[2] E. W. Handley and J. Rea, *B.I.C.S.*, Supplt. 5, 1957, 1.

third play also showed Telephos in a dangerous situation, seeking
to have his wound healed by his enemies. Here all through we have
exciting action ending with success for Telephos. In the *Eurypylos*
Astyoche, Priam's daughter and Telephos' wife, had been bribed
by the present of a golden vine to allow her son to fight for the
Trojans. He was killed by Neoptolemos with the spear which had
wounded Telephos. The long recital of the duel was punctuated
by the lamentations of Astyoche and the Trojan chorus: the play
seems to be in the tradition of the *Persae* and is probably early.
The other plays are not noticeably Aeschylean in style.[1]

The *Nausikaa* has two fragments in Aeschylean language
(439, 440P); the scene must have been the sea-shore; Sophocles, as
Nausikaa, played ball with the chorus of washing-girls and
Odysseus appeared and told his story. Sophocles had evidently
learnt from Homer, as Ion said, but where was the tragedy? The
emergence of Odysseus is illustrated on three vase paintings of the
third quarter of the century (*ARV*[2] 1107, 1177, 1281)[2] and
probably well before 450 on a wall-painting by Polygnotos
(Paus. 1, 22, 6). The *Thamyras*, however, was a tragedy in our
sense. Thamyras challenged the Muses to a contest of song and
they defeated him and blinded him. According to the *Life* (5)
Sophocles 'played the lyre, for which reason he was painted with a
lyre in the Stoa Poikile'. It seems a safe deduction that Sophocles
played Thamyras and that the picture showed him in this part.
Wilamowitz[3] was surely right to give him the two hexameter lines
reciting his genealogy (242P). The anapaestic fragments naming
Athos (237P) and listing musical instruments (238P) may belong to
either Thamyras or the Muses. The difficult ionic fragment
(245P) is sung by a sympathiser, whose identity depends on the
view we take of the chorus: if the Muses formed the chorus, then
the sympathiser was Argiope, Thamyras' mother; otherwise the
sympathisers were the chorus. The Muses struck Thamyras blind.

---

[1] The Telephos satyr-play recorded by an inscription belongs to the
younger Sophocles (Moretti, *Athenaeum*, 38, 1961, 267).

[2] Fuller references for the vases quoted in this Appendix will be
found in *B.I.C.S.*, Supplt. 20, 1968, Appendix.

[3] *Griechische Verskunst* 347.

As Thamyras had a special mask[1] with one black and one grey eye, this was evidently done on the stage and he lost his power of song (241P) and in fury broke his lyre (244P). The last fragment is in aeolo-choriambic: could Thamyras nevertheless still sing, or should this again be given to the sympathiser?

This scene was evidently represented by Polygnotos in his Nekyia at Delphi (Pausanias 10, 30 2), and on a hydria of about 450–40 B.C. in Oxford (*ARV*[2] 1061), which adds to Thamyras with the lyre at his feet a Muse on the right and a Thracian woman tearing her hair on the left; she must be the sympathiser. The six vases showing Thamyras singing in the presence of the Muses have naturally been connected with Polygnotos, who painted the Sack of Troy in the Stoa probably before 461 B.C. If Polygnotos was possibly inspired by Sophocles to paint a Nausikaa picture and two Thamyras pictures, it is perhaps worth noting that his Sack of Troy in the Stoa Poikile had 'the Kings assembled because of Ajax' attempt on Kassandra, including Ajax, the captive women and Kassandra', which may have been the subject of Sophocles' play *Ajax of Lokroi*; the picture of the Sack of Troy in Delphi included the leopard skin over the house of Antenor which was mentioned in that play (11P) and the picture gallery of the Propylaia had a sacrifice of Polyxena, probably by Polygnotos: Sophocles' *Polyxene* was in any case earlier than Euripides' *Hecuba* (between 428 and 424 B.C.). In Sophocles' play Menelaos and Agamemnon quarrelled about the time of sailing back from Troy; Menelaos went on (522P), and only then Agamemnon saw Achilles' ghost (like the ghost of Dareios in the *Persae*) appear above his tomb (523P) to demand the sacrifice of Polyxene and prophesy the future, including the death of Agamemnon himself (526P). Euripides started his *Hecuba* with the appearance of the ghost of Polydoros, thus giving the play a startling opening, and Polymestor at the end took over the prophecy. The Stoa Poikile was finished or nearly finished in 462–1 B.C. according to Miss Jeffery's dating (*B.S.A.* 60, 1965, 41) and the other pictures by Polygnotos in Athens were probably painted for a building built before Kimon's ostracism.

[1] Pollux, 4, 141, Cf. A. Lesky, *Anz. Wiener Ak.*, 1951, 105 ff. The Oxford vase quoted below shows the blind side; the other vases the seeing side.

Probably, therefore, if this connection is valid, 460 B.C. is a bottom date for all these plays. I do not deny that the connection is weak: it depends first on the note about a picture of Sophocles playing the lyre in the Stoa Poikile, which is expressly connected with the *Thamyras*, and then on the connection of both Sophocles and Polygnotos with Kimon. And why does Pausanias only mention the assembly of kings to judge the lesser Ajax in the Sack of Troy when he describes it as one scene among twenty others in Polygnotos' Sack of Troy at Delphi? It must have dominated the Athenian picture and Sophocles' play may have been the cause.

The *Ajax of Lokroi* and the *Captive Women* were probably the same play and the Trojan women formed the chorus. It seems clear that Ajax made a great speech defending himself by his military prowess (41, 35P) when he swore that he had not raped Kassandra.[1] The hypothesis of the surviving *Ajax* begins 'the drama belongs to the Trojan operations like the *Antenoridai*, *Captive Women*, *Rape of Helen* and *Memnon*'. Why does he choose precisely these plays unless they made a trilogy? The *Memnon* has been identified with the *Aithiopes* and must have been earlier in the trilogy than the *Ajax of Lokroi*; 'the four-winged black-skinned wasps with pinched backs' (29P) are perhaps a Myrmidon shield-charge, but nothing else useful remains. The subject of the *Antenoridai* is doubtful: (1) Strabo (608) quotes Sophocles as an authority for the leopard-skin over the house of Antenor; 'accordingly Antenor and his sons found their way in safety to . . . Enetica on the Adriatic', but this may have been prophesied in the *Ajax of Lokroi*, which mentioned the leopard-skin (11P). (2) Bacchylides' *Antenoridai or Request for Helen* (15) associates the *Antenoridai* with the embassy of Menelaos and Odysseus to ask for Helen (Sophocles' *Request for Helen* is fixed by 180P to the period of the Sack of Troy). (3) Accius' *Antenoridae*, naturally held to be adapted from a Sophoclean original, has both a reference to the people (1R), which would fit well with the embassy theme, and the arrival of a foreign champion for Troy (IV, VR). Is it possible that Sophocles combined the embassy to demand back Helen with the arrival of Memnon? If so, this would be the first play, followed by the *Memnon* and the *Ajax of Lokroi*. The *Rape of Helen* I take

[1] Or to make atonement (M. Robertson, *B.S.A.*, 62,1967,11)

to be the same as the *Marriage of Helen* and to be the satyr-play of the trilogy.

The most interesting of the Thamyras vases is the hydria (*ARV*² 1020) by the Phiale painter in the Vatican, which can be dated about 450 B.C. Thamyras (inscribed) is seated on a rock in Thracian costume playing his lyre. On the left two Muses are labelled *Choronika*, perhaps a dual rather than a Doric singular, implying that they were victorious in the chorus. On the right an old woman steps up the rock with a spray in her hand with which she is going to crown Thamyras; her hair is white and her face tattooed. She must be Argiope, the mother of Thamyras, and therefore we are justified in supposing that the Muses formed the chorus; it was his mother who sang of the power of his music before the contest and described him breaking his lyre. She joins other disastrously boastful mothers, Niobe and Kassiopeia. Over her head is written *Euaion kalos*.

The full name is given on a white-ground kalyx-krater (*ARV*² 1017) by the same painter in Agrigento: *Euaion kalos Aischylou*. Let us for the moment forget the name and look at the vase. A tall woman in Oriental clothing is tied to a framework of posts. She is labelled Andromeda. And on the left Perseus with his foot upon a rock is watching her with his chin on his hand. This vase has on the back two women, one holding a sceptre. The Andromeda scene connects with four contemporary vases: on the British Museum hydria (*ARV*² 1062) Andromeda is supported by two young Aethiopians; a number more bring funeral offerings from the left; three more plant the posts on the right. Kepheus looks on and Perseus stands beyond him (not belonging to the action but necessary to the story). On a bell-krater in Caltanisetta (*Arch. Rep.* 1963–4) a slave still has his pick raised, Andromeda is tied to one post; Kepheus looks on. On a pelike in Boston (*Boston Bulletin* 61, 1963, 108) the slaves with funeral offerings are shown, one of Andromeda's hands is already tied to a post, the other is being tied. Kepheus looks on. A kalyx-krater in Basel (Schauenburg, *Anlike und Abendland*, 13, 1967, 4) gives Kepheus, Andromeda tied to two posts, Perseus watching. Five contemporary vases giving Andromeda in Oriental dress tied or being tied to posts surely implies a famous recent production (and

Perseus's arrival was parodied in comedy before 420 B.C. (*JHS* 65, 1945, pl. 5, *ARV*² 1215)). This must surely be Sophocles' *Andromeda*. Evidently Sophocles followed the *Prometheus Vinctus* in having the binding scene on the stage. Euripides in 412 B.C. startlingly began the play with the spectacle of Andromeda tied to a rock in front of a cave (just as he transferred the ghost scene from late in Sophocles' *Polyxene* to the beginning of the *Hecuba*); his Andromeda wore Greek dress and there were no posts. The fragments of Sophocles (including *P.Oxy.* 2453, fr. 49) and Accius give very little. We know that Kassiopeia had boasted of Andromeda's beauty to the Nereids and had thereby caused Poseidon to send the monster, to whom Andromeda was to be sacrificed. It looks as if Andromeda first appealed vainly to her local lover to save her (Accius fr. III, IV, VIR). Kepheus lashed his slaves into making the preparations (129P) and other slaves brought the funeral offerings (130P). Then she was tied up. Perseus arrived and thought this was a normal barbarian human sacrifice (126P). Perseus slew the monster, but we do not know how the play ended, except that Perseus and Andromeda presumably married and returned to Argos.

Schmid-Stählin's suggestion that the *Andromeda* was the middle play of a trilogy, which started with the *Akrisios-Danae* (in which the birth of Perseus was discovered and mother and son cast adrift in a chest because of Akrisios' fear of his grandson) and the *Larisaioi* (in which Akrisios was accidentally killed by a diskos thrown by Perseus) becomes even more attractive with the dating of the *Andromeda* to about 450 (before the re-arrangement of the festival) and the attribution of the Agrigento vase to the Phiale painter, who also painted Akrisios inspecting Danae and Perseus in the chest (*ARV*² 1018) and Perseus stealing the eye of the Graiae (*ARV*² 1019), a story which he must have told in the *Andromeda*. If this date is right, the Euripidean *Danae*, though belonging to the first group of plays, is almost certainly later. It is difficult to get the flavour of the Sophoclean play: certainly Akrisios knows from the oracle that his grandson will kill him: 'I don't know about your rape. I understand one thing: if this child here lives, I am lost' (165P). 'For life, my daughter, is the sweetest gift of all. To die twice is not possible' (67P). Danae defends herself with dignity: 'For the modest brief speech to their parents is fitting, particularly for a girl and an Argive, whose glory is silence and few words' (64P). In Euripides Akrisios' wife has a part; he wants a boy, and she says that having children should not be left to old age (316–17N²). When Danae's child is discovered, both her parents are sure that she has been seduced by a rich man (321–2, 324–8N²). Danae pictures the child capturing her by embraces and kisses (323N²). This is the Euripidean formula: a fifth-century family, or 'men as they are'.

A second white-ground kalyx-krater by the Phiale painter is in the Vatican (*ARV*² 1017). On the front Hermes brings the infant Dionysos to Papposeilenos, who sits on a rock between two maenads. On the back are three Muses. Sophocles wrote a satyr-play *Dionysiskos*, in which Papposeilenos describes the baby stroking his nose and bald forehead (171P) and the satyr-chorus rejoice in the discovery of wine. White-ground kalyx-kraters are very rare: was this designed to form a pair with the other and was the *Dionysiskos* the satyr-play of the trilogy?

The Thamyras vase and the Andromeda vase of the Phiale painter both have the name Euaion, and on the Andromeda vase he is called son of Aeschylus. His name is inscribed on ten vases datable within the period 460–40 B.C., three times with 'son of Aeschylus' added, twice without *Kalos*. On a bell krater by the Lykaon painter in Naples (*ARV*² 1045–7) the name is written against the head of a young man in a symposium and must therefore be his name. On the Lykaon painter's bell-krater in Boston (*ARV*² 1045–7, which has a replica in Oxford) *Euaion* is written above the head of Aktaion in a picture of the rending of Aktaion, which is watched by Zeus with his thunderbolt and Artemis with a torch: Lyssa, in a sleeved garment and high boots (which suggest tragedy), drives the hounds on to him: his hair, horns and ears show that they think he is a stag and the small hound above her head shows that she sends them mad. Aeschylus dramatised the story in the *Toxotides*: the death of Aktaion was told in a messenger speech (244–5N), but Lyssa may have appeared on the stage as she did in the *Xantriai*. It is very tempting to suppose that Euaion acted Aktaion in a revival of his father's play, and that he also acted the mother of Thamyras in Sophocles' play and perhaps Perseus in Sophocles' *Andromeda* (the name is written by Perseus' head). All we know about Euaion is that in the Suda life of Aeschylus he is paired with his brother Euphorion as *tragikos*; Euphorion won four victories with his father's plays and in 431 he won the first prize over Sophocles and Euripides' *Medea*, but no trace remains of Euaion's poetic activity. Was he then an actor? The boundary between poet and actor was in any case fluid.

One last hint the white-ground kalyx-kraters of the Phiale painter give: the back of the Dionysiskos krater shows Muses. The back of the Andromeda krater has two women in normal Greek dress, one with a sceptre: they can hardly be Kassiopeia and a member of the chorus because Andromeda on all the vases and Kepheus on the London and Boston vases wear Oriental clothing. Are they also Muses? But why should Muses be associated with a tragedy or a satyr-play? The association is intelligible if Sophocles had already founded his company of actors in honour of the Muses. Euaion as an actor would be a member, and the two white-ground kalyx-kraters and the hydria will have been a special commission for a party to celebrate a present or past production: they were then sold off and reached Agrigento and Vulci, where they were found, through the secondhand market.

We cannot know very much about the early Sophocles. We can say that the earliest plays were significantly Aeschylean in language and that by the time of the Telephos trilogy and the Perseus trilogy that phase was over, and the style has the alluring artificiality that we know from the *Antigone* and *Ajax*. Aeschylean spirit can perhaps be apprehended in the *Thamyras*, *Eurypylos*, *Polyxene*, *Memnon* and *Ajax of Lokroi*, but certainly not in the *Triptolemos* and *Nausikaa*. Perhaps we should think of Aeschylus and Homer as two different influences on Sophocles. If we accept Homer as meaning the Epic cycle as well as the *Iliad* and *Odyssey* the number of Homeric plays is considerable. Ion, in calling Sophocles the pupil of Homer, may have felt that Sophocles, as against Aeschylus, put more emphasis on the plot and less on the ambience of present emotion and past history which characterises the *Oresteia*. In the three possible Sophoclean trilogies (Telephos story, Perseus story, Trojan story) each play seems to have been a chapter in an exciting story. Perhaps by 450 B.C. Sophocles had already developed his own formula. He was a conscious artist with standards: 'If Aeschylus did what was right, he did it without realising it'. 'I make the sort of characters that are right, Euripides makes the sort of people that are.' His final style, he said, gave the most correct *tone* to the speeches. What was this formula? To accept the story with its divine framework and ask what sort of people are needed for it to work out like this. 'The characters that are right' involves a double standard on the evidence of the surviving plays: major characters whose characteristics make the story credible and minor characters who exist chiefly as foils to the major characters. If this is the formula, one understands that Sophocles was concerned with the training of actors: they had to fit in with each other in getting this conception across. Euripides allowed far more scope for interpretation, which explains partly his great subsequent popularity.

INDEX LOCORUM
AJAX

ANTIGONE

TRACHINIAE

OEDIPUS TYRANNUS

ELECTRA

PHILOCTETES

FRAGMENTA

GENERAL INDEX

Ackermann, P., 104.
Aeschylus, 19, 50, 86, 87, 91, 93, 94, 102, 103, 106–12, 114, 116, 117, 119–22, 124, 132, 133, 136, 137, 139, 144 f., 146, 148, 153, 155, 157, 159, 161, 165 f., 173 f., 176 f.
Aexone, 3.
aidos, 26 n.
alliteration, 161.
Aly, W., 7, 53.
ambassador, 11 n., 13.
anapaests, 140, 175, 176.
anaphora, 159.
antispasts, 139.
antithesis, 160.
appeals, 85.
apragmosyne, 17, 37, 45, 163.
Archelaus, 8, 51.
aristocracy, 1, 10, 37, 50, 54, 60, 71, 72, 163 f, 171.
Aristophanes, 12, 15, 18, 54, 163, 164, 172.
Asclepius, 14.
assonance, 161.
asyndeton, 128, 134, 160.
Ate, 30.
Ax, W., 126, 127, 141.

Bethe, E., 119.
Blumenthal, A. von, 1, 7, 12, 15.
blurred transitions, 150, 154.
Bowra, C. M., 35, 38, 49.
Bruhn, E., 6, 53, 155, 160, 161.
Bruns, I., 9.
Busse, W., 52.

Callias, 5.
Cantarella, R., 49.
change of character, 94 f.
change of rhythm, 135, 138.
change of scene, 119.
character contrasts, 85, 87 f.
choriambs, 139.
chorus, 18, 80, 90, 104, 108, 114, 126 ff.
Cimon, 8 f., 163.
circle of fortunes, 31.

circular form, 129, 135, 150, 152.
Company of the Educated, 7.
Cope, E., 13.
correspondence of rhythm and sense, 130, 131, 134, 135.
Cratinus, 15 n.
criticism of myths, 21, 165.
Croiset, M., 76, 88.

dactyls, 136.
Dale, A. M., 131 n.
dating of plays, 2 f., 144.
death, 43.
debates, 85, 86, 148 f.
De Falco, V. 102, 105 n., 109, 116, 117, 127.
Denniston, J. D., 137.
De Ruyt, F., 47.
diptych form, 102, 168, 172 f., 176 f.
divided strophe and antistrophe, 84, 111, 112, 116.
dochmiacs, 141, 174.
Drew, D. L., 12, 49.

eccyclema, 119.
ekplexis, 112, 167.
emotional recapitulation, 116, 126.
emotions of the reader, 114 f.
enumeration, 158.
Errandonea, J., 80, 106, 120.
Euripides, 2, 3 f., 19, 54, 55, 63, 72, 79, 85–7, 91, 95, 103, 106, 110, 112, 113, 116–18, 126, 139, 146, 147, 153, 161, 163, 165, 169.
explanatory speech, 91, 111.

Fate, 24.
first act, 111.
fortitude, 36, 60.
fortune, 25.
Fränkel, H., 82, 155.
free will, 33.
Friedländer, P., 123, 138.
Fritz, K. von, 73, 96.
Fromhold-Treu, M., 3 n.
Furies, 26.